PONGA LA BASURA EN SU LUGAR
Gracias

"WHERE THE SEA MEETS THE BARNYARD"

$1.29

부침가루
OTTOGI KOREAN
PANCAKE MIX

부침가루
OTTOGI KOREAN
PANCAKE MIX

ROSS

CATTLE CROSSING

# MARCUS
## ~OFF DUTY~

# MARCUS
## ~OFF DUTY~

## The RECIPES I COOK at HOME

## MARCUS SAMUELSSON

WITH ROY FINAMORE ★ PHOTOGRAPHS BY PAUL BRISSMAN
★ ILLUSTRATIONS BY REBEKAH MAYSLES

A Rux Martin Book
Houghton Mifflin Harcourt ★ Boston New York 2014

For information about permission to reproduce selections from this book,
write to Permissions, Houghton Mifflin Harcourt Publishing Company,
215 Park Avenue South, New York, New York 10003.

www.hmhco.com

Samuelsson, Marcus.
   Marcus off duty : the recipes I cook at home / Marcus Samuelsson with Roy Finamore ;
photography by Paul Brissman.
      p.  cm.
"A Rux Martin Book."
ISBN 978-0-470-94058-7 (paper over board); 978-0-544-30927-2  (ebk)
1. Cooking.  2. Samuelsson, Marcus.  I. Finamore, Roy.  II. Title.
TX714.S257 2014
641.5—dc23   2014018169

Book design by Endpaper Studio
Typeset in Benton Sans
Hand lettering by Joel Holland

Printed in the United States of America
DOW 10 9 8 7 6 5 4 3 2 1

This book would have only been a cover and blank pages
without the tribe of farmers, butchers, cooks, chefs, mothers,
fathers, artisans, and shack owners I met along the way—
you know who you are. This is a love letter to you.

And to my mom.
Tack!

LEAH CHASE  DANNY BOWIEN
GABRIELLE HAMILTON  ED LEE
JOHN BESH  SCOTT CONANT  ROY CHOI
ERIC RIPERT  AARON SANCHEZ
ANTHONY BOURDAIN  ALEX GUARNASCHELLI  CHRIS SANTOS
NIGELLA LAWSON  LUDO LEFEBVRE  ALEX STUPAK
AMANDA FREITAG  JAMIE BISSONNETTE  GEOFFREY ZAKARIAN
YOTAM OTTOLENGHI  LINTON HOPKINS  MARC MURPHY
ALICE WATERS  HUGH ACHESON  CHARLIE TROTTER  TED ALLEN
JONATHAN WAXMAN  CHRIS COSENTINO

## ACKNOWLEDGMENTS

*To my wife, Maya, thank you for your love, patience, and support of the book.*
*Sorry we messed up the kitchen for a summer. I owe you a lot of dinners at home.*
*To Rux Martin, for keeping us honest.*
*To Kim Witherspoon, for staying with it and moving it forward.*
*To Roy Finamore, your knowledge and wit are unparalleled. We laughed a lot.*
*To Paul Brissman, five years into it and you didn't give up.*
*To Nils and Vicki, thank you for opening your home. Where's my homemade ramen?*
*To Jeannette Park, you put in a lot of tears, love, and dedication to make the book*
*great. I think you're in it four times.*
*To Eden Fesehaye, you got this started.*
*To Ashley Bode, for all your hard work.*

To Meaghan Dillon and Ashley Beck, your contributions were invaluable.

To James Bowen, I think we made you smile one time.

To Rebekah Maysles, for your incredible illustrations and enthusiasm for the project.

To Joel, Mark, and the kitchen team at Red Rooster, thanks for always helping us at the last minute.

To Klancy Miller, your efforts paved the way.

To Veronica Chambers, thank you for all your help.

To Elvis Mitchell and Brian Duncan, who gave us context.

To the Samuelsson tribe: Helga, Anne-Marie, Edwin, Lennart, Anna, Linda, and Vanessa. I love you all.
    Let's eat together soon.

Special thanks to the St. Supéry winery in Napa for their gracious hospitality.

And to the cowboy who held us up at gunpoint in Fort Worth, way to keep it real.

# CONTENTS

# INTRODUCTION

I'VE COME FULL CIRCLE. I STARTED TO LEARN ABOUT COOKING IN MY GRAND-mother's kitchen. But when I started my journey to the professional kitchen, cooking at home wasn't a priority.

I was fifteen when I applied for and was accepted at the local vocational school where my training began. The meals I learned to cook there were straight out of classic French sources like *Larousse Gastronomique,* but not quite as good. (A successful day at this public school was when one kid didn't throw food at another.) It wasn't long before I started wondering about mixing the foods of other cultures—like the Greek dishes my friend's mother would make—with the French food I was learning. I graduated second in my class and set off to conquer the world of restaurants with a set of knives—the gift of my sisters—and the first of a library of journals where I kept notes on everything from the nutty taste of rouget—a fish I had never heard of—to menu items written in French or German or Italian so I could translate them in my room at night (and not have to ask the chef I was working for what *tafelspitz* was).

My first apprenticeship, or *stage*, was in Switzerland at the Victoria-Jungfrau, a hotel with a large international clientele. Although our menu was mostly classic European, sticky rice and exotic mushrooms would appear with contingents of Japanese tourists—my first exposure to Japanese food. Then to Austria, for a short stint at a hotel

that catered to locals where the menu was strictly regional. Here's where I learned to make *tafelspitz*—aged sirloin braised with carrots and parsnips. It's rich and savory and delicious, but I couldn't help thinking how much better it would be if it was served with Swedish lingonberries. I returned to Switzerland, climbing a few steps up the ladder in the kitchen hierarchy.

A *stage* at a three-star spot in France was my dream, but my next port was actually New York City, where I was to spend nine months at a now-famous Swedish restaurant called Aquavit. My chef was Christer Larsson, who showed me how to

I'm constantly asked, "What's the most important tool in the kitchen?" For me, it's hands. They give us the authority to call any dish ours. Think of strudel dough stretched with the back of your hands, couscous rolled between your palms, Chinese noodles pulled to imperfect perfection. We use our hands to mix meatballs, to knead dough, to prod fish or meat, or tap a cake to determine doneness. Cooks on television always taste with a spoon, but at home we know our hands are clean and we taste with our fingers. My grandmother would always ladle her gravy into her palm and slurp it up. "You have to taste a lot of gravy to get it," she'd say.

There's a Korean saying: sson maat. It translates as "hand taste," but the meaning is that the food tastes so good because the cook has the taste in her fingertips.

Our hands are an elemental way of putting food into our mouths, too. You're never closer to your food than when you lick the dripping juices from a burger off the side of your hand. Eating with your hands is also an indication of the greatest trust and sharing. In Ethiopia, eating with your hands is gursha, a sign of the utmost trust and sharing.

elevate regional Swedish classics to new levels. I worked long and hard to refine my craft, but as soon as I had time off I'd put on my Rollerblades and explore the city. I discovered kimchi in Koreatown, found the spice stores in Little India, and got lost in the wonders of Chinatown. I like being lost in a food place. In Chinatown I wandered among dim sum palaces, sidewalk fish shops, and grocery stores whose crowded aisles were filled with ingredients I had never seen.

I was in love with New York, but I knew that to become a chef myself, I needed the authority that experience in France would give me. After all, the French had set the bar in defining and codifying the restaurant kitchen. I finally got an invitation to work in a three-star restaurant in Vonnas, France, but Georges Blanc would only cover room and board. I needed to make money to get to France and live there.

Salvation came from my old boss in Switzerland. Paul Griggs was now working for a Norwegian cruise line and needed a cook. Was I interested? I jumped at the chance. I had been filling my journals with ideas for new combinations of flavors and cultures, and I stole time on the ship to try them out. I was ready when Chef Paul asked for ideas for specials, and for the first time, I found *my* food making it onto a menu. These trips also gave me an introduction to new worlds of food. I ate grilled fish on the beach in Jamaica, and sun-ripe tomatoes rubbed onto a piece of grilled bread and drizzled with olive oil in Spain. I watched women in Acapulco slapping masa between their hands to make tortillas, and I devoured my first tacos. I ate roast pork and sliced onions piled onto a warm tortilla with salsa and avocados and brightened with a squirt of lime. Then we sailed to Southeast Asia, and I found new smells, new tastes, and new flavors to fall in love with. I discovered the sharp bite of ginger that pushes itself forward in a dish—so different from the flavor of dried ginger that I grew up with. I had seen kaffir lime leaves in the spice stores in New York, but in Singapore I *tasted* them in dish after dish. They had that sparkle, but it was so different from the way I had experienced limes in Mexico. I chewed on these ingredients, and I liked them. I started to think about how I could take the flavors of the world and apply them to a different cuisine. It was something I put into practice when I became chef at Aquavit.

I came back to New York after a year working with Georges Blanc. I had never seen such ingredients; everything was perfect. Blanc's approach to his restaurant was a

major influence on me. He honored the rustic heritage of his mother (La Mère Blanc created the chicken dish that was one of his signatures), he explored new techniques and ingredients, and he kept a high level of elegance.

At last I took the role of restaurant chef, at Aquavit. My life was like that of most restaurant chefs: I explored flavors and textures and I built on all my experiences to

When I think about a pantry shot fifty years—even twenty years ago—I imagine it like an iconic Andy Warhol painting—tomato soup, corn flakes, ketchup, and shortening. An American pantry today reflects where we are now and where we are going. Our tastebuds are changing to reflect a more culturally diverse palate.

create signature dishes. I reveled in the craftsmanship and precision—like a ballerina *en pointe*—of cooking in a fine-dining restaurant. I was living in a tiny apartment with no real kitchen; I did no cooking at home. When money allowed, I'd eat at my friends' restaurants—like Jean-Georges Vongerichten's Vong, where he was doing amazing things with the tastes of Southeast Asia—for research, and I kept up with my love affair with street food. I was always on duty. Even when I traveled to Ethiopia to find my family there, I brought back the spice mix berbere with thoughts about how I would use it in the restaurant—not how I might just stir it into rice at home.

Things started to change around 2000. I moved into a larger apartment with a real kitchen and would host the cooks from the restaurant who had no place to go. I was the only one with a place to myself. And there's no doubt that the events of 9/11 were a marker. Like many of us, I started to look for things I could place more trust in and things that gave me comfort. I'd make something at home and found that being off duty had a lot to say for itself.

More important, though, was getting married. With my wife, Maya, I have made a *home*. Home was something

The beauty of cooking at home is that you don't need to spend lots of money on a variety of tools. A really good chef's knife, heavy-duty pots and pans, a high-efficiency blender, and sturdy wooden spoons are really all you need to create gorgeous dishes in your kitchen. Use your hands, get creative, and don't feel you need to spend money on things like a strawberry huller. A paring knife and some imagination will take you a long way.

I thought about a lot when I was chosen to be chef for the Obamas' first state dinner. The White House may be a national symbol, but it was also the Obamas' home, where they sat down with Sasha and Malia for breakfast. I didn't want this to be yet another French dinner—it felt like all state dinners were French dinners, with chefs presenting their "best" dishes. Couldn't it be more like a house party? The dinner was to honor Prime Minister Manmohan Singh of India and his wife, Gursharan Kaur, who are both vegetarian. So I started to put together a menu of dishes that reflected both American and Indian tastes. There would be greens from Michelle's garden (it doesn't

get more homey than that) with a vinaigrette featuring onion seed—a very Indian ingredient. Both Indians and Americans eat lentils, so I made red lentil soup. A vegetarian main course, with a prawn option for the omnivores. And for dessert, pumpkin tart scented with garam masala.

I started the meal with a bread basket. The White House had never seen such a thing at a formal dinner, but there is no better way to break down barriers than by breaking bread together. We put out corn bread and naan, chutney and sambal, and instructed the servers to just place the bread on the table. So the meal began with the feeling of home, with guests passing the bread to each other and creating a community.

A few hours before the meal, I called my mother in Sweden from the White House kitchen. I told her where I was and what I was doing, and she said, "Ah. What an excellent opportunity for a screwup." Mothers are always right. This was the night of the party crashers. They were discovered and ejected before everyone was seated, but they captured all the press about the event. No matter, I had prepared humble food that spoke of home in the highest of settings.

Here's my full circle: I understand that I belong in a kitchen at home. And I have homes in many places. When I'm in Sweden, I'll cook meatballs in my mother's kitchen and we'll eat them together the same way we did in Göteborg thirty years ago. And like any Swede, I make herring or mackerel for the sisters I grew up with, and it will be as salty as our conversations. When I visit my daughter, we hike in the mountains, and when we come back to her mother's house she'll help me make something warming, with sauerkraut and apples. There isn't really a kitchen in my father's house in Ethiopia. There I'll cook with my sisters over an open fire, and Maya will help, and the food will taste of Africa, and I won't want it to end.

Maya and I cook for each other often in our Harlem brownstone, which has a rich history of people who lived here before us. Legend has it that rapper Heavy D lived here, and I know Kareem Abdul-Jabbar was an owner, because everything in the place is tall. (Music and sports? I had to buy this place.) The kitchen has some problems. The refrigerator door hits the island when I open it, and there's a cabinet above the refrigerator that no one can reach without a big stepladder. But the stove works, and that's what matters. When I redo the kitchen, I want to put a pantry downstairs—like the shelves my grandmother had in her basement, laden with her preserves and jams with their paper labels. I want to run up and down the stairs like I did when I was a kid, and I want kids to run up and down, too.

I improvise dinner for Maya after she's been away for work. Maybe it will be some rice with berbere and spiced butter, a roast apple salad with bitter frisée, some roasted vegetables, and a little bit of meat—a few Korean short ribs. Whatever it is, when Maya opens the door, she's greeted by aromas that tell her, "You're home." To me, this is the highest way of saying, "I love you. I care." And we can remember the meal the next day and smile. The leftovers—however we reinvent them—are delicious.

Maya is exacting when she makes the food of her childhood, and it's like a cooking class for me. When her sisters come to visit—with gifts of food from Ethiopia, the way my grandmother would bring the gifts from her basement shelves—the kitchen turns into an episode from *Chopped*. But there is always a reason. "Our friend has just had a baby and this dish is what we have to make for her." It's the spiritual compass that started for me in Sweden but, through Maya, has become a part of my life.

Home cooking is now where many of my restaurant dishes start. I ask my cooks what they make at home and how they make it. There's a sign—H. Jönsson—over the kitchen at the Red Rooster, my restaurant in Harlem. That way I am reminded every day of my grandmother Helga, whose second name was Jönsson and with whom my journey into the kitchen began. I remember what I eat—there are still journals— and use those memories to make food where the comfort of home is an ingredient.

When I'm frying something at home, I may throw a garlic clove or a sprig of rose- mary into the oil. Not because it's in a recipe; I think I may want it later. Or if the chicken came with a liver, I cook it and chop it up for the gravy or a salad. That's not something I can do in a restaurant, where consistency is the goal. But this kind of improvisation is exciting. It's me being off duty. I hope these recipes from my home inspire you to create your own vocabularies and memories.

★   ★   ★

Our ethnicity has always been one of our **comforts of home**. It's a good thing, it's a great thing that we pay homage to our heritage at the table, like when an Irish girl marries the Italian boy and it's mash-up time. But why stop there, now that we're exposed to such a wider mix of influences in our lives? I start as an Ethiopian raised in Sweden and trained in French techniques, but I bring the flavors of many cultures to my table. Let's all take advantage of as many food cultures as we can. We live in the United States of Flavor.

Maybe because owning a restaurant is so much about entertaining, I don't throw many big parties at home. But it was actually thanks to a home party that I met my wife, and I am grateful for that. Maya and I do a lot of cooking now for **friends and family**. This isn't "entertaining." It's just cooking those comfortable dishes—maybe something we can eat with our hands—that brings us all together.

My customers come to the restaurant for **special days**, so you could say that celebrations are my business. "It's my birthday." "We just got married." "I'm bringing Mom for Mother's Day." If we in the hospitality business ever get tired of catering those celebrations, it's time for us to close our doors. It shouldn't be any different when you're cooking at home; you are spending special days with loved ones. Keep joy in your heart. When you're preparing for Father's Day, start by asking yourself, "What is the food Dad really likes?" And when the big days are approaching, keep your soul in mind. Hold back on what you eat before, so when the day arrives,

it can be like the pop when you pull the cork from a bottle of Champagne.

I'm comfortable at home and impressed at a good restaurant, but when I eat **street food**, I get excited. There's the noise of traffic, the chance I might get jostled. It doesn't matter. I'm almost giddy when it's my turn to order. There's no category of food that's more "feel-based"—it's bold. It creates an instant reaction, a feeling. And it's such good food to cook at home.

We all carry images in our minds and hearts of dads at the grill, **playing with fire**, and grilling is one of these instances where home cooks have taught restaurants. These days, the first thing to go into the kitchen plan of a new restaurant is a top-of-the-line grill. And we're all learning more about technique. Fire doesn't always do what we want it to, so we need to learn to respect it and to manage it. Different levels of heat let us sear, then slow things down, and maybe have a warm spot where meat can rest.

One of the things I think about when I'm **cooking with kids** is that there's no kids' music in Africa or in Jamaica or in India. There's no kids' food, either. You find several generations together—all experiencing the same thing at the same time. And American kids today have been exposed to a world of flavors that I had never even heard of when I was young. So I don't cook down to kids, and I don't think the idea of making something different for them is a good one. Bring kids into the kitchen; expand their knowledge of food and techniques. I would bet that you'll learn from them, too, as I do.

**Soups** have taken the elevator up from being a poor folk's dish made with the ingredients you have on hand to being food you shop for and serve to company. I'm not talking about old-school consommé here, but something both elegant and humble—like a bowl of fresh pea soup garnished with seared scallops. Take pride in your soups.

Think about a meal of curried lentils, rice, stewed eggplant, and potatoes. You wouldn't say that you just ate "side dishes" for dinner; you had a very satisfying meal. I wish we had a better word to describe these dishes. Look to the seasons when you make **sides and condiments**. Capture the incomparable flavor of summer tomatoes by slow-roasting them and freezing them. Make the most of winter with a salad of oranges and fennel, crunchy with pecans. And please make pickles. Pickled cabbage. Pickled cucumbers. Pickled beets. We need that bit of tang on our plates.

Desserts at home should make you happy, and if they don't you haven't done your job. I don't like to toot my own horn, but I think my Lipstick Cobbler is amazing, and it always makes me smile. It also succeeds in the other way that **something sweet** should seduce you. You say to yourself, "No, I shouldn't," but you do. You have one more bite.

Food has a different taste in different places. My mother made fish and boiled potatoes a lot when I was a kid. When we were at the summer house, we'd eat them outside, with the smell of salt in the air; if it rained, we moved inside and looked out the windows at the sea. That meal never tasted the same in the city. After dinner at my grandmother's, my grandfather would go to sit by his radio and drink his coffee. He didn't drink coffee like anyone else I've ever seen. He would pour hot coffee into his saucer, put a sugar cube in his mouth, and slurp the cooled coffee from the plate. We'd keep him company and eat something sweet, so when I remember that radio room, I can taste dessert.

This book can be eaten all over the house. Let different spaces have their own tastes. Enjoy making the food. And enjoy eating it.

# ONE THING THAT USED TO SET CHEFS

apart was that we could get better ingredients. It's great that things have become more democratic. But we still have an edge when it comes to technique. Part of it is training and part of it is repetition, and it's really the repetition that makes a chef great. There's nothing technically complicated in the recipes in this book, but here are some things to keep in mind.

Pay attention to how you use your stove. I use the front right burner for the hottest stuff—when I'm searing or sautéing and using the handle of the pan; you might use the other front burner if you're left-handed. Keep the slow stuff on the back burners. And have respect for your oven. Always protect your hands, and don't stick your face in. The oven temperature drops quickly when you open the door, so when you're basting or checking an internal temperature, take the roasting pan out of the oven and close the door.

Pots and pans are like shoes; you have different ones for different moments. Take a skillet: Cast iron performs differently from nonstick. And since our home stoves never produce the blast of heat that Chinese cooks get from their wok stoves, use the largest skillet you have when you stir-fry—or work in batches. If the ingredients are crowded, they'll steam, not fry.

Sautéing—cooking over pretty high heat in a little bit of fat—is like being in the fast lane on the highway of cooking. Keep focused and make adjustments. You might need a little more heat if something's sticking, or you may just need to release it with the back of your spatula. Here's when you might find that your fish isn't as fresh as you thought it was or that the scallops have been dipped in preservative because they release so much water.

You are working fast when you sear over high heat. Tell yourself, "I'm going in!" and get the pan and oil screaming hot, but not so hot that the oil is smoking. Listen for the sound of an immediate sizzle. If you don't hear it, get the pan hotter before adding anything else.

I can't imagine a spice-driven cuisine where spices aren't toasted to release their essence. Even though you won't be using high heat, they can go from toasted to burned quickly. Use your nose and eyes and get the spices out of the pan as soon as they're fragrant; even if you take the pan off the heat the spices will continue to toast.

Sometimes you need rapidly boiling water. Use high heat, a big pot, and a lot of water when you blanch vegetables. The temperature won't drop as much when you add the veggies, and the water will come back to the fast boil you need to set the color.

When you simmer, look for steady bubbles, not a sputtering fury. And gentler still is poaching, when the bubbles are slow and lazy, quietly transforming a protein to tender doneness. Cook aromatics over medium or medium-low heat. It's a first step, softening the onion, taking the bite out of garlic, or coaxing flavor from a bell pepper.

ORGANIC WHOLE GRAIN BREAD

Cooking for me is like jazz. You start with a solid base and add riffs and beats as you feel the need. Music has always been at the core of who I am and how I entertain. I never hosted anything—from my dorm room in Switzerland to parties at home where my mom and I would make mix tapes to every night at Red Rooster—without a great playlist. I've included music to cook by in every chapter. Feel free to add your own beats and have fun doing it.

# COMFORTS OF HOME

I'VE KNOWN SEVERAL HOMES. THERE IS MY CHILDHOOD HOME IN GÖTEBORG, on the west coast of Sweden, where I learned to roast chicken with my grandmother Helga and where childhood fishing trips with my dad and uncles gave me a lifelong love of seafood. As a boy, being out on a fishing boat with the men in my family made me happy and grateful to eat anything and everything we caught.

There is New York City, the city of many neighborhoods where I live and work. Here's where I discovered the basement grocery stores of Chinatown and the spice shops of Little India on Lexington Avenue and the smells of kimchi and barbecue in Koreatown. And where, on the streets of Harlem, I discover more every day—like our new farmers' market.

And there is Ethiopia, the land of my birth. I can still remember the shock of my first sniff of berbere, the spice mix that Ethiopians use in everything. I visit Ethiopia every year now, but I learn much more about the food from my wife, Maya. She not only teaches me how to make dishes, but also why we eat them.

Every dedicated home cook is a compendium of influences that start from childhood. What I think is interesting is that we're at a moment when our home cooking styles not only reflect our childhood, but the increasing diversity of our adult lives as well. In addition to my three homes, I worked in Switzerland and France. I cooked on cruise ships that ran from the Caribbean to St. Petersburg. And I travel for work and for play. All of these experiences have had an effect on my food. And on my soul.

DILL-SPICED SALMON  30

SKIN-ON MACKEREL (OR SALMON) WITH LIME-SOY SAUCE  32

STEAMED CATFISH WITH CITRUS-SOY VINAIGRETTE  34

BOURBON SHRIMP WITH BABY SPINACH  36

BACK-IN-HABANA GRILLED HAM & CHEESE  37

SERVE-THEM-UP FRIED-SNAPPER TACOS  38

CHICKEN-FRIED STEAK ON A SALAD  40

ORANGE-CURRY BEEF STIR-FRY WITH BROCCOLINI  42

CRAB FRIED RICE  44

QUINOA WITH BROCCOLI, CAULIFLOWER & TOASTED COCONUT  46

COCONUT-LIME CURRIED CHICKEN  48

CHICKEN & GRAVY, FOR AUNT GINNY  50

SEARED SCALLOPS WITH BACON & EGG  52

THE-DAY-AFTER PASTA FRITTATA  54

PYTT I PANNA (THAT'S HASH, TO YOU)  56

STICKY BACON SANDWICHES  58

# MUSIC TO COOK BY

Push It ★ Salt-n-Pepa

Fame ★ David Bowie

Giant Steps ★ John Coltrane

Electric Relaxation ★ A Tribe Called Quest

Never Miss the Water ★ Chaka Khan
   featuring Meshell Ndegeocello

Heart of Glass ★ Blondie

I Would Die 4 U ★ Prince

Hey Ya! ★ Outkast

Open the Door ★ Betty Carter

Got 'til It's Gone ★ Janet Jackson featuring Q-Tip
   and Joni Mitchell

Chicken (Kikirikiki) ★ Miriam Makeba

Jungle Love ★ The Time

Here Comes the Sun ★ Nina Simone
   (François K. remix)

Angie ★ Rolling Stones

# DILL-SPICED SALMON

**SERVES 4**

Salmon with dill is the Swedish equivalent to American meat loaf. When I was growing up in Sweden, it was the weeknight dish that every family had almost every week. I still love the simplicity of this dish, although I now kick up the heat a few notches with a few dashes of chile powder. I love to pair this salmon with Raw Kale Salad (page 276); the mix of kale and root vegetables makes a salad that's not only healthy, but restaurant-level impressive.

This cooking technique will give you salmon that's creamy, almost custardy. If you prefer it more well done, leave it in the skillet for a few more minutes.

4 tablespoons olive oil

Juice of 1 lemon

1 tablespoon Dijon mustard

2 tablespoons chopped fresh dill

2 garlic cloves, thinly sliced

4½ teaspoons chile powder

1 tablespoon coriander seeds, finely ground

1 teaspoon cumin seeds, finely ground

Freshly ground black pepper

4 (6-ounce) skin-on salmon fillets

Kosher salt

1 tablespoon unsalted butter

I was taught to pick herb leaves, but one day I saw a Mexican cook chopping cilantro, stems and all. And it hit me—stems have a lot of flavor. So use the dill stems; just chop them fine.

1. In a mini food processor, blend 2 tablespoons of the olive oil, the lemon juice, mustard, dill, garlic, chile powder, coriander, cumin, and ¼ teaspoon pepper into a paste. Transfer the paste to a bowl.

2. Season the salmon fillets with salt and pepper.

3. Heat the remaining 2 tablespoons olive oil in a large skillet over medium-high heat. When it shimmers, add the salmon fillets, skin side down, and brush half of the paste on the fillets. Cook for 4 minutes, then add the butter. Continue to cook, spooning the oil and butter over the salmon, for 2 minutes. You'll see the color changing as the salmon cooks from the bottom. Flip the salmon and brush the remaining paste onto the other side. You just want the heat to kiss the salmon on this side, so take it out after a few seconds. Let the salmon rest for a few minutes before serving.

Coming up in the kitchens throughout Europe, I rarely saw female chefs. But Amaryll Schwertner of Boulettes Larder at San Francisco's Ferry Building impressed me with her attention and skill.

# SKIN-ON MACKEREL (OR SALMON) WITH LIME-SOY SAUCE

**SERVES 6**

Mackerel is the fish I caught the most when I was a kid. I'd ride out in the boat with my dad and Uncle T. They'd drop the anchor, and we'd set out the four rods on each side of the boat. I always used to wonder, "How do they know where the fish are?" but soon I'd be running from one side of the boat to the other, reeling in mackerel. It was a great job for a kid like me; it kept me busy. But I have to admit that taking the fish off the hook intimidated me. We'd usually catch thirty fish. We'd eat ten for lunch, Uncle Torsten would smoke ten, five would go to the neighbors, and I'd have five to sell—that was my pocket money.

I love the fattiness of mackerel, and I'm game for any recipe that pairs it with salty and citrusy components. Add honey to soy sauce and lime juice and you have a glaze reminiscent of teriyaki. I introduced this dish, which speaks so much to me of home, to Maya. We turn to it whenever we want to make a quick but impressive dinner.

1 tablespoon soy sauce

1 tablespoon honey

Zest of 1 lime

1 tablespoon fresh lime juice

2 teaspoons sesame seeds

1½ teaspoons sesame oil

12 (3- to 4-ounces each) skin-on mackerel fillets or salmon fillets

Note: You can substitute 7-ounce center-cut salmon fillets for the mackerel. They'll broil in about 6 minutes.

1. Position an oven rack 6 inches from the heating element and preheat the broiler.

2. Stir the soy sauce, honey, lime zest, lime juice, sesame seeds, and sesame oil together in a small bowl.

3. Put the fish, skin side down, on a baking sheet and brush with the soy-lime mixture.

4. Broil until almost cooked through, about 3 minutes. It should have just a little give when you prod it and the surface will be caramelized and sticky—like a toffee. You can serve the mackerel immediately or at room temperature.

F CERTIFIED ORGANIC

VEET LIME
(PERSIAN LEMON)

$2.00 pound

*Broiling fish isn't a good time for multitasking. Pay attention, and keep your eye on the fish.*

*I played a lot of soccer when I was growing up. My team was called GAIS and our symbol was a mackerel.*

# STEAMED CATFISH
## WITH CITRUS-SOY VINAIGRETTE

**SERVES 4**

Catfish is like an old jazz standard. It's familiar—and you think you're kind of tired of it. Then you hear someone play it in an entirely new way, and you remember that it's a standard not because someone famous wrote it, or because someone famous sang it. It's a standard because, at the heart of it, there's something universal and true and good. Catfish has been part of the home cook's repertoire for hundreds of years. It's as popular in Europe and Asia as it is in North America and Africa.

My favorite way to prepare catfish is to steam it. Steaming is quick, and it adds some elegance to this common fish. (You can buy a stack-and-steam pot or a bamboo steamer in most kitchenware stores, Chinese markets, and online.) But what really sets this recipe apart is the citrus-soy vinaigrette; it infuses the delicate fillets with a bright, slightly spicy, Asian flavor.

**FOR THE VINAIGRETTE**
**1 garlic clove, minced**
**1 (1-inch) piece ginger, peeled and grated**
**Zest and juice of 1 lime**
**Zest and juice of 1 orange**
**2 tablespoons soy sauce**
**1 teaspoon sesame oil**
**½ teaspoon fish sauce**
**½ teaspoon sugar**
**2 tablespoons olive oil**

**FOR THE FISH**
**4 (6-ounce) catfish fillets**
**Peels from the garlic and ginger**
**Shells from the lime and orange**
**Coarse sea salt**

Save the lime and orange shells and the ginger and garlic peels when you prep the vinaigrette and drop them into the steaming liquid for the fish. They all add flavor.

**MAKE THE VINAIGRETTE**

1. Put all the ingredients except the olive oil in a jar, cover, and shake vigorously. Strain the solids through a fine-mesh sieve. Reserve the solids and liquid.

2. Heat the olive oil in a small saucepan over medium-low heat. Add the solids and cook until the garlic is fragrant, 1 to 2 minutes. Add the reserved liquid, bring to a boil, and cook for 1 minute. Set aside to cool.

**STEAM THE FISH**

3. Place 1 inch of water in the bottom of a steamer, along with ginger and garlic peels, lime and orange shells, and sea salt to taste. Cover the steamer and bring the water to a boil. Remove the lid, lay the fish on the steamer racks, making sure the rack is elevated above the water, and cover again. Steam until the fish is opaque and flaky, about 4 minutes.

4. To serve, plate the fish and drizzle with the vinaigrette.

# BOURBON SHRIMP WITH BABY SPINACH

**SERVES 4 AS AN APPETIZER OR 2 AS A MAIN DISH**

I learned about layering flavors watching my grandmother roast chicken; layering textures came later. Here the sweet bourbon glaze reinforces the natural sweetness of the shrimp, while tender, silky spinach provides the counterpoint.

If you can find them, use head-on shrimp. Eating them with their heads on changes the whole dining experience. It makes it more of a feast. I grew up eating crayfish and shrimp this way in Sweden, holding the heads in our fingers and sucking what we called "the good stuff."

Whatever shrimp you cook, eat them with your fingers. This is not the time for refinement.

**12 jumbo (U10, see page 77) shrimp, peeled, tails left on**
**3 tablespoons olive oil**
**½ teaspoon smoked paprika**
**Kosher salt**
**2 tablespoons bourbon**
**1 tablespoon honey**
**1 tablespoon unsalted butter**
**2 cups baby spinach**
**2 tablespoons chopped fresh mint**
**2 tablespoons chopped fresh basil**
**2 tablespoons fresh lemon juice**
**Freshly ground black pepper**

1. Toss the shrimp with the olive oil, paprika, and salt to taste in a large bowl.
2. Heat a large sauté pan over high heat. Add the shrimp in batches and sauté until pink and curled, about 2 minutes on each side. Transfer to a platter.
3. Add the bourbon, honey, and butter to the skillet. Cook for 1 minute, then remove from the heat. Stir in the baby spinach, mint, basil, and lemon juice. Give it a taste and season with salt and pepper.
4. Spoon the spinach and any glaze in the pan over the shrimp and serve.

# BACK-IN-HABANA GRILLED HAM & CHEESE

**SERVES 4**

Thanks to my Swedish passport, I was able to visit the magical island of Cuba a few years ago where I stayed with a family. The husband was a lawyer and doctor who rented rooms in their home; the wife ran a *paladar*—a family-owned restaurant where tourists can find real Cuban food. I had a long bus trip planned for one day, and she made me this sandwich for the road. The toasty, buttery bread, the salty ham, the tangy mustard and pickles. For a more hearty meal, serve the sandwich with a cup of Pickled Tomato Soup (page 246).

**4 tablespoons (½ stick) unsalted butter, softened**
**1 loaf Italian or Portuguese bread, sliced lengthwise**
**1 tablespoon yellow mustard**
**1½ pounds leftover country ham or baked ham, thinly sliced**
**1 pound Swiss cheese, sliced**
**1 cup dill pickle chips, or more to taste**

Try making this with big potato rolls. They're soft and sweet and get deliciously crunchy. And if you have some leftover roast pork, by all means add it to the sandwich.

1. Preheat a gas grill to high.

2. Spread 2 tablespoons of the softened butter on the bottom half of the bread and the mustard on the top. Layer the ham, cheese, and pickles on the buttered side and top with the mustard-spread bread.

3. Smear the remaining 2 tablespoons butter on the exterior of the bread and wrap the sandwich completely in aluminum foil. Press down firmly on the sandwich to flatten it.

4. Place the wrapped, flattened sandwich on the grill and top with a couple of bricks, a cast iron skillet, or any other heavy, heat-resistant object. Close the lid and grill the sandwich for 5 minutes. Flip it, weight it again, and grill for 5 minutes on the other side.

5. Using tongs, remove the wrapped sandwich from the grill and take off the foil. Return the sandwich to the grill and grill until the outside is crisp and golden brown, 2 to 3 minutes per side.

6. Carefully take the sandwich from the grill and cut it at an angle into small triangles. Place the sandwiches on a large platter and serve them hot.

# SERVE-THEM-UP FRIED SNAPPER TACOS

**SERVES 4**

I had the amazing opportunity to cook fish tacos
with tennis greats Serena and Venus Williams
in a cooking demo. We dusted snapper with a
smoky-tomatoey spice mix, fried it, and topped
it with an heirloom tomato, mango, and avocado
salsa. This is a pretty simple dish to demo, but I
couldn't stop thinking about the wobbly table we
were working at and the hot oil and how I didn't
want to see the pot knocked over onto Venus or
Serena the day before the U.S. Open. But we pulled
it off without a hitch, and I could relax and enjoy
these flavorful tacos.

Use what heirloom tomatoes
you can find, but think about a
variety of colors and flavors, from
Black Galaxy to Green Zebra to
Sun Gold to Brandywine.

**Note:** Tomato powder,
dehydrated tomatoes
ground to a fine powder,
has an intense flavor. It
is available in specialty
stores and online. You
can use it whenever
you need a little tomato
paste and don't want
to open a can. Store it
in the refrigerator so it
won't clump.

### FOR THE FISH SPICE

¼ cup tomato powder (see Note)

¼ cup smoked paprika

¼ cup Wondra flour

3 tablespoons chipotle chile
   powder

1 tablespoon kosher salt

### FOR THE SALSA

1 small red onion, finely chopped

1½ pounds chopped (¼-inch dice) heirloom tomatoes

1 mango, peeled and cut into
  ¼-inch dice
1 jalapeño, seeds removed, minced
2 tablespoons chopped fresh mint
2 tablespoons chopped fresh cilantro
2 avocados, halved, seeded, and cut
  into ¼-inch dice
Juice of 2 limes
Kosher salt

### FOR THE FISH TACOS
Canola oil, for frying
2 garlic cloves, peeled
1 pound snapper fillets, cut into
  strips
Kosher salt
8 corn tortillas
2 limes, cut into eighths

### MAKE THE FISH SPICE
1. Whisk all the ingredients together in a shallow bowl.

### MAKE THE SALSA
2. Rinse the chopped onion in a small strainer under cold water and shake off the excess water. Put the onion in a bowl and add the tomatoes, mango, jalapeño, and herbs. Stir to combine. Fold in the avocados (gently, to preserve their texture) and lime juice. Taste and season with kosher salt—about ½ teaspoon.

### MAKE THE TACOS
3. Pour about 1 inch oil into a cast iron skillet. Add the garlic and heat to 350°F.
4. Dredge the snapper strips in the fish spice, patting off the excess, and place on a plate.
5. Fry the fish in batches until golden brown, 2 to 3 minutes. Transfer with a skimmer or slotted spoon to paper towels to drain. Sprinkle with a little kosher salt.
6. Heat the tortillas in a hot, dry skillet until pliable and browned in spots, about 20 seconds a side.
7. To serve, break the snapper up with a fork. Pile onto the tortillas and top with the salsa. Serve immediately with lime wedges.

# CHICKEN-FRIED STEAK ON A SALAD

**SERVES 4**

Although I'm not a Southern chef, soul food has had a tremendous influence on me. My mentor Leah Chase has been a legend in New Orleans for more than seven decades now. From her I've learned that the best soul food not only tastes good, but also makes you feel good. I start by layering the garlic powder and celery salt you'd usually find in fried chicken coating with smoked paprika and the Ethiopian spice mix berbere for an uptown edge.

Traditionally, this steak would be served with heavy sides: some mac and cheese, buttery mashed potatoes, and some greens cooked with a ham hock—and gravy. Pairing it with a salad of arugula and tomatoes makes it not only an easier weeknight meal but a healthier, more balanced dish. And the smoky Caesar dressing is my nod to that ham hock in the greens.

## FOR THE SMOKY CAESAR DRESSING

**2 large egg yolks**
**1 tablespoon Dijon mustard**
**1 teaspoon liquid smoke**
**2 garlic cloves, peeled**
**3 anchovy fillets**
**½ cup olive oil**
**Juice of 2 limes**

## FOR THE STEAK

**1 pound flank steak or top round steak**
   **(London broil), brought to room temperature,**
   **or leftover steak**
**Kosher salt and freshly ground white pepper**
**Olive oil, for brushing**
**1 large egg**
**1 large egg white**
**1 cup panko bread crumbs**
**2 tablespoons cornstarch**
**2 teaspoons Berbere (page 297)**

*If you have a sprig of rosemary, throw it into the oil while you fry the steaks. Drain it on paper towels, then strip the crisp needles off the stem and scatter them over the salad.*

2 teaspoons smoked paprika

1 teaspoon celery salt

1 teaspoon ground cumin

½ teaspoon garlic powder

½ teaspoon kosher salt

1 teaspoon freshly ground white
  pepper

½ cup canola oil

**FOR THE SALAD**

4 cups arugula

½ cup cherry tomatoes, halved

½ cup grape tomatoes, halved

½ red onion, thinly sliced

*The incomparable Leah Chase*

**MAKE THE DRESSING**

1. Combine the egg yolks, mustard, liquid smoke, garlic, and anchovies in a blender and puree until smooth. With the motor running, add the ½ cup olive oil and the lime juice in a slow, steady stream and blend until emulsified, about 1 minute. Set aside.

**MAKE THE STEAK**

2. If using uncooked steak, place a grill pan over high heat. Season the steak with salt and white pepper or whatever spice blend you like. Brush the steak with olive oil and grill until medium-rare, about 5 minutes on each side. Remove from the heat and let rest for 5 minutes. Cut the grilled or leftover steak into thin strips.

3. Whisk the egg and egg white together in a shallow bowl. Put the panko, cornstarch, berbere, smoked paprika, celery salt, cumin, garlic powder, salt, and white pepper in another shallow bowl and whisk to combine.

4. Dip the steak strips into the egg, then dredge them in the seasoned panko, coating them completely. Set the breaded steak on a rack.

5. Meanwhile, heat the oil in a heavy skillet over medium heat until it shimmers. Working in batches so you don't overcrowd the skillet, fry the steak until the breading is golden brown. Drain on another rack while you finish cooking the remaining strips.

**MAKE THE SALAD**

6. Toss the ingredients together in a large bowl.

7. Divide the salad among four dinner plates and top with the steak. Pass the dressing at the table.

# ORANGE-CURRY BEEF STIR-FRY
## WITH BROCCOLINI

**SERVES 6**

One of the favorite cooking segments I've ever done was cooking this dish on *Good Morning America* with Michelle Obama when Robin Roberts first returned from her battle with cancer. What could be more exciting than preparing this Asian-inspired stir-fry with two strong women whom I truly admire?

If I can, I make the marinade, slice the beef, and chop the broccolini in the morning to make my job in the evening quicker. I love the slight bitterness of broccolini, which cooks much more quickly than broccoli. Serve with some soft flatbread so you can scoop the stir-fry up with your fingers.

**FOR THE STIR-FRY**

**1 cup orange juice**

**2 teaspoons sesame oil**

**2 garlic cloves, chopped**

**2 pounds flank steak, cut across the grain into ½-inch-thick strips**

**1 teaspoon cornstarch**

**3 tablespoons olive oil**

**1 red onion, thinly sliced**

**2 teaspoons mild Madras curry powder (or green curry paste)**

**2 ripe tomatoes, chopped**

**2 tablespoons soy sauce**

**2 tablespoons chopped fresh cilantro**

**1 tablespoon chopped fresh parsley**

**Kosher salt and freshly ground black pepper**

*Pre-chop all your herbs for easy assembly once you start cooking.*

**FOR THE BROCCOLINI**

**1 bunch broccolini, chopped (about 2 cups)**

**2 tablespoons olive oil**

**½ red onion, sliced**

**1 (2-inch) piece ginger, peeled and minced**

**2 garlic cloves, chopped**

**1 tablespoon sesame seeds**

**2 teaspoons mild Madras curry powder or green
   curry paste**

**2 teaspoons tomato paste**

**Juice of 1 lime**

**2 tablespoons soy sauce**

**2 tablespoons rice wine vinegar**

**2 teaspoons sesame oil**

**2 Anaheim chiles, seeds and ribs removed, chopped**

**2 scallions, chopped**

**Kosher salt and freshly ground black pepper**

*If you don't have a large wok, use your largest skillet or sauté pan. You need surface area when you stir-fry. And get the pan smoking hot!*

**MAKE THE STIR-FRY**

1. Combine the orange juice, sesame oil, and garlic in a large bowl. Add the flank steak, turning to coat. Cover and refrigerate for at least 20 minutes or up to 2 hours.

2. Drain the steak, reserving 2 tablespoons of the marinade and discarding the rest. Mix the reserved marinade with the cornstarch to make a slurry.

3. Heat a wok or a large sauté pan over high heat. When the pan is hot, add the olive oil, onion, and curry powder and stir-fry until the onion is translucent, about 3 minutes. Add the flank steak and stir-fry until browned, about 5 minutes. Add the marinade slurry, tomatoes, and soy sauce; bring to a boil and stir-fry until the sauce thickens, about 1 minute. Remove from the heat and add the cilantro and parsley. Taste the sauce and season with salt and pepper.

**MAKE THE BROCCOLINI**

4. Bring a large pot of salted water to a boil. Add the broccolini, bring back to a boil, and cook for 1 minute. Drain.

5. Heat the olive oil in a large skillet over high heat. When it shimmers, add the onion and cook until translucent, about 3 minutes. Add the ginger, garlic, sesame seeds, curry powder, and tomato paste and cook, stirring, for 2 minutes. Add the broccolini, lime juice, soy sauce, vinegar, sesame oil, chiles, and scallions and cook, stirring, until the broccolini is hot and the flavors have melded, about 2 minutes. Season with salt and pepper. Serve with the beef stir-fry.

# CRAB FRIED RICE

**SERVES 4**

As a young chef just starting out in New York, I had limited time and money. One of my favorite things to do on my rare days off was to Rollerblade down to Chinatown and explore the amazing ingredients in the markets. While I was there, I would usually get a bowl of fried rice, which was warm, comforting, and filling. In those days, I couldn't afford to get it with a luxe ingredient like crab—I added that later on. By including it in a simple bowl of fried rice, I'm reminded how one special ingredient can make an ordinary dish extraordinary.

**6 tablespoons olive oil**

**4 garlic cloves, chopped**

**1 (½-inch) piece ginger, peeled and minced**

**2 stalks lemongrass, finely chopped (see Box)**

**4 fresh curry leaves (optional; see Note)**

**½ cup diced Chinese duck sausage or dry Spanish chorizo**

**2 teaspoons curry powder**

**2 cups cooked jasmine rice**

**¼ cup soy sauce**

**2 teaspoons sambal oelek (see Note)**

**Pinch of sugar**

**Kosher salt and freshly ground black pepper**

**4 large eggs, beaten**

**6 scallions, cut into ½-inch pieces**

**8 ounces jumbo lump crabmeat**

**2 tablespoons chopped fresh cilantro**

**2 limes, quartered**

**Boston, Bibb, or iceberg lettuce**

1. Heat the olive oil in a large skillet over medium heat. When it shimmers, add the garlic, ginger, lemongrass, curry leaves, sausage, and curry powder and cook, stirring, for 5 minutes, or until very fragrant.

2. Add the rice to the skillet and stir until all the rice is separated into grains. Cook, stirring occasionally, until the rice is hot, 2 to 3 minutes.

3. Combine the soy sauce, sambal oelek, sugar, and a pinch each of salt and pepper in a small cup, then add it to the rice. Cook, stirring, for another minute.

4. Pour the eggs over the rice and let them sit for about a minute. Stir the eggs into the rice and turn off the heat (you're not making scrambled eggs; you just want the eggs to make the rice creamy). Fold in the scallions and half of the crabmeat. Let sit for another minute. Taste the rice and season it with salt and pepper or more soy sauce.

5. Spoon the rice onto a platter. Scatter the remaining crab and the cilantro over the top and garnish with the lime wedges. Set out a plate of lettuce leaves so you can spoon rice into the leaves, wrap, and enjoy.

Notes: Look for fresh curry leaves—which add a warm, slightly bitter, slightly citrusy flavor—in specialty and Indian markets. They freeze beautifully. You can substitute the zest of ½ lime and ¼ teaspoon minced fresh mint in this recipe.

Sambal oelek, a Southeast Asian chile paste, is available in the Asian section of many markets.

## PREPPING LEMONGRASS

Lemongrass doesn't give up its flavor easily. You have to be brutal with it.

Trim off the root, cut off the top two-thirds, and pull off the tough two outer layers. Then smash—and I mean smash—the core with the heel of a chef's knife, breaking down as many of the fibers as possible. Once you've done that, you can chop the lemongrass.

Don't throw the trimmings away. Keep them in the freezer and use them for stock—especially fish or shrimp stock—or tea.

# QUINOA WITH BROCCOLI, CAULIFLOWER & TOASTED COCONUT

**SERVES 4**

I learned about quinoa from my Ecuadorean friend Papi, who told me that it was a superfood full of nutrients. Ecuador is one of the places where quinoa was first domesticated, about 3,000 years ago, so I guess he knows what he's talking about.

People may say quinoa is like a blank canvas, but I think it holds its own with bold flavors. Here I mix garlic and ginger, parsley and mint, with Aleppo pepper to heat things up a little and some smoked paprika. Add some vegetables, top it with toasted coconut, and you've got an extraordinary every-day dish.

1 cup quinoa

1½ cups water

½ cup coconut milk

Kosher salt

½ cup small broccoli florets

½ cup small cauliflower florets

1 medium carrot, peeled and thinly sliced

2 tablespoons olive oil

2 celery ribs, finely chopped

4 scallions, thinly sliced

1 tablespoon minced peeled ginger

2 garlic cloves, minced

3 ripe tomatoes, chopped

2 tablespoons chopped fresh parsley

1 tablespoon chopped fresh mint

½ teaspoon smoked paprika

½ teaspoon Aleppo pepper (see Note) or
   hot red pepper flakes
Freshly ground black pepper
2 tablespoons unsweetened coconut flakes,
   toasted (see Note)

1. Rinse the quinoa well in a fine-mesh sieve, then drain. Combine the quinoa, water, coconut milk, and ½ teaspoon salt in a medium saucepan and bring to a boil over high heat. Reduce the heat to low, cover, and cook until the quinoa has absorbed the water and milk, about 15 minutes. Remove from the heat.

2. While the quinoa cooks, bring a saucepan of water to a boil over high heat. Add the broccoli and cauliflower, bring back to a boil, and cook for 2 minutes. Remove with a skimmer or slotted spoon. Add the carrot to the water, bring it back to a boil, and cook for 1 minute. Drain and add to the other vegetables.

3. Heat the olive oil in a large skillet over medium-high heat. When it shimmers, add the celery, scallions, ginger, and garlic and cook, stirring often, until fragrant, about 2 minutes. Add the broccoli, cauliflower, carrot, and the tomatoes to the skillet and mix well. Add the parsley, mint, smoked paprika, and Aleppo pepper and stir once or twice, until everything is heated through and combined. Season with salt and pepper.

4. Spoon the quinoa into a wide bowl and fluff it with a fork. Add the vegetables and the coconut flakes and mix well. Serve hot.

Notes: Aleppo pepper is a distinctive chile from the Middle East, usually sold as crushed flakes or a ground powder. It has a robust flavor, with a hint of fruitiness, and it is milder than hot red pepper flakes, which can be used as a substitute.
   Toast the coconut in a small, dry skillet over medium heat, stirring, until golden.

# COCONUT-LIME CURRIED CHICKEN

**SERVES 4**

As an up-and-coming chef, I did several stints cooking on cruise ships in the Caribbean. I loved getting out at each port and tasting the local food. That's when I discovered Trinidadian curry, which I've re-created here, adding touches of Asia with the ginger and lime. You can serve it with noodles, couscous, quinoa, rice—whatever you've got on hand that is quick and delicious—but my choice would be roti (Indian flatbread, page 175).

2 tablespoons canola oil

1 medium yellow onion, sliced

2 garlic cloves, minced

1 (1-inch) piece ginger, peeled and minced

Kosher salt and freshly ground black pepper

1 tablespoon red curry paste (see Note)

4 boneless, skinless chicken breasts
    (about 1½ pounds)

Grated zest and juice of 1 lime

1 (15-ounce) can coconut milk

½ cup water

1 tablespoon raisins

4 fresh mint leaves, chopped

1 teaspoon chopped fresh
    parsley

2 tablespoons toasted (see
    page 47) unsweetened
    coconut flakes

**Note:** You'll find red curry paste in most supermarkets.

1. Put the oil in a large skillet and turn the heat to medium-high. When the oil is shimmering, add the onion, garlic, and ginger. Season with salt and pepper and cook, stirring occasionally, until the onion is translucent and the garlic is slightly golden, about 5 minutes. Reduce the heat to medium. Add half of the curry paste and continue to cook for another minute or two.

2. Meanwhile, season the chicken breasts with salt and pepper on each side and rub them with the remaining curry paste and the lime zest. Move the onion to one side in the skillet and add the chicken in one layer. Return the heat to medium-high and brown the chicken, about 3 minutes per side.

3. Reduce the heat to medium-low and stir in the coconut milk and water. Add the raisins, mint, parsley, and lime juice and cook, turning the chicken once, until the sauce is slightly thickened and the chicken is cooked through, about 10 minutes. Taste and adjust the seasonings as needed.

4. To serve, spoon the chicken and sauce over rice (or noodles or any other starchy side) and garnish with the coconut.

# CHICKEN & GRAVY, FOR AUNT GINNY

**SERVES 2**

Back in cooking school, I was taught that a sauce was always strained, always smooth. But this is *gravy*, and this gravy is all about texture. Shredded chicken, some corn and peas, and chopped hard-boiled eggs in a creamy, garlicky gravy—these are leftovers of the highest level.

You've got two biscuits per serving here, so you have one to wipe your plate with. If you're like me, you won't want to leave a bit of the gravy behind.

**2 tablespoons unsalted butter**
**1 small yellow onion, finely chopped**
**1 garlic clove, minced**
**2 tablespoons all-purpose flour**
**1 cup milk**
**½ cup heavy cream**
**1 cup cooked shredded chicken**
**2 tablespoons cooked corn kernels**
**2 tablespoons blanched peas**
**2 hard-boiled eggs, chopped**
**Kosher salt and freshly ground black pepper**
**4 buttermilk biscuits (page 310, without the cinnamon and cardamom)**

> If you're roasting a chicken with the idea of using the leftovers to make this, save the liver. Sauté it in a little butter, chop it up, and add it to the gravy with the chicken.

1. Melt the butter in a skillet over medium heat. Add the onion and garlic and cook just until softened, 2 to 3 minutes. Stir in the flour and cook for 1 to 2 minutes more. Slowly add the milk, stirring constantly to prevent lumps from forming, then add the cream. Simmer for 3 minutes.

2. Add the chicken, corn, peas, and eggs. Season to taste with salt and pepper and cook until heated through.

3. Split 2 of the biscuits and put them in soup dishes. Spoon the chicken and gravy over them. Add the other biscuits to the dishes and serve.

Aunt Ginny raised my business partner Andrew Chapman. She was one of the six million African-Americans who migrated North in the early part of the last century, one of the many who introduced Southern food to Northerners—the food that had to taste like the home they remembered. The day Aunt Ginny came to visit Rooster, we poured Champagne and sat around listening to her stories. She was at the core of how and why we created the Red Rooster, and a deep font of information about recipes just like this. She passed away last year. Rest in peace, Aunt Ginny. I know you're looking down at us and nodding in approval.

# SEARED SCALLOPS WITH BACON & EGG

**SERVES 4**

Scallops are one of those ingredients that travel easily between high cuisine and rustic home cooking. This dish is a combination of both. Perfectly seared scallops have a natural nuttiness that's enhanced by the crisp, smoky bacon. With crunchy brioche toast and a soft creamy poached egg, you've turned a classic breakfast pairing into a festival of tastes and textures.

4 slices bacon
2 garlic cloves, minced
½ cup chopped frisée
8 sea scallops
1 tablespoon unsalted butter
2 tablespoons olive oil
1 teaspoon soy sauce
4 large eggs
1 tablespoon red wine vinegar
1 teaspoon kosher salt
1 teaspoon smoked paprika or ground sumac
   (see Note)
4 slices brioche, toasted

I have a long history with scallops. When I was working at Georges Blanc in France, we would each have to open at least a hundred or so a night. As young cooks, we would always try to see if we could pre-open them to get ahead of our tasks, but whenever we would ask Chef, the answer was always a stern "No." Scallops are best when fresh out of their shell, and no compromises were permitted.

1. Cook the bacon in a large skillet over medium heat until the fat has rendered, about 4 minutes. Add the garlic and continue to cook until the bacon is crisp, another 4 to 5 minutes. Add the frisée and cook, stirring, until the frisée starts to wilt, about 2 minutes. Transfer the bacon, frisée, and garlic to a plate with a slotted spoon, leaving the fat in the skillet.

2. Place the skillet over high heat. When the bacon fat is hot, add the scallops and sear them for 1 minute. Add the butter to the pan and cook until the scallops have a rich brown crust, about

1 minute more. Flip the scallops over to sear the other side and baste them with the fats. The scallops are done when they give just a little when you prod them with your finger. Add the frisée-bacon mix back into the pan. Drizzle with the olive oil and soy sauce and remove from the heat.

3. Meanwhile, fill a wide saucepan about half full with water and bring to a boil over high heat. Crack the eggs into four cups. When the water's boiling, add the vinegar and salt and reduce the heat. Ease the eggs into the simmering water and poach until the whites are set, about 4 minutes. Remove the eggs with a slotted spoon and dip them into a bowl of salted ice water to stop the cooking.

4. Arrange the poached eggs on four plates and divide the bacon, frisée, and scallop mixture evenly among them. Sprinkle with smoked paprika and serve the brioche toast on the side.

Note: **Look for lemony ground sumac in Middle Eastern markets or online.**

# THE-DAY-AFTER PASTA FRITTATA

**SERVES 4**

Frittatas could be called the Italian way with an omelet, and they're often made with leftovers. I first learned about them in Sweden, from my sister's Italian friends. Following the Italian tradition, I start with leftover tomato-spinach spaghetti, add eggs, bacon, and Parmesan, and season with garlic and thyme—turning last night's dinner into an entirely new meal. Eat it for breakfast, eat it for lunch, or eat it for dinner.

**2 slices bacon, diced**
**2 garlic cloves, halved**
**2 sprigs fresh thyme or oregano**
**3 tablespoons olive oil**
**2 cups leftover Red, White & Green Spaghetti (page 217)**
**¾ cup freshly grated Parmesan cheese**
**6 large eggs, lightly beaten**

1. Preheat the oven to 350°F.
2. Cook the bacon in a 10-inch oven-safe nonstick frying pan over medium heat. Once the fat starts to render, add the garlic and thyme and continue to cook until the bacon is browned and crisp. With a slotted spoon, transfer the bacon to a large bowl. Transfer the garlic and thyme to a plate, leaving the rendered fat in the pan.

3. Add 1 tablespoon of the olive oil, the pasta, Parmesan, and eggs to the bowl with the bacon and stir until the pasta is evenly coated.

4. Add the remaining 2 tablespoons olive oil to the bacon fat in the skillet. Pour the pasta mix into the pan. Shake the pan so that the pasta levels out. Put the skillet over medium heat and cook until the frittata firms on the bottom, about 3 minutes. Chop the garlic and strip the thyme leaves, scatter on top of the frittata, and slide the skillet into the oven. Bake until the frittata is golden and puffed, about 25 minutes.

5. Serve hot or at room temperature.

When I serve this for lunch or dinner, I put out some okra pickles wrapped in prosciutto, grilled sausages, and a big green salad.

# PYTT I PANNA (THAT'S HASH, TO YOU)

**SERVES 4**

On Fridays in Sweden, you eat what you have left from earlier in the week, and this leftover-friendly hash defines Swedish home cooking even more than meatballs. Although it's a dish that comes from thrift, nowadays you'll find people buying the ingredients for it. I make mine with brisket and ham. It's a simple dish, but it wants the refinement that comes from dicing all the ingredients the same size. Put out Pickled Beets (page 299) to serve with this.

**3 tablespoons olive oil**
**1½ cups diced Yukon Gold potatoes (skin on)**
**1 large yellow onion, diced**
**1 cup diced leftover brisket**
**1 cup diced leftover cooked ham**
**Kosher salt and freshly ground black pepper**
**2 tablespoons unsalted butter**
**4 large eggs**
**Kosher salt and freshly ground black pepper**

1. Heat the olive oil in a large frying pan over medium heat and cook the potatoes, stirring occasionally, until tender, about 8 minutes. Add the onion and continue to cook, stirring often, until it is golden and the potatoes have crispy edges, about 6 more minutes. Add the brisket and ham and cook, stirring often, until they're heated through. If things begin to stick to the pan along the way, add a little water to release them. Taste and season with salt and pepper.

2. Melt the butter in a large nonstick skillet over medium-high heat and fry the eggs sunny-side up: You want the tops set and the yolks still runny.

3. Divide the hash among four plates and put a fried egg on top. Season with salt and pepper and serve.

# STICKY BACON SANDWICHES

**SERVES 2**

When I was traveling through Southeast Asia, I discovered Singapore's ultimate breakfast treat called *kaya* toast. An aromatic jam of coconut milk is spread on toast, topped with slivers of cold butter, and served with an egg. It's a wonderful dish, and it started me wondering: What would it be like if I married this idea to a PB & J?

This sandwich hits all those good spots on your tongue. The coconut peanut butter is a little spicy; the grape jam is sweet; the bacon is salty; the egg is creamy; and the toast is crunchy.

### FOR THE COCONUT PEANUT BUTTER

½ cup coconut milk

1 (½-inch) piece ginger, peeled and grated

½ teaspoon ground cloves

½ teaspoon freshly grated nutmeg

1 small red chile, minced

1 tablespoon grated orange zest

2 tablespoons creamy peanut butter

### FOR THE EGGS

2 large eggs

1 tablespoon red wine vinegar

1 teaspoon kosher salt

### FOR THE SANDWICHES

4 slices Texas toast or thick-cut sliced white bread

3 tablespoons Concord grape jam

2 slices thick-cut bacon, cooked until crisp

Kosher salt and freshly ground black pepper

### MAKE THE COCONUT PEANUT BUTTER

1. Combine the coconut milk, ginger, cloves, nutmeg, and chile in a small saucepan over medium heat. Bring to a boil and reduce by half, 3 to 5 minutes. Remove from the heat and stir in the orange zest and peanut butter.

### POACH THE EGGS

2. Fill a wide saucepan about half full with water and bring to a boil over high heat. Crack the eggs into two cups. When the water's boiling, add the vinegar and salt and reduce the heat. Ease the eggs into the simmering water and poach until the whites are set, about 4 minutes. Remove the eggs with a slotted spoon and dip them in a bowl of salted ice water to stop the cooking.

### MAKE THE SANDWICHES

3. Meanwhile, toast the bread until golden brown. Spread the Coconut Peanut Butter on two pieces of toast and the jam on the other two. Break the bacon in half and put on the toasts with the peanut butter. Top with the poached eggs. Season with salt and pepper. Cut the jelly toasts in half and serve on the side; they're for dipping into the egg yolk.

# FRIENDS & FAMILY

I'M NOT BIG ON "ENTERTAINING." YES, I DO THROW SOME BIG PARTIES A FEW times a year, and an end-of-the-year thank-you bash for my staff. Now that Maya and I have a house, though, with a few extra rooms, we have regular visitors. From Ethiopia, from Sweden, from Canada—makes no difference. They're all welcome. But cooking for these people isn't "entertaining"; it's cooking for family and friends.

What I look for on these occasions is feel-good food. Dishes that are relaxed, that make sense depending on my mood or feeling, or on the mood or feeling I want to create at the table. And what I want to do as often as possible is break down that knife-and-fork barrier. There are so many people in this world who eat with their hands; why shouldn't we? It's a great way to get things relaxed and bring us closer to the food. How can you not feel good when you're looking across the table at a friend who's picking meat out of a lobster knuckle and then licking her fingers?

I like the way food brings us together. Maybe it's the smell of the spice-rubbed brisket slow-roasting in the oven, or red shrimp and spicy grits, or the unmistakable aroma of bacon biscuits first thing in the morning—there's something about the scents of cooking that draws people into the kitchen.

You could say that in my home kitchen I love to be the DJ, mixing flavors and recipes, the way a DJ at a nightclub or on the radio mixes melodies and beats.

SPICED NUTS  64

SPICY & SWEET POPCORN  65

MAC & CHEESE & GREENS  66

TWICE-FRIED CHICKEN BREASTS WITH RAINBOW SLAW  69

RED ROOSTER SANGRIA  73

SWEET POTATO GNOCCHI  74

COUSCOUS "PAELLA" WITH SHRIMP, CHICKEN & CHORIZO  76

SOMETIMES I'M A VEGETARIAN POTATO-SPINACH PIE  78

ROAST CHICKEN WITH VINAIGRETTE & COUSCOUS  80

BLOOD-ORANGE DUCK WITH WATERCRESS-CHICKPEA
    SALAD  82

HABESHA LAMB CHOPS WITH APPLE-MANGO CHUTNEY  86

MAYA'S LAMB LASAGNA  88

SPICE-RUBBED TEXAS BRISKET FROM THE OVEN  90

    BARBECUE SAUCE  92

KOREAN-STYLE SHORT RIBS  93

CRISPY SUCKLING PIG  94

BACON BISCUITS WITH JALAPEÑO
    SCRAMBLED EGGS & GRILLED CORN  96

RED SHRIMP & SPICY GRITS  99

STICKY-FINGERS CURRIED LOBSTER STEW  101

WHOLE ROASTED TROUT WITH HERB DRIZZLE & SCARLET
    SALAD  104

MONTEREY SARDINES WITH BURNT LEMONS & HERBS  106

# MUSIC TO COOK BY

Why Can't This Be Love ★ Van Halen

Teardrops ★ Womack & Womack

Use Somebody ★ Kings of Leon

Everyday People ★ Sly and the Family Stone

We Are One ★ Maze, featuring Frankie Beverly

As ★ Stevie Wonder

Watch What You Say ★ Guru, featuring Chaka Khan

B.U.D.D.Y ★ Musiq Soulchild

Far Away ★ Kindred the Family Soul

Feels Good ★ Tony! Toni! Toné!

Shake Your Body (Down to the Ground) ★ The Jacksons

A House Is Not a Home ★ Luther Vandross

You Are My Heaven ★ Roberta Flack, featuring
   Donny Hathaway

Family Affair ★ Mary J. Blige

Good Times ★ Chic

# SPICED NUTS

**MAKES 1½ CUPS**

When you have houseguests coming in and out of your house, it's a good thing to have a bowl of nuts on hand for people to nibble on. The combination of cinnamon, paprika, cayenne, and brown sugar makes these particularly addictive. And there's no need to wait for guests to make them.

**2 tablespoons olive oil**
**½ cup unsalted raw cashews**
**½ cup peeled and blanched whole almonds**
**½ cup walnut halves**
**1 teaspoon ground cinnamon**
**1 teaspoon kosher salt**
**1 teaspoon paprika**
**½ teaspoon cayenne**
**1 tablespoon light brown sugar**

1. Heat the olive oil in a large skillet over low heat. Add the cashews, almonds, walnuts, cinnamon, salt, paprika, and cayenne and cook, stirring often, until the nuts are fragrant and golden, 8 to 10 minutes. Crumble the sugar over the nuts and cook, stirring constantly, until the sugar is melted and coats the nuts, about 3 minutes.

2. Transfer to a bowl and serve warm, or cool and store in an airtight container at room temperature for up to 1 week.

# SPICY & SWEET POPCORN

This gets a lot of mileage in my house.

Mix cinnamon, salt, paprika, cayenne, and light brown sugar—the same amounts as in Spiced Nuts (see opposite). Pop ½ cup popcorn kernels, put them in a bowl, and toss with the spice mix.

# MAC & CHEESE & GREENS

**SERVES 10 TO 12**

Mats Carestam is my oldest friend, and his mother was especially modern—she made American dishes that few Swedish mothers did. I lived for the days when I was invited to dinner at Mats's house and his mother would plop a giant plate of creamy mac and cheese in front of me. I still love pasta covered with cheese. In this version, I've added collard greens—that soul-food influence again—but I cook the greens in coconut milk and flavor them with soy and mustard to add more layers of flavor to what's become a familiar casserole. No matter how many times my friends have had this, they smile like kids when I serve it.

## FOR THE COLLARD GREENS

½ cup coconut milk

2 tablespoons soy sauce

1 tablespoon grainy mustard

6 slices bacon, cooked, drained, and crumbled

3 tablespoons olive oil

1 tablespoon unsalted butter

4 garlic cloves, peeled and halved

4 cups chopped well-washed collard greens

## FOR THE MAC AND CHEESE

8 tablespoons (1 stick) unsalted butter

½ cup thinly sliced shallots

2 garlic cloves, minced

2 tablespoons all-purpose flour

3 cups heavy cream

1 cup whole milk

8 ounces cheddar cheese, grated

4 ounces Gruyère cheese, grated

4 ounces Parmesan cheese, freshly grated

½ cup crème fraîche

1 teaspoon freshly grated nutmeg

1 teaspoon mustard powder

Kosher salt and freshly ground white pepper

1 pound orecchiette or other small, sturdy pasta, cooked until just tender

## FOR THE TOPPING

⅓ cup toasted bread crumbs

¼ cup chopped fresh parsley

2 tablespoons chopped fresh basil

2 tablespoons freshly grated Parmesan cheese

1 tablespoon grated Gruyère cheese

¼ teaspoon kosher salt

⅛ teaspoon freshly ground black pepper

All over the Caribbean, it's not a party without a macaroni pie, their version of mac and cheese. Macaroni pie is always served alongside some kind of chicken, and you know what island you're on based on the hot sauce that's served with the meal.

If you want to go fancy with this, add some cooked lobster or sautéed mushrooms.

## MAKE THE COLLARD GREENS

1. Bring the coconut milk and soy sauce to a boil in a small saucepan. Remove from the heat and stir in the mustard and crumbled bacon.
2. Heat the olive oil and butter in a large pot over low heat. Add the garlic and slowly toast to flavor the fats, about 5 minutes, then discard. Add the collard greens to the pot and cook, stirring frequently, until the greens start to wilt. Stir in the coconut milk mixture and cook, partly covered, until the greens are tender and the sauce has thickened, about 20 minutes.

## MAKE THE MAC AND CHEESE

3. Preheat the broiler. Oil a 9-x-13-inch baking dish.
4. Melt the butter in a large pot over medium-low heat. Add the shallots and cook until they're tender and golden brown, 8 to 10 minutes. Add the minced garlic and flour and cook, stirring, for 1 minute. Slowly whisk in the heavy cream and milk, making sure there are no lumps. Bring to a boil. Reduce the heat to low, then add all the cheeses and the crème fraîche. Whisk until the cheeses are melted and fully incorporated into the sauce. Mix in the nutmeg, mustard, and salt and white pepper to taste.
5. Add the cooked pasta and collard greens to the sauce and toss to combine. Transfer to the baking dish.

## MAKE THE TOPPING

6. Put all the ingredients in a food processor and process until the herbs are minced. Sprinkle the topping over the pasta. Broil until the topping is golden brown, 5 to 8 minutes. Serve immediately.

1. cornbread
2. mac + cheese
3. helga's
4. short ribs
5. pizza
6. chicken soup
7. ambrosia

Chef's Tip: Plan your meal days in advance and figure out what you can make before your guests arrive. That way you won't be spending the whole night behind a stove.

# TWICE-FRIED CHICKEN BREASTS WITH RAINBOW SLAW

**SERVES 4**

So many of my significant food memories have to do with chicken, starting with my grandmother Helga teaching me how to roast one. I've worked to perfect my fried chicken. The trick is frying it twice. The first fry gets the cooking started, and while the chicken rests, the residual heat continues the cooking. The second fry browns the crust, which has semolina and cornstarch for a crunch. Oh, and you've flavored the oil with garlic that you can squeeze out onto bread, just like roasted garlic.

Grilling the vegetables for the slaw gives them a smoky edge, and the bright citrus dressing makes it a perfect companion to the fried chicken.

Go on: Eat this with your hands.

## FOR THE RAINBOW SLAW

¼ head red cabbage

¼ head Napa cabbage

2 thin carrots, peeled

1 red onion, halved

2 tablespoons olive oil

Segments and juice of 1 grapefruit
    (see page 85)

Segments and juice of 1 orange

Juice of 1 lemon

1 tablespoon cottage cheese

1 tablespoon mayonnaise

1 tablespoon raisins

Chile powder

Celery salt

Kosher salt


## FOR THE FRIED CHICKEN

2 tablespoons kosher salt

2 cups water

4 bone-in, skin-on chicken breasts

16 fresh sage leaves, torn

2 cups buttermilk

2 dashes Tabasco sauce

½ teaspoon freshly ground black
    pepper

½ teaspoon chile powder

1 teaspoon celery salt

1 cup all-purpose flour

½ cup semolina flour

2 tablespoons cornstarch

Peanut oil, for frying

1 garlic bulb

Lemon wedges, for garnish

### MAKE THE RAINBOW SLAW

1. Preheat a gas grill to medium-high. Brush the cabbages, carrots, and onion with the olive oil and then grill, turning a few times for even cooking. You're looking to soften the vegetables and to get some good grill marks. The Napa cabbage should take about 5 minutes; the rest, about 10 minutes. (You can also do this indoors on a grill pan.)

2. When the vegetables are cool enough to handle, shred the cabbages and chop the carrots and onion.

3. Mix the grapefruit segments and juice, orange segments and juice, lemon juice, cottage cheese, mayonnaise, and raisins in a large bowl. Add the cabbage, carrots, and onion and toss. Season to taste with chile powder, celery salt, and salt. Cover and refrigerate.

### MAKE THE FRIED CHICKEN

4. Dissolve the salt in the water in a large bowl. Add the chicken, cover, and refrigerate for 1½ hours.

5. Remove the chicken from the brine, carefully separate the skin from the flesh, and place the torn sage leaves underneath the skin. Pat the skin back down.

6. Discard the brine and, in the same bowl, combine the buttermilk, Tabasco, black pepper, chile powder, and ½ teaspoon of the celery salt. Add the chicken, making sure it's covered with the marinade. Cover and refrigerate for 2 hours, or as long as overnight.

7. Take the chicken out of the refrigerator about 15 minutes before you're ready to fry. In a shallow bowl, whisk the flours, cornstarch, and remaining ½ teaspoon celery salt.

8. Fill an 8-quart pot half full with peanut oil and heat it to 340°F. Slice off and discard the top quarter of the garlic bulb; put the large piece in the hot oil. When the garlic is a rich golden brown, 8 to 10 minutes, remove it and drain it on a rack.

Double the recipe if you're serving a crowd or if you want leftovers. There's nothing better than leftover fried chicken. Eat it cold, turn it into a salad, or make Chicken & Gravy (page 50).

9. Wipe the excess marinade off the chicken and roll in the flour mixture; shake off the excess. Fry the chicken for 10 minutes, turning occasionally. Transfer to a rack set over a baking sheet and let it rest for 15 minutes.

10. Heat the oil to 360°F and fry the chicken again, until the crust is a deep golden brown, 3 to 4 minutes.

11. Serve the chicken with lemon wedges and rainbow slaw and the garlic.

At Harlem's Charles' Country Pan Fried Chicken, Charles uses a long-handled cast iron pan to scoop up his fried chicken from the hot oil. I think that pan has been in his family for more than fifty years.

# RED ROOSTER SANGRIA

You can't be a wine snob when you're wearing your sangria hat. Sangria is a celebration, and this one has more body than most because of the sweet mango puree. There's a sophisticated tartness from a mix of citrus juices and layers of flavor thanks to pear brandy. We serve it at my restaurant Red Rooster, but Maya and I also serve it at home when it's jump-up time. That's what Trinidadians call having a party.

And you know, if you don't have a punch bowl, you can mix this in a stockpot, then transfer to pitchers to serve.

Bring ½ cup water, ½ cup sugar, 1 star anise, and ½ vanilla bean (split and scraped) to a simmer in a small saucepan over medium heat. Stir until the sugar dissolves, then let the syrup cool for at least 30 minutes.

Discard the star anise and vanilla pod. Mix the syrup with 3 bottles Cabernet Sauvignon, ¼ cup pear eau de vie (like Poire William), 1 cup mango puree, ¾ cup blood orange juice, and the juice of 1 lemon and 1 lime.

Peel and cut 2 mangoes into 1-inch cubes, then peel and cut ¼ honeydew melon into 1-inch cubes. Put the fruit into a bowl, ladle in enough sangria to cover the fruit, and let it macerate for at least 10 minutes before serving.

To serve, start by filling a large wineglass with ice. Pour in the sangria, leaving room at the top of the glass. Top it off with a splash of cold seltzer and garnish with a cocktail pick of the fruit.

This makes enough for 24 servings.

# SWEET POTATO GNOCCHI

**SERVES 4**

I give these little Italian dumplings a twist. Sweet potatoes are a soul-food staple, so I use them instead of russets to give the dish both color and sweetness. Then I finish with a tomato and almond sauce. The acid of the tomatoes and lemon offsets the sweetness, and there are some almonds for a hint of crunch.

**FOR THE GNOCCHI**

**1 pound sweet potatoes, peeled**

**½ cup all-purpose flour**

**1 large egg**

**1 large egg yolk**

**Kosher salt and freshly ground black pepper**

**FOR THE SAUCE**

**1 tablespoon chopped almonds**

**1 jalapeño, seeds removed and coarsely chopped**

**Grated zest and juice of 1 lemon**

**2 tablespoons olive oil**

**4 plum tomatoes, coarsely chopped**

**1 cup arugula**

**Freshly grated Parmesan cheese, for serving**

You can serve the gnocchi as a first course, but I think it needs to go with something. Here are some ideas:
★ Monterey Sardines with Burnt Lemons & Herbs (page 106)
★ Habesha Lamb Chops with Apple-Mango Chutney (page 86). Use lemon instead of lime in the marinade.
★ Slow-Grilled Lamb Patties (page 200)
★ Sautéed shrimp

## MAKE THE GNOCCHI

1. Place a large pot of salted water over medium-high heat and bring to a boil.

2. Meanwhile, finely grate the sweet potatoes onto a kitchen towel. Gather up the towel and squeeze as much liquid out of the potatoes as possible. Place in a bowl with half of the flour, the egg, yolk, and salt and pepper to taste and mix the ingredients to combine. Continue mixing and adding the remaining flour just until the dough holds together.

3. Roll out a piece of dough into a ¾-inch-wide log on a floured work surface. Cut into 1-inch pieces and push them off to the side while you shape the rest of the gnocchi.

4. Adjust the heat so that the water is at a steady simmer. Slip the gnocchi into the water. They will sink to the bottom; stir gently so they don't stick. When they rise to the top, let them cook for 3 minutes longer. Transfer to a bowl with a skimmer or slotted spoon and keep warm.

## MAKE THE SAUCE

5. Toast the almonds in a large, dry skillet over medium-low heat until golden brown. Transfer to a food processor and add the jalapeño, lemon zest and juice, and oil. Process until smooth.

6. Scrape the sauce back into the skillet and bring to a simmer over medium heat. Add the toma-toes and cook for a minute or two to let the flavors marry. Add the gnocchi and cook, stirring gently, until heated through. Just before removing from the heat, gently toss in the arugula.

7. To serve, divide the gnocchi among four plates and sprinkle with Parmesan.

# COUSCOUS "PAELLA" WITH SHRIMP, CHICKEN & CHORIZO

**SERVES 6**

I was lucky enough to learn how to make couscous from scratch in Morocco. To tell the truth, I wasn't very good at it—not like my friend's aunt, who taught me. She had been rolling the semolina dough between her palms for years, as she had learned from her mother, who learned from her mother before her. When I ate the couscous later that day I could taste the care she had taken with those fluffy grains.

I fell in love with couscous then, and I keep improvising with it. Here I use it as the backbone of a vibrant paella, rich with chorizo and chicken and shrimp and all the traditional flavors of Spain. I love how the couscous soaks up the sauce. The hint of harissa is my nod to Morocco. This is a beautiful dish that you can serve to family and friends with pride.

**4 tablespoons olive oil**

**½ pound dry Spanish chorizo, cut into chunks**

**½ pound boneless, skinless chicken thighs, cut into 1-inch cubes**

**1 medium red onion, thinly sliced**

**1 red bell pepper, chopped**

**2 garlic cloves, crushed**

**1 (8-ounce) jar roasted red peppers, drained and sliced**

**2 teaspoons Harissa (page 245)**

*If you have preserved lemon (see page 123) in the refrigerator, chop up about 2 table-spoons and add it with the shrimp.*

**3 ripe tomatoes, chopped**

**1 cup canned crushed tomatoes**

**1½ cups couscous**

**1 cup chicken broth or dry white wine**

**1 cup water**

**1 pound jumbo (U10) shrimp, shell-on but deveined**

**Juice of 1 lemon**

**1 tablespoon chopped fresh cilantro**

**1 tablespoon chopped fresh parsley**

Buy shrimp by count rather than by a size designation like "jumbo," which can change from market to market. U10 means there are under 10 shrimp per pound.

1. Heat 3 tablespoons of the olive oil in a large skillet over medium heat. Add the chorizo, chicken, onion, bell pepper, and garlic and cook until the onion and pepper are starting to soften and the chicken is starting to brown, about 5 minutes. Add the roasted peppers and harissa and cook for 3 minutes to develop the flavors.

2. Add the chopped tomatoes, crushed tomatoes, couscous, broth, and water. Bring to a boil, cover, reduce the heat, and simmer for 3 minutes. Add the shrimp, pushing it down into the couscous. Cover and simmer for 2 minutes. Turn off the heat and let the paella sit for 10 to 15 minutes to absorb the liquids.

3. Combine the remaining 1 tablespoon olive oil, the lemon juice, cilantro, and parsley in a small bowl. Spoon the couscous into serving bowls, drizzle the oil on top, and serve.

# SOMETIMES I'M A VEGETARIAN POTATO-SPINACH PIE

**SERVES 12**

Potatoes are part of the fabric of life in Sweden. In fact, my grandfather never ate a meal without a potato. Potatoes paired with spinach make one of the best treats ever, a potato-spinach pie. Lots of cultures have a version of this. This one, with its dill, mint, and feta, is kind of Greek—but with puff pastry. This pie makes a great weekend lunch or a satisfying weeknight vegetarian meal when paired with a green salad. It tastes great the next day, too. Reheat it in the oven or even in a skillet to get it crunchy.

1 pound red-skinned potatoes, scrubbed

4 garlic cloves, peeled

3 tablespoons olive oil, plus more for brushing

6 leeks, white and light green parts, sliced and well rinsed

2 pounds baby spinach

½ teaspoon freshly ground black pepper

2 cups crumbled feta cheese

½ cup finely chopped fresh dill

½ cup finely chopped fresh mint

Kosher salt

3 large eggs, lightly beaten

2 frozen puff pastry sheets, thawed but kept cool

1. Preheat the oven to 350°F. Oil a 9-x-13-inch baking dish.

2. Put the potatoes and garlic in a large saucepan and cover with water by at least an inch. Bring to a boil, reduce the heat, and cook until the potatoes are tender, about 20 minutes, Drain. Peel all, some, or none of the potatoes. Return them to the pot with the garlic and mash well with a fork or potato masher. Set aside.

3. Heat the oil in a large skillet over medium-high heat. When it shimmers, add the leeks and cook, stirring, until they're tender and starting to brown, about 10 minutes. Add the spinach in handfuls, stirring it into the leeks with a wooden spoon. Let each handful wilt and cook down before adding more. Once all the spinach is in the pan, season with pepper. Scrape the spinach and leeks into a sieve set over a bowl. Let it cool for about 15 minutes, then gently press out all of the excess liquid.

4. Add the spinach and leeks, the feta, dill, mint, and 1 teaspoon salt to the potatoes and mix well. Taste and adjust the seasoning, adding more salt if needed. Stir in the eggs.

5. Put 1 sheet of puff pastry on a lightly floured surface and roll it out slightly to fit the baking dish. Transfer it to the dish and press the dough into the corners. Trim off any excess with a paring knife. Spread the spinach filling evenly over the dough. Roll out the other sheet of pastry and cover the filling. Trim any excess. Brush the top with olive oil.

6. Bake until the pastry is puffed and golden brown, 30 to 35 minutes. Let stand for 10 minutes before cutting into squares. Serve the pie warm or at room temperature.

# ROAST CHICKEN WITH VINAIGRETTE & COUSCOUS

**SERVES 6 TO 8**

When I was an apprentice in Interlaken, Switzerland, the smell of roasted chicken and the fragrance of herbs—sometimes rosemary, at other times lavender or sage—would hit me every time I walked into the restaurant where I worked. It was a simple dish, but I revisit it often. For this version, I marinate chicken halves in lemon juice, garlic, and herbs, broil them to get the skin extra crisp, then finish the roasting in the oven. Drizzled with vinaigrette and served with couscous, it is light and has familiar flavors.

**FOR THE CHICKEN**

2 small whole chickens, about
    2½ pounds each
Juice of 4 lemons
½ cup olive oil
Leaves from 2 sprigs fresh sage,
    chopped
Needles from 2 sprigs fresh
    rosemary, chopped
4 garlic cloves, halved
Kosher salt and freshly ground
    black pepper
3 carrots, peeled and cut into large
    chunks (2–3 inches)
1 medium onion, cut into large
    chunks (2–3 inches)

**FOR THE COUSCOUS**

4½ cups water
½ teaspoon kosher salt
1 tablespoon olive oil
3 cups couscous

*This is a great dish for large groups because it tastes great after it sits for a while. You have more time to mingle with your friends.*

## FOR THE VINAIGRETTE

**1 tablespoon balsamic vinegar**

**Juice of 1 lemon**

**3 tablespoons olive oil**

**1 tablespoon chopped pitted kalamata olives**

**1 tablespoon chopped fresh rosemary**

**½ teaspoon chopped fresh sage**

**1 garlic clove, chopped**

**1 tablespoon raisins**

**Kosher salt and freshly ground black pepper**

### MAKE THE CHICKEN

1. Rub the chickens inside and out with the juice of 2 of the lemons and pat them dry. Cut the chickens in half lengthwise, using kitchen shears to cut along both sides of each backbone and a chef's knife to cut through the breastbone. Put the chicken halves in a large bowl.

2. Whisk the olive oil, sage, rosemary, garlic cloves, and the juice from the remaining 2 lemons together in a small bowl. Pour over the chicken halves and turn the chicken to coat it with the marinade. Cover the bowl and refrigerate for 30 minutes.

3. Preheat the broiler.

4. Transfer the chicken, skin side up, and the marinade to a roasting pan and season the chicken generously with salt and pepper. Slide the pan under the broiler to brown the chicken, about 15 minutes. The skin should crackle. Turn off the broiler, set the oven temperature to 350°F, and roast the chicken for 5 minutes.

5. Add the carrots and onion to the roasting pan and continue roasting until the juices of the chickens run clear when a knife is inserted near the thighs and the vegetables are tender, 25 to 30 minutes. Remove the pan from the oven and let the chicken rest for 15 minutes.

### MAKE THE COUSCOUS

6. While the chicken rests, bring the water to a boil in a large saucepan. Add the salt and olive oil. Pour in the couscous, stir, cover the pot, and turn off the heat. When the water is absorbed, about 15 minutes, fluff the couscous with a fork.

### MAKE THE VINAIGRETTE

7. Put the balsamic vinegar and lemon juice into a medium bowl. Whisk in the olive oil, followed by the olives, rosemary, sage, garlic, and raisins. Season to taste with salt and pepper.

8. Spoon the couscous and vegetables onto a large serving platter. Cut the chicken into pieces, place on the couscous, and drizzle with the vinaigrette.

# BLOOD ORANGE DUCK WITH WATERCRESS-CHICKPEA SALAD

**SERVES 4**

Duck, with its rich dark meat and crackling skin, is really a celebration dish, something elegant for New Year's Eve or a birthday. Citrus juices help cut the richness of the meat; blood oranges have an almost floral taste, so if you can find them, use them. The miso, chile paste, and soy give this duck an Asian feel. Think Duck à l'Orange without the usual suspects.

**FOR THE DUCK**

1 (4½-pound) duck

Zest and juice of 1 grapefruit

1 cup blood orange juice (or fresh orange juice)

1 blood orange (or Valencia, Cara Cara, or navel orange), zested and cut into quarters

2 tablespoons soy sauce

1 tablespoon white miso

1 teaspoon sambal oelek (see Note) or Harissa (page 245)

1 teaspoon sesame oil

1 tablespoon kosher salt

1 red onion, chopped

2 garlic cloves, peeled

2 sprigs fresh thyme

Note: Sambal oelek, a Southeast Asian chile paste, is available in the Asian section of many supermarkets.

### FOR THE SALAD

½ cup cooked chickpeas

Segments and juice from 1 blood
  orange (see page 85)

2 tablespoons olive oil

1 tablespoon balsamic vinegar

2 cups watercress

2 tablespoons toasted pine nuts

1 shallot, very thinly sliced

### MAKE THE DUCK

1. Pull the excess fat from the cavity of the duck. (Freeze it so you can render it later.)

2. Put ½ cup grapefruit juice (drink the rest) in a bowl with the grapefruit zest, blood orange juice, blood orange zest, soy sauce, miso, sambal oelek, sesame oil, and salt and whisk until smooth. Set the duck in a large bowl, then pour the citrus-soy marinade over it. Cover and marinate for 1 hour in the refrigerator.

3. Preheat the oven to 300°F.

4. Remove the duck from the marinade and place it on a rack in a roasting pan. Poke the skin all over the duck with a skewer or the tip of a small knife. Place the blood orange quarters, onion, garlic cloves, and thyme in the duck's cavity. Tie the legs together with butcher's twine and roast the duck for 1 hour. Bail out any fat that has rendered from the duck. (Strain the fat and freeze it.)

Use duck fat to fry potatoes, or when you're cooking greens.

5. Increase the oven temperature to 450°F and roast the duck for another 45 minutes, basting every few minutes with the marinade while it roasts. If the duck is burning, lower the heat to 350°F. The duck is done when the legs move easily and an instant-read thermometer inserted into the thickest part of the thigh registers 160°F. Let the duck rest on a cutting board for 30 minutes.

**MAKE THE SALAD**

6. Warm the chickpeas in a small pot over medium heat.

7. Whisk the orange juice, olive oil, and balsamic vinegar together in a small bowl.

8. Put the chickpeas, watercress, orange segments, pine nuts, and shallot in a salad bowl. Toss with the vinaigrette. If you want, strip the leaves from the thyme in the duck cavity and add them to the salad.

9. Carve the duck and serve it with the watercress-chickpea salad.

Don't waste any of that duck! Put the neck in the roasting pan with the duck for the first hour. Let it cool and pull off the meat. Season the liver with salt and pepper, dust it with flour, and sear it in some of the duck fat. Chop it up. Toss the liver and neck meat into the salad.

# CITRUS SEGMENTS AND JUICE

★ Cut off the top and bottom of whatever citrus you're segmenting to expose the flesh.

★ Stand the fruit on one flat end and use a small, sharp knife to follow the shape of the fruit and cut off the zest and cottony pith. Turn it over and trim off any bits of pith that you've missed.

★ Hold the fruit over a bowl and cut between the membranes and the flesh to release the segments. Let them drop into the bowl.

★ Squeeze the membranes over the bowl to get out all the juice that's left. And if there's any flesh on the peel, squeeze that in, too.

# HABESHA LAMB CHOPS
## WITH APPLE-MANGO CHUTNEY

**SERVES 4**

*Habesha* is what Ethiopians call each other as a term of collective pride and to celebrate unity. The inspiration for this dish comes from East Africa, where I was born, and where Indian immigrants brought their cooking. The apple-mango chutney gets a little spice from the ginger and chile, but the sweetness is layered and complex. Mango can sometimes take over in a chutney; here the apple and mint make the flavors bright. Marinating the lamb in yogurt and garam masala is another nod to Indian immigrant cooking, and the yogurt also tenderizes the meat and keeps it moist when you grill it.

**FOR THE APPLE-MANGO CHUTNEY**

**2 Granny Smith apples**

**2 ripe mangoes, pitted, peeled, and cut into cubes**

**½ cup mango juice (see Note)**

**½ cup apple juice**

**2 garlic cloves, chopped**

**1 teaspoon minced peeled ginger**

**1½ teaspoons minced serrano chiles, with seeds**

**2 teaspoons mustard seeds**

**Kosher salt and freshly ground black pepper**

**Juice of 2 limes**

**2 tablespoons chopped fresh mint**

**FOR THE LAMB CHOPS**

**1 cup plain whole-milk yogurt**

**1½ tablespoons fresh lime juice**

**2 tablespoons chopped fresh mint**

**1½ teaspoons garam masala**

**8 T-bone loin lamb chops, each about 1-inch thick**

**Vegetable oil spray**

**Kosher salt and freshly ground black pepper**

## MAKE THE CHUTNEY

1. Peel, core, and cut one of the apples into cubes. Put it into a medium saucepan with the mangoes, mango juice, apple juice, garlic, ginger, serrano chiles, and mustard seeds. Season to taste with salt and pepper. Bring to a simmer and cook over low heat until the mangoes break down but still have a little texture, 1 hour. In the last 10 minutes of cooking, peel the second apple and grate it into the chutney. Remove from the heat and stir in the lime juice and mint.

## MAKE THE LAMB CHOPS

2. Spray the grill rack with vegetable oil spray and preheat the gas grill to medium-high.

3. Whisk the yogurt, lime juice, mint, and garam masala together in a large bowl. Add the lamb chops and turn to coat them with the yogurt marinade. Let stand at room temperature for 15 minutes.

4. Remove the lamb chops from the yogurt mixture and season generously with salt and pepper. Grill the lamb to the desired doneness, about 5 minutes per side for medium-rare.

5. Place 2 lamb chops on each plate and serve with the chutney.

Note: **Find mango juice in the grocery store, Latin markets, and online.**

# MAYA'S LAMB LASAGNA

**SERVES 6 TO 8**

My wife Maya is one of the best Ethiopian cooks I know. Then she ventured into Italian food—not unusual, really, given Ethiopia's Italian population resulting from Italy's attempts at colonization. From the first time she prepared this lasagna, it's been one of my favorite dishes. I love the richness that the lamb adds and the creaminess that the ricotta lends to the sauce. I eat it as often as she'll make it.

You can make this on Sunday and have it on hand throughout the week. I think it tastes even better a day or two later.

1 pound dried lasagna noodles (not no-boil)

2 tablespoons olive oil

1 pound ground lamb

2 garlic cloves, minced

1 large yellow onion, chopped

1 (28-ounce) can crushed tomatoes

½ cup water

1 (15-ounce) container ricotta cheese

1 teaspoon dried oregano

½ teaspoon kosher salt

8 fresh basil leaves, chopped, plus more for serving

2 cups grated mozzarella cheese (8 ounces)

*If you've got leftovers, add a layer of Smoky Collards & Kale (page 282). Or some sautéed zucchini.*

1. Bring a large pot of salted water to a boil. Add the lasagna noodles and cook until al dente, about 10 minutes. Drain, rinse in cold water, and set aside on kitchen towels.

2. Meanwhile, heat the oil in a large skillet over medium heat. Add the lamb, garlic, and onion and cook, stirring often, until the lamb is browned and the onion is tender, 8 to 10 minutes. Add the crushed tomatoes, water, ricotta, dried oregano, and salt. Bring the sauce to a simmer and cook, stirring occasionally, to marry the flavors, about 10 minutes. Stir in the chopped basil.

3. Preheat the oven to 350°F.

4. Spoon some of the lamb sauce into the bottom of a 9-x-13-inch baking dish and top with a layer of the lasagna noodles. Spread a layer of the sauce over the pasta and scatter with some of the mozzarella. Continue to layer the pasta, sauce, and cheese, ending with the sauce and mozzarella. You may not need all of the lasagna noodles.

5. Bake the lasagna until it's hot and bubbling, about 40 minutes. Let the lasagna rest for 10 minutes or up to 30 minutes. Rip up some fresh basil leaves and scatter them over the lasagna before serving.

# SPICE-RUBBED TEXAS BRISKET FROM THE OVEN

**SERVES 6 TO 8**

Texas is one of my favorite places to cook—and eat. There's nothing like Texas barbecued brisket. But smoking a piece of beef for hours isn't the easiest thing, so I rub the meat with chile powder, smoked paprika, cumin, sage, and oregano, wrap it tightly in foil, and roast it low and slow for a brisket that's moist and succulent and packed with smoky spice. The sweet tanginess of the barbecue sauce, which has a little heat from the chipotles and ginger, is the perfect accompaniment.

You could serve this with spongy sliced white bread like they do in Texas. Sometimes something so wrong can be so right.

### FOR THE SPICE RUB
**1 tablespoon chile powder**
**1 teaspoon smoked paprika**
**1 teaspoon kosher salt**
**½ teaspoon ground cumin**
**½ teaspoon dried sage, crumbled**
**½ teaspoon sugar**
**½ teaspoon ground oregano**
**¼ teaspoon cayenne**
**¼ teaspoon freshly ground black pepper**

### FOR THE BRISKET
**2 large garlic cloves, minced**
**1 (5-pound) beef brisket, flat cut**
**Barbecue Sauce (page 92)**

1. Preheat the oven to 325°F.

**MAKE THE SPICE RUB**
2. Mix the seasonings together in a small bowl.

**MAKE THE BRISKET**
3. Rub the garlic into both sides of the brisket, then rub in the spice rub. Set the brisket, fat side up, on two large overlapping pieces of heavy-duty foil. Wrap the brisket tightly in the foil and set it on a rimmed baking sheet. Roast until tender, about 3 hours. Serve hot or cold with warm barbecue sauce.

# BARBECUE SAUCE

You can make this up to 1 week ahead. Keep it covered in the refrigerator, but heat it before serving. It's great with the brisket, but try serving it with chicken or pork or meatballs. Even with roasted vegetables.

Melt 1 tablespoon unsalted butter in a medium saucepan over medium heat. Add 2 minced garlic cloves and cook until fragrant, about 1 minute. Stir in ½ cup ketchup, ½ cup canned crushed tomatoes, ½ cup packed light brown sugar, ½ cup red wine vinegar, ¼ cup fresh lemon juice, 2 tablespoons Worcestershire sauce, 2 chopped chipotles in adobo, 2 teaspoons mustard seeds, 1 teaspoon grated fresh ginger, and a pinch of cayenne.

Bring the sauce to a boil. Reduce the heat to medium-low and simmer, stirring occasionally, until the sauce is thickened and reduced to about 1½ cups, 15 to 20 minutes. Give it a taste and season with salt and pepper.

I had so much fun at Angelo's when I was in Fort Worth, Texas. They wouldn't share all the secrets to their sauce, but I think mine is pretty close.

# KOREAN-STYLE SHORT RIBS

**SERVES 4**

This recipe is inspired by the *bulgogi*—barbecued beef—that I get in Koreatown. Actually, it's a Korean version of steak fajitas, but instead of tortillas, I serve the meat in lettuce leaves. The dish is traditionally served with kimchi, but any kind of vinegar slaw works well. Short ribs have a reputation for being time-consuming, but these marinate for as little as 10 minutes and broil to perfection in the same amount of time.

**2 pounds bone-in beef short ribs or country-style ribs**
**¾ cup soy sauce**
**1½ teaspoons sesame oil**
**1 teaspoon honey**
**1½ teaspoons ground coriander**
**¾ teaspoon ground cumin**
**¾ teaspoon chile powder**
**3 garlic cloves, minced**
**Lettuce leaves and kimchi (see Note), for serving**

> Make a quick drizzling sauce with ¼ cup soy sauce, 2 teaspoons Ginger Simple Syrup (page 339), and some finely chopped scallions.

1. Cut the rib meat in half almost all the way through lengthwise, so you can open it like a book. Put the ribs in a single layer in a baking dish.

2. Whisk the soy sauce, sesame oil, honey, coriander, cumin, chile powder, and garlic together to make a marinade. Pour the marinade over the short ribs, turning the ribs to coat completely. Cover and marinate for 10 minutes to 1 hour.

3. Set an oven rack 6 inches from the broiler, set the broiler pan on the rack, and preheat (you want the broiler pan very hot so the meat will start to sear immediately).

4. Remove the pan from the broiler and carefully lay the short ribs on it. Broil the ribs until they are caramelized and the meat has just a little give when you prod it with your finger, 5 to 6 minutes, turning once. Be careful when you check the ribs; the fats and sugar can pop. And don't overcook the ribs or they will get tough and chewy.

5. To serve, cut the meat off the bone into bite-sized pieces and serve alongside lettuce leaves and kimchi for guests to make their own short rib lettuce wraps.

**Note:** Look for kimchi in Korean markets, in some grocery stores and farmers' markets, or online.

# CRISPY SUCKLING PIG

**SERVES 8 TO 10**

This is a fantastic dish to make whenever you're feeling ambitious and having a big gathering of folks who love pork. Part of the reason you want to do something like this is that you'll have the best leftovers, which can lead into ten other dishes for later. You'll have to special-order the whole pig from a butcher and make sure it's thoroughly cleaned inside and out (with the eyeballs removed). Rub the pig with caraway to start infusing it with flavor, then make a mop sauce with garlic, ginger, cumin, chile paste, soy sauce, miso, and coffee for a succulent East-meets-West flavor combination. This one makes me think of my friends Christian from Ecuador and Sweet Joy from the Philippines—they both come from countries that are big on pork.

Don't carve this. Just put it out on a big platter with a knife and let your guests go for the bits they want.

1 (10-pound) whole suckling pig (see above),
    prepped for roasting by your butcher

1 cup canola oil

2 tablespoons caraway seeds

4 garlic cloves, peeled

1 (2-inch) piece ginger, peeled and chopped

1 teaspoon cumin seeds

1 cup coffee

1 cup chicken broth

½ cup soy sauce

2 tablespoons dark miso

2 bay leaves

2 tablespoons kosher salt

1 tablespoon chile paste

*Make this the centerpiece of a feast. Put out bowls of salsa verde (see page 184), Plátanos Mash (page 288), Pickled Cabbage (page 294), watercress, slivered onions, limes, and bottles of hot sauce. Beer goes without saying.*

1. Wash the pig well, inside and out, and pat it dry.

2. Rub the pig all over with ½ cup of the canola oil and 1 tablespoon of the caraway seeds. Set it on a platter, cover with plastic wrap, and refrigerate for 12 hours. Take it out of the refrigerator 1 hour before roasting.

3. Set a rack in the lowest position and preheat the oven to 300°F.

4. Put the remaining ½ cup canola oil and remaining 1 tablespoon caraway seeds in a blender with the rest of the ingredients and puree.

5. Wrap the pig's ears with aluminum foil to prevent them from scorching and score the body all over with a sharp knife, cutting through the skin but not into the flesh. Rub the pig inside and out with three-quarters of the puree, put it in a roasting pan, and roast for 4 hours. Baste with the rest of the puree, increase the heat to 400°F, and roast until an instant-read thermometer inserted in the thickest part of the leg registers 160°F, about 1 hour. Transfer the pig to a carving board and let it rest for 30 minutes before serving.

# BACON BISCUITS WITH JALAPEÑO SCRAMBLED EGGS & GRILLED CORN

**SERVES 8, WITH LEFTOVER BISCUITS**

I made this for myself for breakfast once and realized it was too good not to serve to friends. Bacony biscuits, loaded with cheese and chives and brushed with maple syrup, next to a bowl of spicy scrambled eggs and grilled corn. Could there be a better brunch? Now I whip up a batch of these whenever we have houseguests and leave the extra biscuits on the counter so my guests can nibble on them whenever they are feeling hungry. I promise you there are never any left at the end of the day.

**FOR THE BISCUITS**

**6 slices thick-cut bacon**

**3¾ cups all-purpose flour**

**1½ tablespoons baking powder**

**1½ teaspoons baking soda**

**1¼ teaspoons kosher salt**

**8 tablespoons (1 stick) cold unsalted butter, cut into ½-inch cubes, plus 1 tablespoon, melted**

**1½ cups grated cheddar cheese (6 ounces)**

**½ cup crumbled blue cheese**

**¼ cup chopped fresh chives**

**¾ cup buttermilk**

**2 tablespoons pure maple syrup**

**FOR THE CORN**

**4 medium ears corn, cut in half**

**2 tablespoons olive oil**

### FOR THE EGGS

**4 slices thick-cut bacon, chopped**
**3 jalapeños, chopped**
**12 large eggs**
**1 cup half and half**
**Pinch of cayenne**
**Kosher salt and freshly ground black**
**    pepper**

### MAKE THE BISCUITS

1. Preheat the oven to 425°F. Line a baking sheet with parchment.

2. Cook the bacon in a large skillet over medium heat until it's crisp and brown, about 5 minutes. Transfer to paper towels to absorb the excess fat, then crumble.

3. Combine the flour, baking powder, baking soda, and salt in a food processor and process for 5 seconds. Add the cold butter. Process until the mixture begins to resemble coarse meal, about 30 seconds. Transfer to a large bowl. Add the bacon, cheddar cheese, blue cheese, and chives. Toss to blend. Gradually add the buttermilk, mixing with your hand until the liquid is fully incorporated into the dough.

4. Lightly flour your hands, grab about ½ cup of dough, and pat it into a rough round. Put the biscuit on the baking sheet. Continue with the remaining dough, placing the biscuits 2 inches apart on the baking sheet.

5. Bake the biscuits until they are golden and a knife inserted into the center comes out clean, 18 to 20 minutes. Combine the melted butter and maple syrup and lightly brush on the biscuits.

**GRILL THE CORN**

6. Preheat a gas grill to high.

7. Brush the corn with the olive oil, put it on the grill, and grill until the corn is caramelized and some of the kernels have popped, 10 to 15 minutes, turning every 5 minutes.

**MAKE THE EGGS**

8. Cook the bacon in a large skillet over medium-high heat until it starts to brown, about 5 minutes. Add one of the chopped jalapeños and sauté until the jalapeño is tender and the edges are brown, about 4 minutes.

9. Beat together the eggs, half and half, and the remaining jalapeños. Season with cayenne, and salt and pepper to taste. Pour into the skillet with the bacon and turn the heat down to low. Cook, scraping the eggs across the bottom of the skillet to make large curds, until the eggs are cooked but still moist, about 5 minutes.

10. Serve the biscuits warm or at room temperature, split and topped with the scrambled eggs, and a piece of corn per person.

# RED SHRIMP & SPICY GRITS

**SERVES 4**

There are countless ways of cooking the shrimp for this classic Low Country dish.
I add some andouille, cherry tomatoes for a burst of fresh flavor, and paprika and chile
powder to amp up the red color (and the heat).

I didn't grow up eating grits, so I didn't know about a "right" way to make them.
I make them my way. I start by toasting them with an onion and garlic and some curry,
paprika, and chile powder to infuse them with the spices, then I cook them with tomatoes, corn kernels, and wine. It's a mash-up that's a huge hit whenever I make it for
friends who come over to watch a football game (the name for soccer in our house).

**FOR THE GRITS**

¼ cup olive oil

1 medium red onion, chopped

2 garlic cloves, minced

½ teaspoon paprika

½ teaspoon chile powder

½ teaspoon curry powder

1 cup stone-ground grits

1 bay leaf

1 cup canned crushed tomatoes

1 cup corn kernels (fresh or frozen)

¼ cup dry white wine

3 cups water

**FOR THE SHRIMP**

Juice of 2 lemons

2 tablespoons olive oil

½ teaspoon paprika

½ teaspoon chile powder

½ teaspoon curry powder

1 pound extra-large (12–15) shrimp,
    peeled and deveined

8 ounces andouille or other smoked sausage, cut into ½-inch-thick pieces

2 garlic cloves, minced

¼ cup dry white wine

1 tablespoon chopped fresh parsley

1 tablespoon chopped fresh cilantro

Kosher salt and freshly ground black pepper

8 cherry tomatoes, halved, or 1 ripe tomato, chopped

2 tablespoons freshly grated Parmesan cheese (optional)

### MAKE THE GRITS

1. Heat the olive oil in a saucepan over medium heat. Add the onion, garlic, paprika, chile powder, and curry powder. Cook until the onion is slightly softened, 2 to 3 minutes.

2. Add the grits and bay leaf and cook, stirring, for 30 seconds. Add the canned tomatoes, corn kernels, white wine, and water. Simmer, partly covered and stirring once or twice, until the grits are smooth on your tongue, 25 minutes. Discard the bay leaf.

### MAKE THE SHRIMP

3. Put half the lemon juice and 1 tablespoon of the olive oil into a bowl with the paprika, chile powder, and curry powder. Stir to combine, add the shrimp, and toss. Let sit for 15 minutes.

4. Heat a skillet over medium-high heat. Add the andouille and sauté until golden brown, about 5 minutes. Remove the sausage from the pan and fold it into the cooked grits.

5. Add the remaining 1 tablespoon olive oil to the same skillet over medium-high heat. Add the shrimp and garlic and sauté until pink and almost cooked through, about 3 minutes. Pour in the wine and bring it to a boil as you scrape the bottom of the skillet. Add the remaining lemon juice and the parsley and cilantro. Remove from the heat. Season to taste with salt and pepper. Stir in the tomatoes.

6. To serve, divide the grits among four bowls. Top with 3 or 4 shrimp and spoon the tomatoes and pan juices over all. Sprinkle with grated Parmesan, if you'd like.

Leftover grits make great fritters. Chop up some shrimp and mix them into the grits. Make patties, flour them, and deep-fry.

# STICKY-FINGERS CURRIED LOBSTER STEW

**SERVES 4**

I love to cook lobster for friends—and I've never heard anyone say, "Lobster? Again?" There's nothing like walking into a kitchen and seeing a big pot of stew simmering on the stove. The Asian flavors—red curry, coconut milk, lemongrass—make this stew feel sophisticated and complex. Eating with your hands immediately transforms the meal into something more rustic, more casual, and more fun. Serve with a baguette for mopping up every last drop of sauce.

**2 tablespoons olive oil**

**2 tablespoons red curry paste**

**1 teaspoon mustard seeds**

**1 teaspoon coriander seeds**

**1 stalk lemongrass, smashed (see "Prepping Lemongrass," page 45)**

**2 kaffir lime leaves (see Note)**

**4 garlic cloves, minced**

**1 cup coconut milk**

**4 cups water**

**1 cup dry white wine**

**4 ripe tomatoes, chopped**

**2 cups basmati rice**

**6 fingerling or creamer potatoes, scrubbed and quartered**

**2 tablespoons kosher salt**

**1 tablespoon sugar**

**2 (2-pound) lobsters**

**2 red finger chiles (or other small red chiles), thinly sliced**

**Juice of 2 limes**

> Note: If you find kaffir lime leaves in an Asian or Indian market—or in your supermarket—buy them and freeze them. If not, you can substitute the grated zest of 1 lime and ½ teaspoon minced fresh mint.

1. Heat the olive oil in a medium skillet over medium-high heat. Add the curry paste, mustard seeds, coriander seeds, lemongrass, kaffir lime leaves, and garlic and cook, stirring, until fragrant, about 3 minutes. Remove from the heat and cool.

2. Discard the lime leaves and lemongrass. Scrape the remaining contents of the skillet into a blender. Add the coconut milk and blend. Set the curry sauce aside.

3. Bring the water to a boil in a large saucepan over medium heat. Add the white wine, tomatoes, rice, and potatoes. Bring back to a boil, turn the heat to low, cover the pot, and cook until the potatoes are tender and the rice is done, 12 to 15 minutes.

4. Meanwhile, fill a stockpot with water, add the salt and sugar, and bring to a boil. Add the lobsters, headfirst. Cover the pot and cook the lobsters for 7 minutes.

5. Lift the lobsters out of the pot with tongs (reserve the lobster water) and let them cool. When you can handle them, pull off the claws and crack the shells with the back of a heavy knife. Separate the bodies from the tails and cut each in half lengthwise. Remove and discard the sand sac and vein.

6. While the lobsters cool, pour the curry sauce into a large saucepan over medium heat. Add 2 cups of the lobster water. Bring to a simmer and cook until reduced and slightly thickened, about 15 minutes. Add the lobster pieces and cook for a few minutes, to warm the lobster.

7. Spoon the rice and potatoes into four small bowls and the lobster and curry sauce into a big serving bowl. Sprinkle the lobster with the chiles and lime juice and let your guests help themselves.

For even more flavor, chop up the trimmings from the lemongrass, tie them in cheesecloth, and cook them with the rice.

# WHOLE ROASTED TROUT
## WITH HERB DRIZZLE & SCARLET SALAD

**SERVES 4**

Trout became a favorite of mine after I moved to the United States. It's great cooked whole as it is here: painted with an Asian rub of miso, soy, herbs, sesame oil, and a bit of chile heat, grilled on the stovetop to set the skin, then roasted. Once it's filleted, it's drizzled with the flavors of the rub for instant freshness. With a brilliant red salad of radicchio and pomegranate and that herb drizzle, it makes an impressive but not labor-intensive meal to share with friends.

**FOR THE HERB DRIZZLE**
**Juice of 1 lemon**
**1 tablespoon sesame seeds**
**1½ teaspoons white miso**
**1½ teaspoons soy sauce**
**1½ teaspoons chopped fresh parsley**
**1½ teaspoons chopped fresh cilantro**
**¼ teaspoon sesame oil**

**FOR THE TROUT**
**1½ teaspoons chopped fresh parsley**
**1½ teaspoons chopped fresh cilantro**
**1½ teaspoons white miso**
**1½ teaspoons soy sauce**

1 teaspoon chile paste

¼ teaspoon sesame oil

1 garlic clove, minced

2 whole trout

FOR THE SALAD

Juice of 2 limes

2 tablespoons pomegranate juice

1 tablespoon soy sauce

1 teaspoon sugar

1 tablespoon olive oil

½ teaspoon sesame oil

3 tablespoons pomegranate seeds

1 tablespoon chopped fresh chives

1 head radicchio, torn into small pieces

2 romaine hearts, torn into small pieces

Leaves from 4 cilantro sprigs, chopped

Leaves from 2 parsley sprigs, chopped

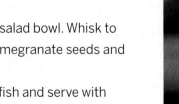

**MAKE THE HERB DRIZZLE**

1. Mix all the ingredients together in a small bowl. Set aside.

**MAKE THE TROUT**

2. Preheat the oven to 375°F. Heat a grill pan over high heat.

3. Mix the parsley, cilantro, miso, soy sauce, chile paste, sesame oil, and garlic together and rub all over the fish. Grill the fish for 3 minutes on each side, then put the grill pan into the oven and roast until the fish is cooked through, 18 to 20 minutes. Let rest for 10 minutes.

**MAKE THE SALAD**

4. Combine the lime juice, pomegranate juice, soy sauce, and sugar in a salad bowl. Whisk to dissolve the sugar, then whisk in the olive and sesame oils. Stir in the pomegranate seeds and chives. Add the radicchio, romaine, cilantro, and parsley and toss.

5. Fillet the trout and put it on a platter. Spoon the herb drizzle over the fish and serve with the salad.

# MONTEREY SARDINES WITH BURNT LEMONS & HERBS

**SERVES 6**

You don't have to have an outdoor grill to get that special charred flavor—particularly when you're cooking fish. You can use a grill pan or a cast iron skillet on your stovetop, which is what I do here with one of my favorite fish, the meaty sardine. A little relish of green olives and red onion, the herbs, and the caramelized lemon make this dish bright and lip-smacking good.

2 lemons, scrubbed and cut into 6 wedges each
Kosher salt
3 tablespoons plus 2 teaspoons coarsely chopped fresh cilantro
18 fresh sardines, gutted, scaled, and rinsed
3 tablespoons coarsely chopped fresh parsley
2 garlic cloves, sliced
2 teaspoons finely chopped lemon zest
⅓ cup brine-cured green olives, pitted and coarsely chopped
3 tablespoons finely chopped red onion
1 tablespoon olive oil, plus more for drizzling
1 tablespoon unsalted butter
2 teaspoons soy sauce
Freshly ground black pepper

*If you have any sardines left over, break up the fish, scramble it with some eggs, and hit them with hot sauce.*

*I call sardines a graduation dish. When you discover that you <u>like</u> dealing with all those little bones, you've graduated to being a true fishhead.*

1. Toss the lemons with 2 teaspoons salt and 2 teaspoons of the chopped cilantro. Set aside.

2. Put the sardines in a single layer in a 9-x-13-inch baking dish. Sprinkle the fish with salt. Cover with plastic wrap and refrigerate for 30 minutes.

3. Meanwhile, combine the remaining 3 tablespoons cilantro, the parsley, garlic, and lemon zest in a small bowl. In a separate bowl, mix the olives and onion together.

4. Drizzle the sardines lightly with olive oil. Sprinkle half of the herb mixture over the sardines, turning to coat.

5. Heat a cast iron skillet over high until just about smoking. Add the sardines in batches, searing them for 2 minutes on one side. Flip and sear for 1 minute on the other side. Transfer the blackened sardines to a serving platter and keep warm while you cook the remaining fish, making sure the skillet is smoking hot again before adding more sardines.

6. Get the skillet hot again and add the lemon wedges. Sear until caramelized on both cut sides, 2 to 3 minutes. Transfer the lemons to the platter. Turn off the heat, add the butter, soy sauce, and the 1 tablespoon olive oil to the skillet and swirl the pan until the butter melts. Drizzle over the sardines.

7. Scatter the onion-olive relish and the remaining herb mixture over the sardines, season with freshly ground black pepper, and serve.

# SPECIAL DAYS

THE MOST SPECIAL DAY IN MY LIFE WAS THE DAY MAYA AND I celebrated our wedding in the countryside in Ethiopia. There was the excitement of waiting for everyone to meet each other—this mash-up of my mother, friends from the U.S., U.K., and Sweden, my family in Africa, and the hundreds of people from Maya's village. There was the drama of the generator that kept breaking down; there was the joy of constant music. And the food. There were sides of beef, each with a butcher who would shave off slices to order and dip them in berbere for a version of that very Ethiopian raw beef dish called *kitfo*. There were vats of *doro wat,* goats roasting over an open fire. It wasn't a day for a vegetarian (though vegetables were served). But I learned something from Maya's tribe. Eating relates to our spiritual conscience, and there is always a reason. We eat *this* way because *this* is happening.

This chapter is a collection of dishes inspired by celebrations I've thrown and celebrations I've attended. I've adopted many special days here in America—as many of us have. Thanksgiving, of course, but there's so much more. I'll make dumplings to welcome Chinese New Year, and I'll listen to jazz and cook a New Orleans–inspired andouille stew for Mardi Gras. And I'll do a stovetop clambake for the Fourth of July, while my neighbors in Harlem head to the parks for their incredible—and illegal—cookouts. I hope these dishes inspire you when you're preparing for an old, familial celebration or when you're heralding a holiday for the first time.

Life moves quickly. These special days, the ones we take time to mark with our hearts—and our meals—are the ones we remember and treasure.

## ★ CHINESE NEW YEAR ★

POACHED CHICKEN WITH GINGER-SCALLION SAUCE   114

SHRIMP & PORK DUMPLINGS   116


## ★ MARDI GRAS ★

ANDOUILLE SAUSAGE & OYSTERS   118


## ★ EASTER ★

YOGURT-MARINATED LEG OF LAMB   121

  PRESERVED LEMONS   123


## ★ PASSOVER ★

FENNEL—MATZO BALL CHICKEN SOUP   124


## ★ MOTHER'S DAY ★

ISN'T SHE LOVELY CREPES WITH RHUBARB-STRAWBERRY
    COMPOTE   126

ROAST BEEF TENDERLOIN WITH A COFFEE-CHOCOLATE
    CRUST   128


## ★ FATHER'S DAY ★

DREAMING OF AUSTRIA   130

★ FOURTH OF JULY ★
FIREHOUSE STOVETOP CLAMBAKE  132

★ THANKSGIVING ★
HARISSA-CRUSTED TURKEY  134

★ CHRISTMAS ★
HELGA JÖNSSON'S ROAST CHICKEN  136
  HOT SPICED WINE  139

★ KWANZAA ★
SOHA CHICKEN JOLLOF RICE  140

# MUSIC TO COOK BY

China Girl ★ David Bowie

Hijo de Africa ★ MC Solaar

The Star Spangled Banner ★ Marvin Gaye

It Ain't Over 'til It's Over (Mama Said album)
   ★ Lenny Kravitz

This Christmas ★ Cee Lo Green

Black Cow ★ Steely Dan

No Water ★ Bob Marley and the Wailers

The Good Life ★ Frank Sinatra and Count Basie
   and His Orchestra

Harvest for the World ★ Isley Brothers

Little Red Rooster ★ Big Mama Thornton

Poached Chicken
with Ginger-Scallion
Sauce (page 114)

# POACHED CHICKEN
## WITH GINGER-SCALLION SAUCE

**SERVES 4**

One of my favorite things to do is to visit Chinatown during Chinese New Year. The meals during this holiday are symbolic, with dishes designed to bring good luck and prosperity for the coming year. But you don't need to be super-educated about the traditions to enjoy them. This whole poached chicken symbolizes joy and togetherness of family.

**1 (3½-pound) chicken**

**1 red chile**

**2 garlic cloves, thinly sliced**

**3 tablespoons sesame oil**

**6 tablespoons peanut oil**

**3 scallions, cut into thin strips**

**1 (3-inch) piece ginger, peeled and minced**

**2 tablespoons light soy sauce**

**1 tablespoon dry sherry**

**2 teaspoons brown sugar**

**1 lemongrass stalk, pounded (see "Prepping Lemongrass," page 45)**

**FOR THE GARNISH**

**2 scallions, thinly sliced on the bias**

**1 cucumber, peeled, halved, seeded, and cut on the bias**

**Fresh cilantro leaves**

**1 teaspoon sesame seeds**

1. Put the chicken in a large stockpot and add just enough water to cover. Add the red chile and garlic. Bring to a boil, reduce the heat, and simmer for 20 minutes. Turn off the heat and let the chicken sit until the broth is lukewarm. Transfer the chicken to a carving board (reserve the broth for another use). Pat the chicken dry with paper towels and rub it lightly all over with the sesame oil. Cut the chicken into 8 serving pieces, arrange on a serving platter, and keep warm.
2. Heat the peanut oil in a small saucepan over high heat. When it shimmers, add the scallion strips. Sauté for 30 seconds, stirring constantly. Remove with a slotted spoon, drain on paper towels, and set aside for the garnish. Add the ginger to the pan and sauté for 30 seconds. Add the soy sauce, sherry, brown sugar, and lemongrass and bring to a boil. Remove the sauce from the heat and discard the lemongrass.

**GARNISH THE CHICKEN**
3. Scatter the sliced scallions, cucumber, cilantro, and sesame seeds around the chicken. Top with the fried scallions and drizzle the sauce over all. Serve warm.

# CHINESE NEW YEAR
# SHRIMP & PORK DUMPLINGS

**MAKES ABOUT 30 DUMPLINGS**

When I worked the cruise ships traveling to Southeast Asia, I was in awe of the Filipino line cooks. Not only did they know Western and Chinese cooking equally well, they made killer dumplings. And it was in Singapore that I experienced the sharp flavor of fresh ginger—so unlike the ground ginger I knew from home. There's ginger in both the dumpling filling and the dipping sauce here, but shrimp and pork are the stars. The pork (a symbol of strength and wealth) is tender; the shrimp (a symbol of happiness and good fortune) gives the filling density and some chew. It's a combination both elegant and humble.

Dumplings are an important part of the New Year's meal in Northern China. There, you might find some peanuts in the filling—for health and long life. Have family and friends pitch in when you're assembling them.

**FOR THE DUMPLINGS**

½ pound shrimp (any size), peeled and minced or ground
    in a food processor
¼ pound ground pork
1 tablespoon soy sauce
2 teaspoons finely chopped scallion
1 teaspoon chopped fresh cilantro
1 garlic clove, minced
½ teaspoon grated peeled ginger
½ teaspoon sesame oil
30 round dumpling wrappers
15 medium (31–35) shrimp,
    peeled

*Grate ginger on a Microplane.*

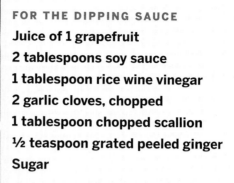

### FOR THE DIPPING SAUCE

**Juice of 1 grapefruit**
**2 tablespoons soy sauce**
**1 tablespoon rice wine vinegar**
**2 garlic cloves, chopped**
**1 tablespoon chopped scallion**
**½ teaspoon grated peeled ginger**
**Sugar**

### MAKE THE DUMPLINGS

1. Put the ground shrimp, pork, soy sauce, scallion, cilantro, garlic, ginger, and sesame oil in a bowl and mix well.

2. Spoon about 1 tablespoon of the filling onto the center of a wrapper. Brush the edge with water. Pick up the wrapper, fold it into a half-moon, and pinch to seal. Repeat to make all the dumplings, setting them on a lightly oiled baking sheet.

3. Add about 1 inch of water to a pot and fit in a bamboo steamer. Bring the water to a boil over medium-high heat.

4. When the water is boiling, place the dumplings in the steamer and set a raw shrimp half on top of each (they will stick to the dumplings during steaming). Cover and steam until cooked, about 5 minutes.

### MAKE THE DIPPING SAUCE

5. While the dumplings steam, stir the grapefruit juice, soy sauce, vinegar, garlic, scallion, and ginger together in a small bowl. Taste and add a pinch or two of sugar. Serve alongside the steamed dumplings.

# ANDOUILLE SAUSAGE & OYSTERS

**SERVES 8**

Mardi Gras celebrations culminate on Shrove Tuesday—aka Fat Tuesday. It's the last day before the fasting season of Lent, and it's Fat because we fill our bellies with rich and delicious dishes. This is my version of a New Orleans gumbo—a dish I learned about during my visits with the New Orleans cooking legend Leah Chase. No long-cooked dark roux, just onions and peppers and andouille with some okra to thicken the stock. And yes, fried oysters on top.

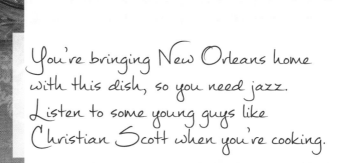

*You're bringing New Orleans home with this dish, so you need jazz. Listen to some young guys like Christian Scott when you're cooking.*

4¼ cups water

2½ cups long-grain white rice

Kosher salt

Peanut oil as needed

1 pound andouille sausage (see Note), quartered lengthwise and cut crosswise into ½-inch-thick pieces

½ pound okra, trimmed and thinly sliced

2 medium onions, chopped

1 celery rib, chopped

1 green bell pepper, seeded and chopped

1 red bell pepper, seeded and chopped

2 large garlic cloves, finely chopped

1¾ cups chicken broth

Freshly ground black pepper

2 scallions, thinly sliced

2 tablespoons cornstarch

1 tablespoon cornmeal

1 teaspoon smoked paprika

8 oysters, shucked

Note: If you can't find andouille in your local stores, you can order it online. Or in a pinch you can substitute another smoked sausage like kielbasa.

1. Preheat the oven to 350°F.

2. Bring 4 cups of the water to a boil in a 4-quart heavy saucepan. Add the rice and ½ teaspoon salt and stir. Cook over low heat, covered tightly, until the water is absorbed and the rice is tender, about 20 minutes. Remove the saucepan from the heat and let it stand, covered and undisturbed, for 10 minutes. Fluff the rice with a fork and keep covered.

3. While the rice cooks, heat 1 tablespoon peanut oil in a 10- to 12-inch heavy skillet—preferably cast iron—over medium-high heat until it's hot but not smoking. Add half of the sausage and sauté, stirring occasionally, until browned, 2 to 3 minutes. Transfer the sausage with a slotted spoon to a bowl. Add a little more oil if needed and brown the rest of the sausage, then transfer to the bowl. Add a little more oil if needed, then add the okra and cook, stirring occasionally, until browned, 2 to 3 minutes. Transfer the okra to another bowl.

4. Heat 1 tablespoon peanut oil in the skillet. Add the onions, celery, and bell peppers and cook, stirring occasionally, until the onions and peppers are softened and browned, about 5 minutes. Add the garlic and sauté until it's fragrant, about 1 minute. Add the remaining ¼ cup water, the okra, broth, black pepper, and 1 teaspoon salt. Bring to a boil, then reduce the heat and simmer, stirring occasionally, until slightly thickened and the liquid has cooked down to just below the surface of the solids, 10 to 15 minutes. Stir in the sausage and scallions. Taste and season with salt and pepper.

5. Heat 2 inches peanut oil in a saucepan to 350°F.

6. Mix the cornstarch, cornmeal, and smoked paprika together in a small bowl. Dredge the oysters, coating them completely. Fry the oysters in batches until golden, 1 to 2 minutes. Remove with a slotted spoon and drain on paper towels.

7. Put a big spoonful of rice into 8 soup plates, ladle on the andouille stew, and top each serving with a fried oyster.

You don't have to be in New Orleans to experience great gumbo. These guys in Charleston know just where to find the best oysters.

# YOGURT-MARINATED LEG OF LAMB

**SERVES 8 TO 10**

Easter is a big celebration in Ethiopia. The Ethiopian Orthodox church follows the Julian calendar, which means that the holiday doesn't always fall on the same day as other denominations' celebrations. As a result, some years I have Easter dinners two Sundays in a row—one Ethiopian, for which we have *doro wat* (see page 159). Our other Easter celebration features this yogurt-marinated leg of lamb, which is moist and full of flavor and inspired by the foods of the Middle East—with just a hint of North Africa. You'll need to start this the night before.

**2 cups plain Greek yogurt**

**2 tablespoons ground coriander**

**1½ tablespoons cumin seeds**

**1 tablespoon caraway seeds**

**2 teaspoons ground turmeric**

**2 teaspoons smoked paprika**

**Juice of 1 lemon**

**5 large garlic cloves, minced**

**Kosher salt and freshly ground black pepper**

**¼ cup olive oil**

**1 (6- to 8-pound) bone-in leg of lamb, fat trimmed**

**2 lemons, halved**

**Vegetable oil, for brushing**

**2 preserved lemons (see page 123), cut into pieces**

1. Mix the yogurt, coriander, cumin, caraway, turmeric, paprika, and lemon juice together in a large bowl. Transfer 1 generous cup to another bowl and stir in 1 minced garlic clove. Season the yogurt sauce with salt and pepper. Cover and refrigerate.

2. To make the marinade, add the remaining 4 minced garlic cloves and the olive oil to the remaining seasoned yogurt. Add salt and pepper to taste. Transfer the marinade to a 2-gallon zip-top bag. Add the lamb, close the bag, and massage to make sure all the lamb is covered with the marinade. Refrigerate overnight.

3. Take the lamb out of the refrigerator and leave it at room temperature for 1 hour. Preheat the oven to 425°F.

4. Set the lamb on a rack in a roasting pan. Roast for 30 minutes. Reduce the heat to 350°F and roast until the lamb reaches 125°F (for medium-rare). Start checking with an instant-read thermometer in the thickest parts of the leg after 30 minutes at 350°F. Let it rest, tented with foil, for at least 20 minutes before carving.

5. Heat a small, heavy skillet over high heat. When it's very hot, brush the lemon halves with vegetable oil and sear in the skillet, cut side down, until dark brown, about 5 minutes.

6. Serve the lamb with the blackened lemons, pieces of preserved lemons, and the yogurt sauce.

# PRESERVED LEMONS

You can find preserved lemons in specialty shops and online, but they're so easy to make at home. You just need to plan ahead, because they take a month to cure. But they last forever, and you want to always have them in your refrigerator.

Cut scrubbed lemons into quarters from top to bottom, leaving them attached at the bottom. Fill the insides of each lemon with 1 tablespoon kosher salt and squeeze closed. Pack the lemons tightly into a sterilized Mason jar, leaving about an inch of headroom. Screw on the top and put someplace out of the light for 3 days. Open the jar, push the lemons down, and add enough fresh lemon juice to cover them generously. Close the jar again and refrigerate for 1 month before using.

When you need them, pull off and discard the flesh. You want the peel— sliced or chopped.

# FENNEL—MATZO BALL CHICKEN SOUP

**SERVES 6**

You find dumplings in the foods of many cultures, like the *kroppkakor* (Swedish Potato Dumplings, page 292) that I grew up with, the *knoedel* (bread dumplings) that I learned about when I was a young chef in Austria, and the gnocchi that I've made with my friend Jonathan Waxman. They're all delicious and I love experimenting with them, making them my own. Here I roast fennel until it's meltingly soft, then puree it and add it to matzo balls that are served in chicken soup. The fennel adds a hint of licorice bitterness to the fluffy matzo balls, along with a richness that almost makes me think I'm eating a protein.

**FOR THE MATZO BALLS**

2 smallish fennel bulbs (about 1 pound)

2 tablespoons olive oil

½ cup chicken broth

2 large garlic cloves, coarsely chopped

¾ teaspoon chopped fresh thyme leaves

Kosher salt and freshly ground black pepper

¼ teaspoon fennel seeds, ground in a spice grinder or with a mortar and pestle (optional)

2 large eggs

½ cup plus 2 tablespoons matzo meal if needed

**FOR THE SOUP**

2 tablespoons olive oil

2 onions, thinly sliced

2 carrots, peeled and diced

2 garlic cloves, chopped

2 quarts chicken broth (homemade or good-quality, low-sodium store-bought)

1 cup dry white wine

¼ pound shiitake mushrooms, stemmed and thinly sliced

Fennel stalks are excellent when you're making a fish or chicken stock. Same goes for the core and tough outer pieces, so don't throw them away. Lock them in a plastic bag and freeze until you need them.

## MAKE THE MATZO BALLS

1. Preheat the oven to 400°F.

2. Cut off the fennel stalks and reserve for another use. If there are some attractive feathery fronds, finely chop and set aside about 2 tablespoons to garnish the soup. Quarter the bulbs and trim away the hard core and any tough outer pieces. Choose a shallow baking pan just large enough to fit the fennel. Drizzle the fennel with 1 tablespoon of the olive oil and toss to coat. Arrange the fennel in one layer and roast until pale gold, about 20 minutes. Turn the fennel over and roast for 10 minutes longer. Pour in the broth, add the garlic and ½ teaspoon of the thyme, and season with salt and pepper. Cover the pan with foil and roast until the fennel is very soft and tender, about 35 minutes. Remove the foil, stir, and roast for a few more minutes to cook off all the liquid. Let the fennel cool slightly.

3. Scrape the fennel and any juices in the pan into a food processor and pulse to chop coarsely. Add the remaining ¼ teaspoon thyme, 1 teaspoon salt (or to taste), a grind or two of pepper, and the fennel seeds, if using. With the machine on, add the remaining 1 tablespoon oil through the feed tube.

4. Measure 1 cup of the fennel puree into a large bowl (any left over is a cook's treat). Whisk in the eggs, one at a time. Add ½ cup of the matzo meal and stir well. If you can form a lump of dough into a very soft walnut-size ball that holds its shape, don't add any more matzo meal (the dough will become firmer when you chill it). If necessary, add just enough meal to enable you to do so. Cover the bowl with plastic wrap and refrigerate for at least 2 hours or up to 4 hours.

5. Bring a large, wide pot of salted water to a boil over high heat.

6. Wet your hands, roll the matzo dough into walnut-size balls, and put them on a plate or baking sheet. When all the balls are rolled and the water is boiling furiously, turn the heat down to a gentle boil. Carefully slide in the balls, one at a time, and cover the pot tightly. Turn the heat down to low and simmer the matzo balls for 30 minutes, without removing the cover. Test a matzo ball by cutting it in half. It should be light, fluffy, and completely cooked through. If it isn't, simmer the matzo balls a few more minutes. Remove them gently with a skimmer or large slotted spoon— they are too fragile to pour into a colander—and put them on a platter. Cover lightly with plastic wrap and let them sit while you make the soup.

## MAKE THE SOUP

7. Heat the oil in a stockpot over medium-high heat. When it shimmers, add the onions, carrots, and garlic and sauté until the onion softens, about 5 minutes. Add the broth and wine and bring to a boil. Turn the heat down and simmer for 10 minutes.

8. Strain the broth and return it to the pot. Add the mushrooms and matzo balls and simmer until the mushrooms are tender and the matzo balls hot, about 5 minutes.

9. Using a slotted spoon, transfer the matzo balls to shallow soup bowls and ladle the hot soup and mushrooms over them. Garnish with the chopped fennel fronds.

# ISN'T SHE LOVELY CREPES WITH RHUBARB-STRAWBERRY COMPOTE

**SERVES 4, WITH 3 CREPES EACH**

Simple crepes can be dressed up in so many ways. They can be doused with orange liqueur and flamed, they can be filled with whipped cream and jam, and I'm not even going to start on the myriad savory fillings. I like them best served with fruit. This simple compote of rhubarb and strawberries stewed in orange juice and flavored with cardamom and ginger is sweet and tangy. I think it tastes like spring.

**FOR THE COMPOTE**

2 rhubarb stalks, peeled and chopped into ¼-inch-thick pieces (1 generous cup)

½ cup granulated sugar

1 cup fresh orange juice

1 teaspoon ground ginger

2 cardamom pods

½ pint strawberries, hulled and coarsely chopped

**FOR THE CREPES**

6 large eggs

1 cup whole milk

2 cups heavy cream

1 teaspoon vanilla extract

1 cup all-purpose flour

1 cup confectioners' sugar

2 teaspoons grated orange zest

⅛ teaspoon kosher salt

Melted butter, for the pan

1 tablespoon Grand Marnier (or other orange liqueur)

Fresh mint leaves, for garnish

*Don't be discouraged if you screw up the first crepe or two. You'll find the right heat.*

## MAKE THE COMPOTE

1. Simmer the rhubarb, granulated sugar, orange juice, ginger, and cardamom in a saucepan over medium-low heat until the rhubarb is very tender and starting to break down, about 30 minutes. Remove from the heat. Remove the cardamom pods and stir in the strawberries. Let the compote sit on the back of the stove while you make the crepes.

## MAKE THE CREPES

2. Put the eggs, milk, ½ cup of the heavy cream, ½ teaspoon of the vanilla, the flour, ¼ cup of the confectioners' sugar, 1 teaspoon of the zest, and the salt in a blender and blend until just smooth. Refrigerate the batter for 1 hour. (You can make the batter the day before and refrigerate it, covered.)

3. Brush a 10-inch nonstick skillet lightly with some melted butter, then heat over medium-high heat until hot. Lift up the skillet, pour in a scant ¼ cup batter, and immediately tilt and rotate the skillet to coat it with batter. If the batter sets before the skillet is coated, reduce the heat slightly for the next crepe. Cook until the underside is golden and the top is just set, 15 to 45 seconds. Loosen the edge of the crepe with a heatproof rubber spatula, then flip the crepe over with your fingertips and cook it for another 15 seconds. Transfer the cooked crepe to a plate. Continue making the crepes, brushing the skillet with butter each time and stacking the cooked crepes.

4. Beat the remaining 1½ cups cream, ½ teaspoon vanilla, ¾ cup confectioners' sugar, 1 teaspoon zest, and the Grand Marnier with an electric mixer in a large bowl until the cream holds stiff peaks.

5. Spread a generous tablespoon of the rhubarb-strawberry compote in the center of each crepe and either roll them up or fold them in quarters. Lay 3 filled crepes on each plate. Serve with a big dollop of the whipped cream and garnish with mint leaves.

# MOTHER'S DAY
# ROAST BEEF TENDERLOIN
## WITH A COFFEE-CHOCOLATE CRUST

**SERVES 6 TO 8**

Sometimes a celebration calls for a big, impressive roast of beef, and what better way to honor Mom than with beef tenderloin? It's an elegant cut, fork-tender, but the flavor is mild so it's an ideal candidate for a zesty rub. I start with Provençal flavors—rosemary, tarragon, mustard, anchovies, garlic—and add coffee and chocolate for rich, deep notes.

1 (3- to 4-pound) trimmed beef tenderloin

Kosher salt and freshly ground black pepper

2 tablespoons coffee beans

2 tablespoons black peppercorns

2 teaspoons grated unsweetened chocolate (100% cacao)

1 tablespoon Dijon mustard

4 anchovy fillets, chopped

3 garlic cloves, minced

3 tablespoons olive oil

1 tablespoon chopped
    fresh tarragon

Needles from 2 sprigs fresh
    rosemary, chopped

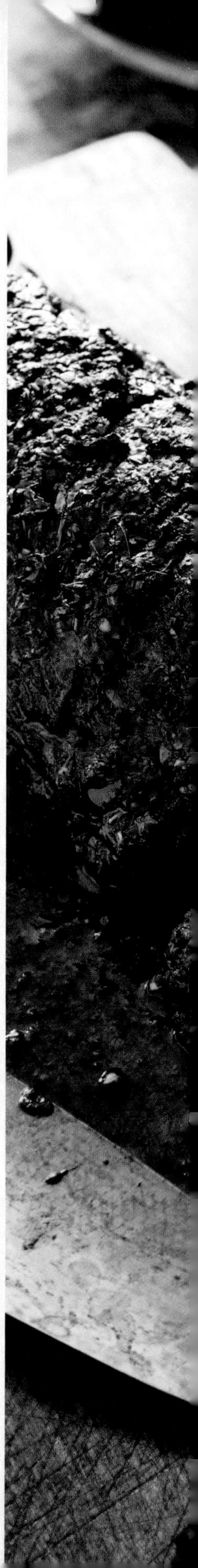

1. Take the beef out of the refrigerator 1 hour before you plan to roast it and season with salt and pepper.

2. Preheat the oven to 425°F.

3. Crush the coffee beans and peppercorns with a mortar and pestle or on the counter with the back of a small, heavy skillet.

4. Mix the coffee bean–peppercorn mixture with the chocolate, mustard, anchovies, garlic, and 1 tablespoon of the olive oil to make a thick paste.

5. Heat the remaining 2 tablespoons olive oil in a large, ovenproof skillet over high heat. When it shimmers, add the beef and sear it on all sides, about 8 minutes. Press down on the beef to get a good crust on it. Slather the paste on the beef and strew the herbs on top.

6. Slide the skillet into the oven and roast until the beef registers 120° to 125°F for medium-rare; start checking with an instant-read thermometer after 20 minutes. Tent the roast loosely with foil and let it rest for 30 minutes before carving.

## FATHER'S DAY
# DREAMING OF AUSTRIA

**SERVES 6**

When I was a young chef, I worked for a short period at Elisabethpark, a hotel in Bad Gastein, Austria. The days were long and grueling, but I learned a lot, particularly about the power of regional cuisine. On my rare evenings off, I'd go to a local bar with a friend or two from the kitchen. We'd drink *Weissbier* or cider, play cards, eat knackwurst with sweet mustard, and sop up sauerkraut stewed with apples and potatoes with bits of soft pretzels. It's a great meal to re-create for dads.

Get the best sauerkraut you can—maybe from a German butcher—for this dish. And don't forget the soft pretzels!

### FOR THE MUSTARD
**6 tablespoons grainy Dijon mustard**
**1 tablespoon chopped fresh dill**
**1 tablespoon honey**

### FOR THE SAUERKRAUT AND KNACKWURST
**2 slices bacon, chopped**
**1 large onion, thinly sliced**
**2 garlic cloves, chopped**
**2 (8-ounce) russet potatoes, peeled and grated**
**2 Granny Smith apples, peeled, cored, and grated**
**2 cups sauerkraut, rinsed and drained**
**2 cups lager-style beer**
**1 cup beef or chicken broth (or water)**
**½ cup apple cider vinegar**
**2 teaspoons caraway seeds**
**1 bay leaf**
**6 links knackwurst**

## MAKE THE MUSTARD

1. Mix all the ingredients together in a small bowl.

## MAKE THE SAUERKRAUT AND KNACKWURST

2. Sauté the bacon, onion, and garlic in a large, heavy pot over medium-high heat until the bacon is crisp and the onion is starting to brown, about 8 minutes. Rinse the potatoes and add them to the pot with the apples, sauerkraut, beer, broth, vinegar, caraway, and bay leaf. Bring to a boil, then cover, reduce the heat, and simmer for 35 minutes. Discard the bay leaf.

3. Meanwhile, preheat a gas grill to high.

4. Set the knackwurst on top of the sauerkraut, cover, and simmer for 10 minutes.

5. Remove the knackwurst and place on the grill to cook until golden brown and lightly charred, turning occasionally, 7 to 8 minutes.

6. Pile the sauerkraut onto a platter, top with the knackwurst, and serve with the mustard.

The butcher in a well-stocked meat market like this one in Clifton, New Jersey, can help you with this recipe.

## FOURTH OF JULY
# FIREHOUSE STOVETOP CLAMBAKE

**SERVES 4 TO 6**

Clambakes are a wonderful American summer tradition and a fantastic way to feed a crowd efficiently. They also remind me of Swedish crawfish parties. But you don't need to dig a pit to cook up the clams, mussels, shrimp, and potatoes—a big pot on top of the stove works great. I'm usually in the city for Fourth of July, not out at the beach as I'd like to be, and this is the dish I prepare for friends—just like firemen would make it for each other.

**4 slices bacon, diced**
**4 garlic cloves, halved**
**2 cups chicken broth**
**2 cups water**
**¼ cup dry white wine**
**8 medium red-skinned potatoes,
    scrubbed and quartered**
**2 medium red onions, coarsely
    chopped**
**4 sprigs fresh thyme**
**Kosher salt and freshly ground black
    pepper**
**1 dozen cherrystone clams, scrubbed**
**1 pound mussels, washed and
    debearded**
**1 pound large (21–25) shrimp**
**3 tablespoons unsalted butter,
    cut into bits**
**Chopped fresh parsley, for
    garnish**
**2 lemons, cut into
    wedges**

1. Cook the bacon in a very large stockpot over medium heat until it renders some fat. Add the garlic and cook until it's fragrant, about 1 minute. Add the chicken broth, water, wine, potatoes, onions, and thyme. Season with salt and pepper. Bring to a boil, reduce the heat, cover, and simmer until the potatoes are tender, 10 to 15 minutes.

2. Add the clams, mussels, and shrimp and scatter the surface with the butter. Cover and cook until the clams and mussels open and the shrimp are pink and opaque, 4 to 5 minutes. If some of the clams and mussels do not open, remove the shrimp and cook for a little longer; discard any that do not open.

3. Use a skimmer or a slotted spoon to divide the seafood and potatoes among deep bowls, then ladle in the fragrant broth and onions. Sprinkle the bowls with chopped parsley and serve with lemon wedges.

# THANKSGIVING
# HARISSA-CRUSTED TURKEY

**SERVES 8 TO 10**

Thanksgiving quickly became my favorite holiday when I moved to New York. I was one of a group of young chefs with small apartments, and we would take turns hosting potlucks. I usually brought gravlax. Or herring. But as soon as I moved into a bigger apartment—with a real kitchen—I wanted to host and cook the turkey. I started by rubbing it with harissa and stuffing it with sweet potatoes and onions. I like making this holiday spicy.

Start this the day before.

**1 (12-pound) turkey (neck and liver reserved)**
**Kosher salt and freshly ground black pepper**
**6 garlic cloves, quartered**
**2 red onions, quartered**
**2 cups cubed (½-inch) peeled sweet potatoes**
**2 sprigs fresh thyme, coarsely chopped**
**1 cup plus ½ tablespoon Harissa (page 245)**
**½ cup olive oil, plus more for the liver**
**3 cups chicken broth**
**1 cup water**
**All-purpose flour**

> *Don't forget to put out some Hot Brussels Sprouts Slaw (page 280). And for dessert? Garam Masala–Pumpkin Tart (page 321) and Buttermilk Sorbet (page 338).*

1. Season the turkey liberally, inside and out, with salt and pepper. Put it on a baking sheet and refrigerate, uncovered, overnight.

2. Position a rack in the lower third of the oven and preheat to 400°F.

3. Toss the garlic, onions, sweet potatoes, and thyme with ½ tablespoon of the harissa. Stuff the vegetables into the large cavity and close with a wooden skewer.

4. Combine 1 cup harissa with the olive oil and generously rub over and under the skin of the bird. Fold the neck skin under the body and secure it with a small skewer; tie the drumsticks together with kitchen string; and secure the wings to the body with small skewers. Put the turkey and the neck in the roasting pan and tent the breast with foil. Roast for 20 minutes. Pour 2 cups of the broth into the pan and stir to scrape up any browned

bits on the bottom. Roast the turkey for 40 minutes. Remove the neck from the pan. Reduce the oven temperature to 350°F. Add the remaining 1 cup broth to the pan and continue to roast the bird, basting occasionally with the pan juices, until an instant-read thermometer inserted into the thickest part of a thigh registers 165°F, 1½ to 2 hours more. Remove the foil during the last 20 minutes of cooking. Transfer the turkey to a cutting board and let rest for 30 minutes.

5. Skim the excess fat from the juices in the roasting pan, then set the pan over medium-low heat. Add the water, stirring to dissolve any browned bits, and simmer the pan gravy until it reduces and thickens slightly.

6. Heat a slick of oil in a small skillet over medium-high heat. When it shimmers, dredge the liver in flour, add it to the skillet, and sear until cooked through but still pink, about 5 minutes. Chop the liver and pull the meat from the neck. Add the liver and neck meat to the pan gravy.

7. Carve the turkey and serve with the gravy and the vegetables in the cavity.

Be quick when you add the broth and when you baste. Oven temperatures drop very quickly.

# CHRISTMAS
# HELGA JÖNSSON'S ROAST CHICKEN

**SERVES 4**

My grandmother Helga Jönsson always salted her chicken and left it in the cool basement for a couple of hours. Then she'd pull out her spices—cardamom, ginger, coriander seeds—to rub over the chicken, and she'd stuff it with apples and onions and rosemary from her yard. Then she'd roast it on a raft of carrots. I honor Helga's traditions with this recipe, but I brine the bird in orange juice and turn to classic Indian spices—turmeric and garam masala—for a golden rub. You know I can't help tinkering, but the spirit is pure Helga.

Helga served her Christmas chicken with potato dumplings (page 292), and so do I, but I mash things up a little by serving the chicken with a roasted garlic and herb vinaigrette and some Smoky Collards & Kale (page 282), too. My Swedish Princess Cake (page 330) is the perfect ending for this meal.

**FOR THE GARLIC-HERB VINAIGRETTE**

**3 tablespoons olive oil**

**3 garlic cloves, peeled**

**2 sprigs fresh rosemary**

**1 tablespoon chopped fresh parsley**

**1 tablespoon chopped fresh cilantro**

**1 tablespoon rice wine vinegar**

**2 teaspoons soy sauce**

**Kosher salt and freshly ground black pepper**
**4 dashes Tabasco sauce**

**FOR THE CHICKEN**
**1 (3½-pound) chicken**
**5 cups water**
**1 cup orange juice**
**½ cup kosher salt**
**5 sprigs fresh rosemary**
**2 tablespoons unsalted butter, softened**
**Grated zest of 1 orange**
**Juice of ½ orange**
**2 teaspoons ground turmeric**
**2 teaspoons garam masala**
**3 carrots, peeled and halved**
**2 tablespoons all-purpose flour, plus more for**
   **dredging**
**Soy sauce**
**Olive oil, for the liver**

**MAKE THE GARLIC-HERB VINAIGRETTE**
1. Heat the oil in a small skillet over low heat. Add the garlic and rosemary and cook, being careful not to burn the rosemary, until the garlic is softened and golden, about 10 minutes. Scrape the garlic and oil into a blender. When the rosemary is cool enough to handle, strip the needles and add them to the blender with the parsley, cilantro, vinegar, and soy sauce. Blend to a smooth puree. Scrape into a small bowl and season with salt, pepper, and the Tabasco. Cover and set aside.

**MAKE THE CHICKEN**
2. Trim off any excess skin from the neck and remove any fat from the chicken cavity (save these as well as the neck and giblets for stock); refrigerate the liver. Combine 3 cups of the water and the orange juice in a

bowl large enough to hold the chicken. Add the salt and stir to dissolve. Submerge the chicken in the brine and refrigerate for 3 hours.

3. Preheat the oven to 350°F.

4. Pull the needles from 3 of the rosemary sprigs. Chop them and put them in a bowl with the butter, orange zest and juice, turmeric, and garam masala. Mix well.

5. Lay the carrots in the middle of a cast iron skillet to make a rack for the chicken. Pat the chicken dry, stuff the cavity with the remaining 2 rosemary sprigs, and rub the chicken with the spiced butter. Set the chicken on the carrots and roast, basting a few times, until the juices run clear when a knife is inserted near a thigh, about 1½ hours.

6. Transfer the chicken and carrots to a carving board and let rest for 30 minutes.

7. Put the skillet over medium heat. Add the 2 tablespoons flour to the drippings and cook, stirring, for 1 minute. Add the remaining 2 cups water and cook, stirring, until it comes to a boil. Reduce the heat and simmer for 10 minutes. Taste and season the gravy with soy sauce.

8. Meanwhile, heat a slick of oil in a small skillet over medium-high heat. When it shimmers, dredge the liver in flour, add it to the skillet, and sear until cooked through but still pink, about 3 minutes.

9. Carve the chicken and put it on a platter. Add the carrots and liver and serve with the gravy and the vinaigrette.

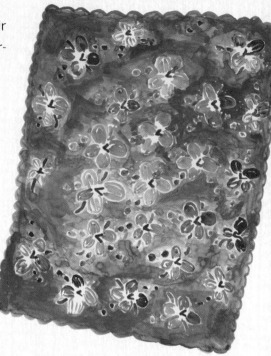

Helga made stock with the neck and skin and gizzards and chicken carcass and whatever vegetable scraps and peelings she had. Nothing went to waste. Later she'd serve the stock with a pot of rice or potatoes and whatever meat was left over from an earlier meal.

# HOT SPICED WINE

Hot mulled wines are common all over Europe, but they are a particular favorite in Sweden. I start making this drink as soon as it gets cold outside. When the days get shorter, there's a natural inclination to retreat a little bit. But when my friends are gathered in my living room and we are all clutching warm mugs of spiced wine, I'm reminded that the colder months—maybe even more so than the summer—are a good time to draw close to the people you love.

Use a mortar and pestle to crush 2 cinnamon sticks and 1 teaspoon cardamom pods; you want to break up the cinnamon and open the cardamom pods to release the seeds. Put the crushed spices, a 1-inch piece of peeled

ginger, the zest from half an orange, 8 cloves, and ⅓ cup vodka in a jar. Cover and infuse for 24 hours.

Strain the vodka through a fine sieve into a large saucepan. Add a bottle of dry red wine, 1 cup of ruby port or Madeira, 1 cup sugar, ½ cup blanched almonds, ½ cup raisins, and 1 star anise. Heat over medium heat until the wine is hot and bubbles start to form around the edges of the pot.

Ladle the hot wine into mugs and garnish with a few blanched almonds and raisins. You can keep any remaining wine in the saucepan, covered, over the lowest-possible heat until ready to serve. Do not let the wine boil.

This makes enough for 8.

# SOHA CHICKEN JOLLOF RICE

**SERVES 6 TO 8**

When I want great Senegalese cooking I head to 118th Street and 8th Avenue—the heart of South Harlem (yes, uptowners call it SoHa) and the center of a huge West African community. It brings back memories of the time I spent with a family in Senegal, when we shared a pot of rice with every meal.

There are as many variations of this one-pot (jollof) meal as there are cooks. I stain my rice red with dende oil and tomatoes, season it with curry and cinnamon and a hot pepper, and pack it with chicken, onions, peppers, cabbage, and green beans. Africa's groundnuts (here in the form of peanut butter) add richness and make the rice even more fragrant.

**¼ cup dende oil (see Note)**

**8 bone-in chicken thighs**

**2 medium onions, chopped**

**1 red bell pepper, chopped**

**1 bird's eye chile (or other small hot chile), chopped**

**1 large carrot, peeled and coarsely shredded**

**4 garlic cloves, minced**

**1½ cups long-grain white rice**

**¼ cup tomato paste**

**¼ cup peanut butter**

**1 large ripe tomato, seeded and chopped**

**3 cups water**

**1 cup canned crushed tomatoes**

**1 cup chopped (1-inch lengths) green beans,
   fresh or frozen**

**1 cup thinly sliced cabbage**

**1 teaspoon curry powder**

**½ teaspoon ground cinnamon**

**Kosher salt and freshly ground black pepper**

**3 hard-boiled eggs, sliced, for garnish**

Note: Rich, red dende oil is a palm oil popular in African and Brazilian cooking. Look for it in African and Brazilian markets and online. In a pinch, you can substitute peanut oil.

1. Heat the oil in a large pot over medium-high heat. When it shimmers, add the chicken and brown on all sides, 5 to 6 minutes. Transfer the chicken to a platter.

2. Add the onions, bell pepper, chile, and carrot to the pot. Cook until the onions are wilted and translucent, 4 to 5 minutes. Add the garlic and cook until fragrant, about 1 minute.

3. Add the rice and cook, stirring, until all the rice is coated with oil, about 1 minute. Add the tomato paste and peanut butter and stir to distribute them evenly. Add the chopped tomato and cook until it starts to soften, 2 to 3 minutes. Add the water, crushed tomatoes, green beans, cabbage, curry powder, and cinnamon. Stir everything together and season well with salt and pepper. Return the chicken to the pot, burying it in the rice. Bring to a boil, reduce the heat to low, cover tightly, and simmer until the rice is tender and the chicken cooked through, 20 minutes.

4. Remove the pot from the heat and let rest for 10 minutes. Pile the chicken and rice on a platter and garnish with the sliced hard-boiled eggs.

# STREET FOOD

STREET FOOD HAS TO BE MY FAVORITE FOOD IN THE WORLD, AND I'VE HAD A long love affair with it. It started in Sweden, with hot dogs and meatballs on the street, and continued in Germany and Austria, where I found wurst. Then I started working on cruise ships. Docks are never in the finest part of town, but there would always be people selling food when I got off the boat. There were the tamale guys in Acapulco. And the hawkers in Singapore—Arabs, Indians, Chinese, Malay people, all cooking on the street. For a few bucks, I could have an Indian breakfast of goat stew and egg and chutney or eat noodles that had been fried right in front of me—so far from the complex dishes that I prepared for the ship's dining room with its sparkling white tablecloths. Now, when I travel to Austin, Texas, I head to the South Congress neighborhood and smile at all the food trucks. Grand Central Market is my happy place in Los Angeles.

The street food of Mexico may be the most exciting of all—the ceviches in shacks on the coast, the *tacos al pastor* I got in a stall in Mexico City. But then I remember the fish fry from Oistin's in Barbados and the docks in Zanzibar, where Africans and Persians and Indians cooked the seafood they had just caught. And there's the Jamaican man not far from where I live now: He cooks up meat and chicken and fish with that spice mix called jerk, and his food is incredible.

On the street, people are selling their culture, and themselves. These are unplugged sessions, not rehearsed performances. And this is the best kind of food to make at home, because these cooks do all their prep in their little home kitchens, just like you will.

# MUSIC TO COOK BY

Sabotage ★ Beastie Boys

California Love ★ 2pac featuring Roger Troutman, Dr. Dre

Oye como Va ★ Santana

Walk on the Wild Side ★ Lou Reed

The Adventures of Rain Dance Maggie ★ Red Hot Chili Peppers

Your Love ★ Frankie Knuckles

What's Happening Brother ★ Marvin Gaye

You're Too Bad ★ Jackie Opel

Get Money ★ Notorious B.I.G.

T.S.O.P (The Sound of Philadelphia) (The Soul Train Song)
    ★ MFSB featuring the Three Degrees

Grazing in the Grass ★ Hugh Masekela

Hard to Handle ★ Black Crowes

Diamonds on the Soles of Her Shoes ★ Paul Simon

Roforofo Fight ★ Fela Kuti

Money Eh No Problem ★ Lord Shorty

The Message ★ Grandmaster Flash

Hey Yah ★ Sean Paul featuring Beenie Man

# LIP-SMACKIN' GOOD CORN ON THE COB

**SERVES 4 TO 8**

I've loved corn on the cob ever since I was a kid. The warm melted butter, the crunch-iness of the corn, the messy deliciousness of eating with my hands. I still love it, but now I use it as a palette for playing with flavor. The corn here is inspired by the street corn of Mexico, where it's charred on a grill, slathered with mayonnaise, and sprinkled with crumbled queso fresco. I keep with the butter of my childhood, but I spice things up with soy sauce and Aleppo pepper. Give it a squirt of lime, and it's one of the best summertime dishes possible.

**8 ears corn, still in their husks**
**6 tablespoons (¾ stick) unsalted butter, softened**
**4 garlic cloves, coarsely chopped**
**1 tablespoon soy sauce**
**1 teaspoon Aleppo pepper (see Note, page 47) or hot red pepper flakes**
**Kosher salt and freshly ground black pepper**
**2 limes, quartered**
**½ cup crumbled queso fresco or mild feta cheese**
**1 tablespoon chopped fresh cilantro**

1. Preheat a gas grill to high. Peel back the husks from the corn but keep them attached at the base. Remove the silk from the corn and pull the husks back up. Put the corn in a stockpot, cover with cold water, and soak for at least 10 minutes.

2. Put the butter, garlic, soy, and Aleppo pepper into a food processor and process until smooth. Season to taste with salt and pepper. (You can also mince the garlic and just beat the garlic butter together with a wooden spoon.)

3. Place the corn on the grill, close the hood, and grill, turning occasionally, until the husks are charred and the corn is steamed through and hot but the kernels are still juicy and crisp, 15 to 20 minutes. Test by piercing the corn with a knife.

4. Pull the husks back and immediately brush the corn with the garlic butter. Squeeze the limes over the corn and sprinkle with the cheese and cilantro. Serve right away.

# SWEDE DOGGY DOGS WITH SHRIMP SALAD

**SERVES 8**

My very first job was at a hot dog stand in Göteborg. It was one of the simplest and most entertaining jobs I had growing up. Nighttime was the busiest. Bar hoppers and club goers were our biggest customers, and because they'd often had a lot to drink, they were gregarious—they tipped super well. I made some dirty-water dogs like they do in New York, but most of the time I'd grill them. But you'll see that there's a big difference between Swedish hot dogs and their American cousins. We serve ours with a sweet shrimp salad on top. This is my mash-up of an American corn dog and a Swedish hot dog. If you want, give them a shot or two of hot sauce.

## FOR THE SHRIMP SALAD

½ pound small (36–45) shrimp, shells on

1 tablespoon mayonnaise

Juice of 1 lime

1 tablespoon chopped fresh dill

1 teaspoon horseradish (preferably freshly grated)

1 small red onion, finely chopped

½ cup coarsely chopped arugula

## FOR THE CORN DOGS

1 cup yellow cornmeal

1 cup all-purpose flour, plus more for dredging

¼ cup sugar

4 teaspoons baking powder

¼ teaspoon kosher salt

1¼ cups milk

2 large eggs

Peanut oil, for frying

8 Popsicle sticks

8 hot dogs (I like Dietz & Watson)

1 romaine lettuce heart, leaves separated

When frying, hold your battered hot dog in the oil for a few seconds before submerging fully. This will result in a fluffy and crisp exterior.

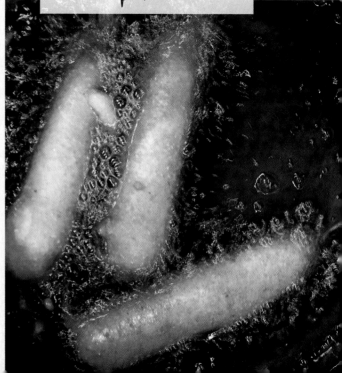

## MAKE THE SHRIMP SALAD

1. Bring a small saucepan of salted water to a boil. Add the shrimp and cook until pink and opaque, 2 to 3 minutes. While the shrimp cook, fill a bowl with ice and cold water. Once the shrimp are cooked, drain, then drop into the ice water to cool. Shell the shrimp.

2. Whisk the mayonnaise, lime juice, dill, and horseradish together in a medium bowl. Add the onion, arugula, and cooled shrimp and mix well. Cover and refrigerate until you're ready to serve.

## MAKE THE CORN DOGS

3. Whisk the cornmeal, flour, sugar, baking powder, and salt together in a medium bowl. In a separate bowl, whisk the milk and eggs. Make a well in the dry ingredients, pour in the wet ingredients, and whisk until no lumps remain.

4. Fill a large, heavy-bottomed saucepan half full with oil and heat to 350°F (you can also use an electric deep-fryer).

5. Push a Popsicle stick into an end of each hot dog, leaving a handle. Place some flour in a shallow bowl. Dredge the hot dogs in the flour. When the oil is hot, use the handle to dip a hot dog in the batter; let the excess drip off. Lower halfway into the oil and hold it there for 10 seconds, then release it (this helps prevent the dog from sticking to the bottom). Work in batches so you don't overcrowd the pan. Fry until the batter is puffed and golden, 2 to 3 minutes. Drain on paper towels.

6. To serve, place a corn dog in a romaine leaf and top with a spoonful of shrimp salad.

Save those shrimp shells in the freezer so you can make stock.

# SPICY SHRIMP FALAFEL

**SERVES 8 (16 FALAFEL BALLS)**

You can find falafel all over New York City—at the halal street carts, in little storefronts. My favorite is at Mamoun's in Greenwich Village, but I hate the long wait. So I make my own at home, where I can experiment with flavors. This version incorporates shrimp and soy sauce in the chickpea batter to up the umami factor. And the chiles, fish sauce, and sesame oil add an Asian twist to a traditional Middle Eastern dish. They're one of my favorite things to serve at parties with a dipping sauce. But they make a great stuffed pita sandwich, too.

1 cup canned chickpeas, rinsed and drained

4 garlic cloves—2 coarsely chopped, 2 minced

2 green Thai chiles, seeds and ribs removed, coarsely chopped

Kosher salt

1 pound shrimp (any size), peeled, deveined, and finely chopped

1 tablespoon chopped fresh chives

2 teaspoons soy sauce

1 teaspoon fish sauce

1 teaspoon sesame seeds

1 teaspoon toasted sesame oil

1½ tablespoons chopped fresh parsley

3 tablespoons cornstarch

½ cup all-purpose flour

Peanut oil, for frying

1 cup shredded iceberg lettuce

1 red onion, thinly sliced

8 cherry tomatoes, cut in half

2 tablespoons plain yogurt

Juice of 1 lemon

Freshly ground black pepper

8 pita breads

New York has no shortage of great, quick bites when you're on the go, which for me is quite often.

1. Put the chickpeas, chopped garlic, chiles, and 1 teaspoon salt in a food processor and pulse until smooth. Scrape into a bowl and stir in the shrimp, chives, soy sauce, fish sauce, sesame seeds, sesame oil, and 1 tablespoon of the parsley. With wet hands to prevent the mixture from sticking, roll into 16 balls, each about 2 inches in diameter. Set on a parchment-lined tray and refrigerate for 20 minutes.

2. Combine the cornstarch and flour in a shallow bowl. Roll the falafel balls in the flour mixture.

3. Fill a large, heavy saucepan half-full with oil and heat to 350°F. Working in batches to avoid overcrowding, fry the falafel balls until golden, 5 to 6 minutes. Drain on paper towels.

4. Toss the minced garlic, remaining ½ tablespoon parsley, lettuce, onion, tomatoes, yogurt, and lemon juice in a medium bowl. Give it a taste and season with salt and pepper.

5. To assemble the sandwiches, cut an end off each pita and open to form a pocket. Stuff the bottoms of the pitas with the lettuce-yogurt salad, then add the falafel. Top with additional salad and serve.

# FISH & CHIPS WITH FRIED PICKLES

**SERVES 4 TO 6**

In 1860, Joseph Malin, a Jewish immigrant from Eastern Europe, opened the first fish-and-chips shop in London's East End. There are now well over 8,000 such shops in Britain. Some of my happiest memories are of afternoons I've spent with friends, eating fish and chips in a British pub and watching soccer. At home, I fry my fish in a beer batter seasoned with Old Bay. And instead of just passing a bottle of malt vinegar, I serve a tarragon–malt vinegar mayonnaise and fried pickles. If you can't find halibut when you're shopping, you can substitute cod, haddock, or whiting and get equally delicious results.

**¾ cup mayonnaise**
**3 tablespoons chopped fresh tarragon**
**1 tablespoon malt vinegar or apple cider vinegar**
**Kosher salt and freshly ground black pepper**
**1 cup all-purpose flour, plus more for dredging**
**1½ teaspoons Old Bay seasoning**
**1 (12-ounce) bottle lager-style beer**
**Peanut oil, for frying**
**3 russet potatoes (8–10 ounces each), scrubbed**
**1½ pounds halibut fillets**
**1 or 2 large dill pickles, cut into ¼-inch-thick rounds**

1. Whisk the mayonnaise, tarragon, and vinegar together in a small bowl. Taste, and season with salt and pepper. Cover and refrigerate until you're ready to serve.
2. Whisk the flour and Old Bay together in a large bowl. Pour in the beer and whisk until the batter is smooth.
3. Fill a large, heavy saucepan half-full with oil and heat to 350°F. Heat the oven to 200°F.
4. While the oil heats, slice the potatoes into ¼-inch-thick rounds. Working in batches, add the potato slices to the oil. Fry, turning occasionally, until the potatoes are tender, cooked through, and just starting to turn golden, 5 to 8 minutes. Drain on paper towels.

*If you're in London, go to Borough Market, grab a beer and fish and chips, and watch the market. It's magical. Don't forget to order the mushy peas.*

5. Cut the fish crosswise into ½- to ¾-inch-thick slices and season with salt and pepper on all sides. Place some flour in a shallow bowl. Dredge the fish in the flour. Working in batches and bringing the oil back up to 350°F between each batch, dip the fish into the beer batter to coat, let excess batter drip back into the bowl, and use a bamboo skewer or your hands to lower the fish halfway into the oil. Hold for 10 seconds, then release (this helps prevent sticking on the bottom). Fry until deep golden and just cooked through, 4 to 5 minutes. Transfer the fish to a rack set over a baking sheet and slide into the oven to keep warm.

6. When you've finished frying the fish, heat the oil to 375°F. Again working in batches, fry the potatoes a second time until puffed and golden brown, 2 to 3 minutes. Pile them in a bowl lined with paper towels.

7. Working in batches, dredge the pickles in flour, dip into the beer batter to coat lightly, let the excess batter drip off, and fry until golden, 3 to 4 minutes. Drain on paper towels.

8. Divide the fish, chips, and pickles among your plates and serve immediately, with the tarragon–malt vinegar mayonnaise on the side.

# CUZ'S FISH BURGERS WITH BAJAN MAYO

**SERVES 4**

I've been obsessed with burgers since my first visit to the United States, and I look for them everywhere. This one, a fish burger with cheese and egg, is my current favorite. Every time I make it, I'm transported back to Barbados—to Cuz's stand in the parking lot between my hotel and the beach where I first had this. There was a line out the door, as people waited while the guy griddled his daily catch and slapped the fillets onto a bun with a piece of cheese and an egg. So fresh. So delicious. I took my fish burger out to the beach and ate it there. And went back the next day for another.

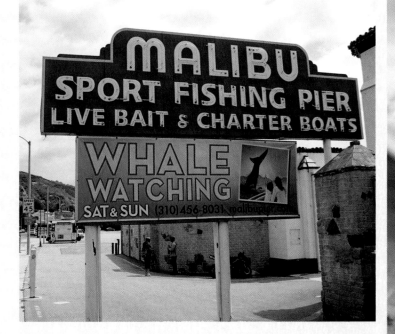

## FOR THE BAJAN MAYO

1 large egg yolk

½ teaspoon kosher salt

½ teaspoon Colman's dry
    mustard

2 pinches sugar

1 tablespoon white wine vinegar

2 teaspoons fresh lemon juice

1 teaspoon Tabasco or other
    hot sauce

1 cup olive oil

## FOR THE GLAZE

1 tablespoon soy sauce

1 teaspoon honey

¼ teaspoon wasabi paste

4 drops sesame oil

4 dashes Tabasco or other
    hot sauce

## FOR THE BURGERS

4 (4-ounce) skinless fish
    fillets (halibut, mahimahi,
    swordfish, and snapper are
    all good choices)

Kosher salt and freshly ground
    black pepper

2 tablespoons vegetable oil

4 sesame buns, split

4 slices cheddar cheese

1 tomato, thinly sliced

4 slices red onion

4 romaine lettuce leaves

About ¼ cup Pickled Cabbage
    (page 294)

4 large eggs, prepared over
    easy

### MAKE THE BAJAN MAYO

1. Whisk the egg yolk, salt, mustard, and sugar together in a glass bowl. Combine the vinegar, lemon juice, and Tabasco in a measuring cup.

2. Whisk half the liquid into the yolk. Then begin whisking in the oil, a few drops at a time, until the mayo begins to emulsify. Continue whisking in the oil—you can add it more quickly now—until the mayo is very thick. Add the rest of the liquid and whisk until well combined. Cover and refrigerate. It will keep for about 1 week.

### MAKE THE GLAZE

3. Stir all the ingredients together in a small bowl.

### MAKE THE BURGERS

4. Heat a cast iron skillet or grill pan over high heat.

5. Season the fish on both sides with salt and pepper. Spoon the vegetable oil into the hot pan. Add the fish, brush the top with the glaze, and sear for 3 minutes. Turn the fish over, paint it with glaze, and sear until the fish feels firm when you prod it, about 3 minutes.

6. To assemble the burgers, spread a thin layer of the Bajan mayo on both sides of the sesame buns. To each, add a cooked fillet, a slice of cheddar cheese, a piece of tomato, a slice of onion, a lettuce leaf, and a tablespoon or so of the pickled cabbage. Top with an over-easy egg.

# ETHIOPIAN (DORO WAT) TOSTADOS

**MAKES ABOUT 32 TOSTADOS**

I love this dish because it's a mash-up of the Latin food that I love and my Ethiopian heritage. I got the idea when I saw a street vendor selling *doro wat* in New York, and I remember thinking how cool it was that the Ethiopian chicken stew had become street food. My version is less traditional than his. I do cook the stew long and slow so the onions melt into the sauce, and the berbere goes in later in the cooking to add body. But I've added a rich chicken liver spread, a garnish of homemade *ayib* (an Ethiopian soft-curd cheese flavored with dried spinach), and I pile it onto a fried corn tortilla for the ultimate street treat.

**FOR THE DORO WAT**

¼ cup olive oil

5 red onions, finely chopped

5 garlic cloves, minced

1 (2-inch) piece ginger, peeled and minced

1 tablespoon tomato paste

½ teaspoon ground cardamom

2 teaspoons kosher salt

8 chicken legs, skin removed

3 tablespoons Spiced Butter (page 160)
   or vegetable oil

2 cups chicken broth

1 cup canned crushed tomatoes

1 cup dry red wine

3 tablespoons Berbere (page 297)

**FOR THE AYIB**

1 cup fresh spinach leaves

2 quarts buttermilk

¼ teaspoon smoked paprika

Kosher salt and freshly ground black
   pepper

*If the city I'm visiting is known for its tacos, you can bet you'll find me at a Mexican restaurant, stand, or taco truck.*

**11 (6-inch) corn tortillas**
**Vegetable oil, for frying**
**Kosher salt**
**Chicken Liver Spread (page 164)**
**Chopped fresh parsley, for garnish**

### MAKE THE CHICKEN *DORO WAT*

1. Heat the olive oil in a Dutch oven over low heat. When it moves easily in the pot, add the onions, garlic, and ginger and cook until very soft, stirring occasionally, about 30 minutes. Stir in the tomato paste and cook for 15 minutes, stirring occasionally.

2. Mix the cardamom and salt and use to season the chicken legs. Add the chicken to the Dutch oven along with the spiced butter, chicken broth, crushed tomatoes, and wine. Bring to a simmer. After 30 minutes, stir in the berbere. Cook until the chicken is fork-tender, 15 minutes longer. Remove the chicken from the sauce. When it's cool enough to handle, pull off the meat and shred it with two forks. Mix the meat with 1 cup of the sauce (save the rest for other uses like pasta, see opposite). Leave the chicken on the bone if you plan to serve this traditionally (see opposite).

### MAKE THE *AYIB*

3. Preheat the oven to 350°F.

4. Spread the spinach leaves on a baking sheet and bake until crisp, 5 to 7 minutes. Keep an eye on them, because the leaves can go from browned to burned in a moment. Remove the baking sheet from the oven as soon as the spinach looks papery and lightly browned on the edges. Let the leaves cool and then crumble into flakes.

5. Bring the buttermilk to a boil in a large saucepan. In a moment or two, it will separate into curds and whey. Remove the saucepan from the heat and set it aside to cool slightly.

6. Pour the curds and whey through a sieve lined with two or three layers of dampened cheesecloth set over a bowl. Let the curds drain for 20 minutes. Gather up the curds in the cloth and turn them out into a bowl. Fold in the spinach and smoked paprika. Taste, then season with salt and pepper.

## TO SERVE

7. Use a 1½-inch biscuit cutter to cut out 32 rounds from the tortillas. Heat about 1 inch of oil in a large, heavy skillet until hot but not smoking. Fry the tortilla rounds in batches until golden brown, 10 to 15 seconds. Drain on paper towels and sprinkle immediately with salt.

8. Divide the chicken among the tostados and top with some of the chicken liver spread and *ayib*. (Leftover *ayib* will keep about 1 week, covered in the refrigerator.) Garnish with the parsley and serve.

> Heat leftover <u>doro wat</u> sauce in a saucepan. Fold in fresh chopped tomatoes and cooked penne or other sturdy pasta. Top each serving with a plop of <u>ayib</u>.

# DORO WAT

**Because this dish is made with chicken, it's a sign of celebration. If you have an Ethiopian restaurant near you, ask to buy some injera and celebrate like an Ethiopian.**

**Injera is a large, spongy and soft, yeast-risen flatbread made of teff flour, and it could be called the national dish of Ethiopia. It serves as platter, fork, and spoon for every meal.**

**To serve a traditional *doro wat*, lay a round of injera on a platter. Put the chicken legs in the center of the bread and spoon on plenty of the sauce. Arrange small piles of collards, lentils, Shiro (page 284), *ayib*, a bowl of Addis Dip (page 303), and a stack of folded injera around the *doro wat*. Guests will rip off pieces of the injera and use them to pick up and eat the food. It is a comforting, and spiritual, way of eating. The injera that served as platter will become soaked with the sauce, the juices from the collards, the lentils, and the *shiro*. It is particularly tasty and should not be left uneaten.**

**Leave some injera out on the counter overnight to dry. Break it into pieces and use it like a cracker, like my wife does.**

# SPICED BUTTER

Make this butter and you have flavor. You can sauté with it because it's been clarified and can take high heat. You can stir it into rice and use it to finish other dishes. Think of it as *the* butter.

Cut 1 pound of unsalted butter into pieces and put in a saucepan with a cinnamon stick, 2 peeled garlic cloves, a 2-inch piece of peeled ginger, a sprig of rosemary, and 1 teaspoon ground turmeric. Turn the heat to low, let the butter melt, then simmer very gently (you don't want the milk solids to brown) for 30 minutes to infuse the flavors into the butter.

Let the butter sit for 10 minutes until the milk solids settle at the bottom. Skim off any froth and pull out the cinnamon, garlic, ginger, and rosemary. Pour the butter into a large measuring cup—be careful to leave all the milk solids behind. Discard the solids. Then pour the butter into ice cube trays and freeze it. Once they're solid, you can put the butter cubes into plastic bags and keep them in the freezer for months. This makes about 1½ cups.

Durban Curry Buns (page 162)

# DURBAN CURRY BUNS

**SERVES 6**

This dish, known in South Africa as Bunny Chow, was created by Indian immigrants in the city of Durban. It's made with lamb, not rabbit, so the name is a bit misleading. It was originally a workman's lunch, a hollowed-out piece of bread filled with a meat curry that you could carry with you to the fields. The curry is dry, so it won't soak through the crusty bread and make it soggy. I like to pack this on the rare occasions when I can steal away to Central Park for a picnic with my wife.

I have to tell you, the aromas that fill my kitchen when I make this transport me right back to the markets and spice shops of South Africa.

2 pounds boneless lean lamb, preferably
    from the leg, cubed

2 teaspoons garam masala

2 tablespoons vegetable oil

1 medium yellow onion, thinly sliced

1 cinnamon stick

4 cardamom pods, lightly crushed

2–3 curry leaves (fresh or frozen; see Note)
    or grated zest of ½ lime

2 large tomatoes, chopped

1½ teaspoons minced peeled ginger

1½ teaspoons minced garlic

4 teaspoons Durban masala (see Note),
    or 4 teaspoons mild curry powder plus
    2 teaspoons paprika

1 teaspoon ground turmeric

4 medium red-skinned potatoes, scrubbed
    and cubed

¼ cup water

Kosher salt

When I cook and eat this dish, I think about all the times I was supposed to cook for Nelson Mandela. That never panned out, but I did have the pleasure of breaking bread with Desmond Tutu, and he told me stories of what he and Mandela did together. The warmth of the curry reminds me of how much I love South Africa, its food, people, and culture. It's like Mandiba is smiling down at us.

*I have to have pickles with this, and like the South Africans, I'd choose achaar, an Indian pickle. These days, South Africa is home to the largest population of Indians outside of India, and their influence on South Africa's cuisine is ever-present.*

**FOR SERVING**
**1 teaspoon vegetable oil**
**½ cup chopped kale**
**¼ cup chopped tomato**
**3 loaves crusty rustic bread, or 6 Kaiser rolls or large brioche buns**
**Fresh cilantro, for garnish**

1. Massage the lamb with the garam masala and leave it on the counter until you need it.
2. Heat the oil in a large saucepan over medium heat. When it shimmers, add the onion, cinnamon stick, cardamom pods, and curry leaves. Cook until the onion is light golden brown, 6 to 7 minutes. Add the tomatoes, ginger, garlic, Durban masala, and turmeric. Cook over medium heat, stirring occasionally, until the tomatoes cook down, about 10 minutes.
3. Add the lamb and cook for another 10 minutes. Stir in the potatoes and water and bring to a boil. Lower the heat, cover the pan partway, and simmer over low heat until the meat is tender and the potatoes are cooked, about 30 minutes. Taste and add salt as needed.

**TO SERVE**
4. Heat the oil in a nonstick skillet over high heat. When it's almost smoking, add the kale and sauté, stirring, just until it starts to wilt, about 2 minutes. Add to the stew, along with the ¼ cup chopped tomato.
5. Split the bread and pull out some of the soft insides (fold it into the stew, if you'd like). Spoon the curry into the hollowed-out loaves of bread, garnish with cilantro, and serve.

**Notes:** Durban masala is a mix of coriander, cumin, and fenugreek seeds, urad dal (Indian black lentils), peppercorns, chile powder, and paprika. If you're lucky enough to have a South African market near you, buy some. You can also find recipes online.

Look for fresh curry leaves—which add a warm, slightly bitter, slightly citrusy flavor—in specialty or Indian markets. They freeze beautifully.

# BANH MI SANDWICH

**SERVES 2**

Banh mi are like Vietnamese hoagies, served on baguette-style bread (bread you can thank French colonization for), with pickled veggies, house-cured or grilled meats, homemade mayonnaise, and hot peppers. The original sandwich was just pâté spread on a sliced baguette with sliced ham. The banh mi I find in my neighborhood—and that I make—is Saigon style. It's a feast of contrasts: creamy chicken liver spread (perfumed with Madeira and bourbon), crunchy vegetables, mild roast chicken, and tangy pickled cabbage. If you really want to go overboard, add some sliced tongue.

**FOR THE CHICKEN LIVER SPREAD (ENOUGH FOR 8 SANDWICHES)**

8 tablespoons (1 stick) unsalted butter, softened

1 pound chicken livers, cleaned

1 shallot, minced

¼ cup bourbon

¼ cup Madeira

¼ cup heavy cream

½ teaspoon kosher salt

⅛ teaspoon ground allspice

⅛ teaspoon freshly ground black pepper

**FOR THE BANH MI**

2 tablespoons mayonnaise

1 teaspoon Sriracha sauce

1 long crisp French bread (baguette, ficelle, or your favorite crusty white bread)

½ pound leftover roasted chicken, shredded

¼ cup grated carrot

¼ cup grated cucumber

¼ cup (or more) Pickled Cabbage (page 294)

Fresh cilantro leaves

### MAKE THE CHICKEN LIVER SPREAD

1. Melt 1 tablespoon of the butter in a large skillet over high heat. Pat the chicken livers dry and add them and the shallot to the pan. Sauté until the livers are cooked but still pink inside, about 3 minutes. Scrape into a food processor.

2. Pour the bourbon and Madeira into the skillet, return to high heat, and reduce to about 3 tablespoons. Stir in the cream and take off the heat. Pour into the food processor. Add the salt, allspice, and pepper and process until finely chopped. With the processor running, drop in the remaining butter by tablespoons and process until all the butter is incorporated and the spread is smooth.

3. Scrape the liver spread into a bowl, cover, and refrigerate until cold and firm. Bring it to room temperature before serving.

### MAKE THE BANH MI

4. Mix the mayonnaise and Sriracha together.

5. Cut the bread in half lengthwise. Slather the chicken liver spread on the bottom half (be generous) and the seasoned mayonnaise on the top half. Pile the chicken, carrot, cucumber, pickled cabbage, and cilantro (again, be generous) on the bottom half. Put the top on, slice the sandwich in half, and serve.

# PHILLY STEAK SANDWICHES MY WAY

**SERVES 6**

Whenever I go to Philadelphia, I make it a point to visit Reading Terminal Market. Everything that Philly has to love can be found there, including that classic: the Philly cheese-steak. I grew up in working-class Sweden, and while I don't have the accent of those Philly cooks, I can relate to the "big" sandwich. I make the sandwich my way. I skip the Cheez Whiz (go on, keep reading) and add a corn mayo that gives my sandwich a little sweetness and crunch. And I love the meatiness of skirt steak and the freshness of the basil and oregano. This may not be the classic, but I tell you, it's good!

**⅔ cup mayonnaise**
**1½ tablespoons red wine vinegar**
**1 tablespoon chopped fresh oregano**
**1 tablespoon chopped fresh basil**
**1 small garlic clove, minced**
**2 ears corn, husks removed**
**2 small red bell peppers, seeds and ribs removed,**
    **quartered lengthwise**
**1 large red onion, cut into ½-inch-thick rounds**
**1¼–1½ pounds skirt steak, cut crosswise into 6-inch pieces**
**6 hero rolls, split**
**Olive oil**
**Kosher salt and freshly ground black pepper**

1. Preheat a gas grill to high.
2. Whisk the mayonnaise, vinegar, oregano, basil, and garlic together.
3. Brush the corn, peppers, onion slices, steaks, and hero rolls with olive oil, then season with salt and pepper. Grill the vegetables,

turning occasionally, until they are charred and tender, 8 to 10 minutes for the peppers and onion and 15 minutes for the corn. Grill the steaks until they are charred and medium-rare, about 3 minutes per side. Let the steaks rest for 5 minutes. Grill the rolls, cut side down, until golden, with grill marks, 2 to 3 minutes.

4. Cut the corn kernels from the cobs and stir them into the herb mayonnaise. Taste and season with salt and pepper if you need to.

5. To make the sandwiches, cut the steaks across the grain into 1-inch-thick strips. Arrange the bottom halves of the rolls on a platter, then top with the steak, peppers, and onion. Spoon on the herbed-corn mayonnaise, top with the other halves of the rolls, pressing gently, and serve.

# PULLED PORK ON A BUN

**SERVES 8, WITH PLENTY OF LEFTOVERS**

All over the South, you'll find roadside stands or trucks off on a shoulder selling pulled pork, however they make it in that state or region. You can buy it by the pound to bring home with the fixings for a meal or you can eat it right there. I think it evokes all the hominess of Southern hospitality, and I make my version when we're expecting a houseful of friends. I braise a Boston butt with bourbon, tamarind, and prunes and throw in smoked paprika and chile powder, so it has that deeply satisfying combination of sweet and spicy and the seductive pull of East-meets-West. If a few unexpected guests turn up, there's plenty to go around—as long as the unexpected guests bring a six-pack of cold beer!

It's a great thing to make ahead. Or make extra for the freezer. It only gets better.

**2 quarts water**

**1 cup molasses**

**1 cup kosher salt**

**1 (8-pound) bone-in Boston butt, rind removed**

**1 teaspoon cumin seeds**

**1 teaspoon fennel seeds**

**1 teaspoon coriander seeds**

**1 tablespoon chile powder**

**1 tablespoon smoked paprika**

**½ cup tamarind paste**

**2 tablespoons tomato paste**

**1 cup bourbon**

**4 cups chicken broth, plus more if necessary**

**10 pitted prunes**

**8 brioche buns, split (see Note)**

> Note: I like to elevate this sandwich by serving it on brioche, but there's no reason you can't use big potato rolls or hamburger buns. And if you want to add some Barbecue Sauce (page 92), go ahead.

1. Put the water, molasses, and salt in a large stock-pot and stir to dissolve the salt. Add the Boston butt, making sure it is completely submerged in the brine (if it's not, add more water). Cover and refrigerate for 12 hours or up to 2 days.

2. Preheat the oven to 250°F.

3. Grind the cumin seeds, fennel seeds, and coriander seeds to a powder in a spice grinder. Transfer to a bowl and add the chile powder, smoked paprika, tamarind paste, tomato paste, bourbon, and chicken broth. Whisk until smooth.

4. Remove the pork from the brine and put in a roasting pan. Pour the braising liquid over it and add the prunes. Bake until the pork is fall-apart tender, about 8 hours, basting every 30 minutes with the liquid. Add a little more chicken broth if you need it.

5. Let the pork rest for at least 20 minutes on a cutting board. Fold a kitchen towel and put it under one end of the roasting pan so the juices all settle on the other end. When the fat rises, skim it off.

6. Pull the pork into pieces with a couple of forks and put it in a bowl. Moisten it with some of the pan juices and pile it into the buns. Serve immediately.

Farmers like Pete Eshelman in Fort Wayne go out of their way to ensure their animals are raised in an all-natural, humane, and stress-free sustainable environment. This is a photo of the beautiful Mangalitsa pigs he has at Joseph Decuis farm.

# K-TOWN NOODLES

**SERVES 4**

When we were filming *Top Chef Masters* in Los Angeles, we ate in Koreatown (known as K-Town to the locals) all the time, and I discovered that L.A. has some of the best Korean street food—not only in the country, but in the world. With some second-generation Korean staff members as my guides, I learned much about the bold and hearty notes of Korean home cooking. To me, this dish is luxury, and it's become my default quick supper instead of pasta.

When I peel the cucumber for these noodles, I do it only partially, leaving strips of peel so the cucumber looks striped. The noodles are equally great hot or at room temperature.

**5–6 ounces very thin bean thread noodles**

**½ cup soy sauce**

**3 tablespoons sesame oil**

**2 garlic cloves, chopped**

**1 tablespoon sugar**

**1 tablespoon canola oil**

**1 medium yellow onion, thinly sliced**

**3 medium carrots, peeled and cut into thin 2-inch sticks**

**1½ cups shiitake mushrooms, stemmed and thinly sliced**

**3 cups baby spinach**

**½ seedless cucumber, peeled so it's striped, and diced**

**½ cup Korean kimchi (see Note)**

**2 scallions, chopped**

Spicy-sour or blisteringly hot, kimchi is fermented—like a classic dill pickle—so it's rich with lactobacilli, the "good" bacteria that aid in digestion. It's packed with vitamins A, B, and C, too. And not all kimchi is made with cabbage. Try other kinds, like radish.

**Note:** Look for kimchi in Korean markets, in some grocery stores and farmers' markets, or online.

1. Put the noodles in a large bowl, cover with warm water, and let soak until softened, about 10 minutes. Drain in a colander.

2. Bring a 4-quart saucepan of water to a boil. Add the noodles and cook until tender, about 2 minutes. Drain in a colander and rinse under cold water until cool. Reserve.

3. Put the soy sauce, sesame oil, garlic, and sugar in a blender and blend until smooth.

4. Heat the canola oil in a deep, 12-inch heavy skillet over high heat until it just begins to smoke. Add the onion and carrots and stir-fry until softened, about 3 minutes. Add the mushrooms and continue to stir-fry until they soften. Add the spinach and stir-fry for about 30 seconds, then add the noodles and the soy sauce mixture and toss to coat the noodles and vegetables. Lower the heat and simmer, stirring occasionally, until most of the liquid is absorbed, 3 to 5 minutes.

5. To serve, toss the cucumber, kimchi, and scallions into the noodles and then divide among four bowls.

# POTATO & SPINACH SAMOSAS
## WITH SPICY BUTTERMILK DIP

**MAKES ABOUT 25 SAMOSAS**

Almost every country has a version of the samosa—a little packet of dough with a delicious filling—whether it's a pierogi, empanada, *pastelito,* or an Ethiopian *sambusa*. In India, samosas are often made with a tender pastry, stuffed with lamb or potatoes, and fried. I make mine with phyllo, fill them with potatoes and spinach and fiery chiles and ginger, and bake them. I love the crunch when my teeth break through the crisp shell. Served with a cool and spicy buttermilk dip that cuts through the spice of the chiles, they're the perfect snack.

### FOR THE SAMOSAS

½ pound red-skinned potatoes, about 2 inches
    in diameter, scrubbed

1 tablespoon ground cumin

1 teaspoon fennel seeds

½ teaspoon curry powder

¼ cup vegetable oil

1 medium yellow onion, chopped

3 small serrano chiles, chopped

1 (2-inch) piece ginger, peeled and grated

3 garlic cloves, minced

10 ounces spinach, stemmed, washed, and
    coarsely chopped

Kosher salt and freshly ground black pepper

8 tablespoons (1 stick) unsalted butter, melted

½ (1-pound) package phyllo, thawed if frozen

### FOR THE SPICY BUTTERMILK DIP

½ cup buttermilk

Juice of 1 lemon

1 teaspoon Sriracha or other hot sauce

**1 garlic clove, minced**

**1 tablespoon chopped fresh parsley**

**1 teaspoon chopped fresh dill**

**1 handful fresh mint**

**Kosher salt and freshly ground black pepper**

### MAKE THE SAMOSAS

1. In a saucepan, cover the potatoes with salted water by at least an inch and bring to a boil. Reduce the heat and simmer until the potatoes are barely tender, about 12 minutes. Drain. When they are cool enough to handle, peel and cut into ¼-inch dice.

2. Toast the cumin, fennel seeds, and curry powder in a large, heavy skillet over medium heat, stirring occasionally, until the spices are fragrant and several shades darker, about 2 minutes. Add the vegetable oil, onion, chiles, ginger, and garlic to the skillet. Cook, stirring occasionally, until the onion is softened, 6 to 7 minutes.

3. Increase the heat to medium-high, add the diced potatoes and spinach, and cook, stirring, until the spinach is wilted but still bright green, about 2 minutes. Taste the filling, then season with salt and pepper. Transfer to a bowl and let cool. (The filling can be made 1 day ahead and kept covered in the refrigerator.)

4. Preheat the oven to 400°F. Brush a baking sheet with some of the butter.

5. Unroll the phyllo onto a sheet of waxed paper. Cover it with a second sheet of waxed paper to keep it from drying out while you work. On a work surface, arrange 1 phyllo sheet with a long end in front of you. Brush the phyllo lightly with melted butter. Top this with a second phyllo sheet and brush lightly with butter. Cut the stacked phyllo in quarters lengthwise to make strips approximately 12 inches long by about 4¼ inches wide. Put 1 heaping tablespoon of filling at the bottom of a strip. Fold one corner of the strip over the filling, forming a triangle. Continue folding the strip, maintaining the triangular shape, as if you were folding a flag. Keep it loose; it you fold too tightly, the samosas will burst.

6. Put the samosa, seam side down, on the baking sheet and cover with plastic wrap. Repeat with the rest of the filling and phyllo in the same manner.

7. Remove the plastic, brush the samosas with butter, and bake them until golden brown, about 10 minutes.

### MAKE THE SPICY BUTTERMILK DIP

8. Meanwhile, whisk the buttermilk, lemon juice, Sriracha, garlic, parsley, and dill together in a small bowl. Right before serving, chop the mint leaves, stir into the dip, then season with salt and pepper.

9. Serve the warm samosas with the dip.

Jackson Heights, Queens, has some of the best food in the whole city.

# AUNT JOSULYN'S ROTI

**MAKES 8 FLATBREADS**

Roti may have begun as an Indian flatbread, but cooks in Trinidad and Guyana started stuffing it and turned it into street food. I work chickpeas into the dough. My version is a perfect trifecta of India, Africa, and the Americas.

Eat these breads on their own with chutney and pickles and hot sauce, use them to sop up Doro Wat (page 159) or Coconut-Lime Curried Chicken (page 48), or make wraps with them. They're meant to be served warm, but you can do what the street vendors do: Reheat them in a dry skillet.

**1 (15-ounce) can chickpeas, rinsed and drained**
**2 heaping teaspoons curry powder or ground turmeric**
**1½ cups water**
**2 cups all-purpose flour, plus more for kneading**
**Kosher salt**
**4 tablespoons Spiced Butter (see page 176 or page 160), melted**

1. Combine the chickpeas, 1 heaping teaspoon of the curry powder, and 1 cup of the water in a small saucepan over medium-high heat. Bring to a simmer, reduce the heat to low, and simmer until the water is almost gone, about 40 minutes. Drain and spread the chickpeas out on paper towels. Cool completely.

2. Whisk together the flour, the remaining 1 heaping teaspoon curry powder, and a pinch of salt. Add the remaining ½ cup water and 1 tablespoon spiced butter and mix with your hands to make a very tight dough that cleans the bowl. Knead the dough on a lightly floured surface until smooth, about 1 minute. Cover it with a towel and let it rest for 15 to 20 minutes.

"Aunt Josulyn" has a roti stand near the beach in Barbados, and she showed me how to make these breads. I even worked at the stand. She's from Guyana—roti country. The Guyanese and Trinidadians will always argue over whose roti is best, though.

3. Put the chickpeas in a bowl, add 1 tablespoon spiced butter, and mash coarsely with a fork. You want some big chunks left.

4. Roll the dough out into a 12- to 13-inch round. Spread the chickpeas over the dough. Roll the dough up loosely into a log, fold the left and right thirds over each other, and roll out again, this time into an 8-inch square. Roll the dough into a tight log, cover it with a towel, and let it rest for 15 to 20 minutes.

5. Cut the dough into 8 pieces. Roll out each piece into a 7- to 8-inch round.

6. Brush a skillet with spiced butter and set it over medium-low heat. When it's hot, add one of the roti, brush the top with spiced butter, and cook until browned in spots, turning once, about 3 minutes a side. Continue with the remaining butter and rounds, stacking the roti on a plate as they're cooked and covering them with a towel to keep them warm.

Note: You can make a quick spiced butter by melting 1 stick of unsalted butter with 2 teaspoons curry powder in a small saucepan. Let it sit for about 5 minutes to let the milk solids settle on the bottom of the pan. Skim any froth from the top, then pour or spoon off the butter, leaving the solids behind.

# PUMPKIN-CINNAMON EMPANADAS

**MAKES 24 EMPANADAS**

Many countries have some form of stuffed pastry. They can be savory or sweet, hot or cold, a snack or a light meal, or a dessert. Empanadas are stuffed pastries from Spain, cousin to Indian samosas (page 172). My friend Andrea Bergquist, who helped me open the Red Rooster in Harlem, makes wonderful empanadas. She starts with a flaky yeast pastry and comes up with the best combinations for fillings. I thought of her as I started to play with the pumpkin, brown sugar, and cinnamon in this recipe. I think these empanadas taste like autumn. I can't resist eating one as soon as they come out of the oven. The rest, I share, or have as a snack throughout the day.

## FOR THE DOUGH

**1 cup milk**

**1 tablespoon unsalted butter**

**¾ cup rendered lard (see Note)**

**1 envelope active dry yeast**

**2½–3 cups all-purpose flour**

**½ teaspoon kosher salt**

## FOR THE FILLING

**1 (15-ounce) can pumpkin puree**

**⅔ cup chopped piloncillo or lightly packed dark brown sugar (see Note)**

**1½ teaspoons ground cinnamon**

**½ teaspoon kosher salt**

**1 large egg, beaten with 1 tablespoon milk, for an egg wash**

**Sugar, for sprinkling**

Notes: Butchers, farmers' markets, and Mexican markets are all good sources for lard. If you can't find it, render the fat from 2 slices of bacon and add enough butter to make ¾ cup.

Piloncillo is a pure, unrefined sugar pressed into a cone shape. You can find it in Mexican markets, some grocery stores, and online.

## MAKE THE DOUGH

1. Bring the milk to a simmer in a small pan over medium heat. Remove from the heat, add the butter and lard, let them melt, and cool to lukewarm. Add the yeast, stir, and let sit until foamy, about 10 minutes.

2. Mix the flour and salt together in a large bowl, then make a well in the center. Pour the wet ingredients into the well. Using your hand, start pulling the flour into the wet ingredients until you've combined the wet and dry and made a ball of dough. Turn the dough out onto a lightly floured surface and knead until smooth and elastic, about 5 minutes. Place the dough in a buttered bowl, cover with a damp cloth, and let rise in a warm, draft-free place until doubled, about 30 minutes.

## MAKE THE FILLING

3. Meanwhile, put the pumpkin, piloncillo, cinnamon, and salt in a saucepan over medium-low heat. Cover and cook, stirring every few minutes, until the sugar is completely melted. Uncover and simmer until the filling is very thick, about 15 minutes. Scrape the filling into a bowl and cool to room temperature.

4. Preheat the oven to 425°F.

5. Divide the dough into 24 pieces and shape into balls. On a lightly floured work surface, roll one ball into a 3½- to 4-inch circle. Brush the edge very lightly with water, then spoon 2 teaspoons of the filling into the center. Fold the dough carefully over the filling and press the edges together to seal. Crimp the edge with the tines of a fork. Repeat to make 24 empanadas, placing them on a baking sheet as you go.

6. Prick each empanada once or twice with a fork. Bake until they begin to color, 15 minutes. Remove from the oven, brush lightly with the egg wash, and sprinkle lightly with sugar. Return to the oven and bake until the empanadas are golden brown, about 5 minutes.

I travel to the West Coast quite often for work and often stop by Downtown L.A.'s Grand Central Market. In the middle of all that history, grit, glamour, and gentrification, there is a diverse food market that has been there since 1917. The West Coast culinary scene is heavily influenced by Latin America and Asia, and it's evident in all the variety of vendors and food stalls here. Walk in and you can eat lengua (tongue) tacos, then papaya salad made to order in a Thai clay mortar and pestle, and finish by picking up some exotic spices from one of the best suppliers in the city.

The best empanada I've ever had was in East L.A. It was big enough for six—almost like a crepe—and filled with pork stew.

# PLAYING WITH FIRE

MAKE A FIRE AND PEOPLE WILL GATHER AROUND IT. YOUR GUESTS MAY NOT PAY attention when you stand at the stove, but the grill is seductive. Sure, it's the oldest style of cooking, but really it's a different kind of cooking. I don't think that any technique compares when it comes to the pure richness and complexity of flavor that you get from grilling. It's about improvisation, it's about responding to what's happening, and it's a little bit about showmanship. Think about it. Put a piece of salmon on a cedar board, cover it with foil, set it on the grill, and in just a few seconds you've made your own piece of cooking equipment, and with that smoker/steamer and fire, you will produce fish that's moist, succulent, and touched by smoke. That is theater, and great cooking.

We didn't grill in Sweden. But we did smoke fish and meat, and so I feel a connection to my youth when I'm at a grill. After I visited Japan, I started to experiment with *robatayaki*, the slow-grilling technique that develops deep flavor.

Successful grilling is all about how you manage heat, and no matter what size grill you're working on, you should always have at least two levels of heat. That way you can move things around when you need to, speeding up the cooking or slowing things down. And do what I do: Use the grill as a stove, too. Make some dirty rice on the grill, or spicy ketchup. Improvise.

# MUSIC TO GRILL BY

Beds Are Burning ★ Midnight Oil

Pull Up to the Bumper ★ Grace Jones

Fu-Gee-La (Sly & Robbie Mix) ★ Fugees

Electric Lady ★ Janelle Monáe featuring Solange

Always on My Mind ★ Willie Nelson

The Passenger ★ The Jolly Boys

I'm on Fire ★ Bruce Springsteen

Fire and Desire ★ Rick James & Teena Marie

September ★ Earth Wind & Fire

Dancing with Myself ★ Billy Idol

Girl on Fire ★ Alicia Keys

Quiet Storm ★ Smokey Robinson

Of Fire ★ Christian Scott

Burning of the Midnight Lamp
★ The Jimi Hendrix Experience

The Glow of Love ★ Change

# ROOF GARDEN FISH TACOS

**SERVES 4**

I'm a huge fan of fish tacos. Fish marinated in onions and a lot of citrus, then grilled, a soft corn tortilla, a slather of lime mayonnaise, a little cabbage and avocado, and salsa verde—it's like bringing a Mexican beach to my roof garden for a sunny afternoon with friends. I love all the green stuff that can go into a salsa verde. This one has a nice balance of heat from the chiles, acid from the tomatillos and lime, creaminess from the avocado, and the freshness of herbs. Try it with grilled pork and chicken, too.

**FOR THE SALSA VERDE**

3 tablespoons olive oil

2 garlic cloves, chopped

2 jalapeños, chopped

2 poblano chiles, seeded and chopped

2 tomatillos, husked, rinsed, and chopped

1 avocado, seeded, peeled, and sliced

1 teaspoon drained capers

2 teaspoons chopped fresh mint

2 teaspoons chopped fresh cilantro

2 teaspoons chopped fresh parsley

Juice of 2 limes

2 teaspoons red wine vinegar

### FOR THE TACOS

2 medium white onions, chopped
½ cup chopped fresh cilantro
¼ cup olive oil
5 tablespoons fresh lime juice
3 tablespoons fresh orange juice
2 garlic cloves, minced
1 teaspoon dried oregano, preferably Mexican
1 pound tilapia, striped bass, or sturgeon fillets
Kosher salt and freshly ground black pepper
1 cup mayonnaise
1 tablespoon milk
Corn tortillas
2 avocados, seeded, peeled, and sliced
½ small head green cabbage, cored and thinly
    sliced
Lime wedges, for garnish

### MAKE THE SALSA VERDE

1. Put the olive oil, garlic, and jalapeños into a skillet over medium heat and cook until the garlic starts to turn golden. Add the poblanos and tomatillos and cook until the chiles soften, about 5 minutes.
2. Scrape the cooked vegetables into a food processor. Add the avocado, capers, mint, cilantro, parsley, lime juice, and vinegar and process until almost smooth. Scrape the salsa into a bowl, cover, and refrigerate until you're ready to serve.

### MAKE THE TACOS

3. Combine 1 cup of the onions, ¼ cup of the chopped cilantro, the olive oil, 3 tablespoons of the lime juice, the orange juice, garlic, and oregano in a medium bowl to make a marinade.

4. Season the fish with salt and pepper. Spread half of the onion marinade in a 7-x-11-inch glass baking dish. Set the fish on top and spoon the remaining marinade over the fish. Cover and refrigerate for 1 hour.

5. Whisk the mayonnaise, milk, and remaining 2 tablespoons lime juice in a small bowl and refrigerate.

6. Preheat a gas grill to medium-high and brush the grates with oil.

7. Scrape the marinade off the fish and grill until it is just opaque in the center, 3 to 5 minutes per side. Transfer to a serving platter. Warm the tortillas on the grill (getting some grill marks is good).

8. To serve, use two forks to break the fish into chunks. Spread some of the lime mayonnaise onto the tortillas, top with the fish, avocados, cabbage, and remaining chopped onion and cilantro. Pass the lime wedges and salsa verde.

Here's an easy way to get delicious tortillas. Combine 1½ cups masa harina (do not use cornmeal), ¼ teaspoon salt, ¼ teaspoon ground cumin, and 1 teaspoon Aleppo pepper (see page 47), in a bowl. Stir in 2 tablespoons vegetable oil, then slowly stream in 1 cup hot water until a dough forms. Knead well on a floured surface, cover in plastic wrap, and let sit at room temperature for 30 minutes to 1 hour. Take small pinches of dough, roll in flour, then press or roll into a small disk (I use a cutting board and a heavy frying pan, both wrapped in plastic, to shape the tortillas.) Fry for 45 seconds on each side in a pan that has been lightly coated with vegetable oil. It's as easy as that.

Grilled Shrimp & Sausage Skewers
with Extra-Dirty Rice (page 188)

# GRILLED SHRIMP & SAUSAGE SKEWERS WITH EXTRA-DIRTY RICE

**SERVES 6**

This dish doesn't require a lot of effort, but it always brings the wow factor when I make it for friends. The sweet shrimp and smoky sausage (marinated with lime and chile), the dirty rice (a little sticky but with a nice surprise crunch from the almonds), and the cooling yogurt sauce (with just a kick of heat)—it all transports me back to the Caribbean.

I use a gas grill at home, and I'll always heat the entire grill to high heat, or to medium heat—depending on what I'm grilling. But once it's hot, I turn half the grill down to a lower temperature, so I can move whatever I'm grilling to that side if things are happening too fast.

You can do the same thing with charcoal. Just bank the coals on one side of the grate.

**FOR THE DIRTY RICE**

1½ cups basmati rice
2 tablespoons olive oil
2 tablespoons chopped blanched almonds
1 teaspoon minced peeled ginger
1 garlic clove, chopped
1 teaspoon garam masala
1 teaspoon curry powder
2 cardamom pods
1 cup coconut milk
2 cups chicken broth
1 teaspoon kosher salt

**FOR THE CILANTRO-YOGURT SAUCE**

6 tablespoons plain yogurt
Juice of 1 lime
½ tablespoon chopped fresh cilantro
½ tablespoon chopped fresh parsley
Dash of Tabasco sauce

**FOR THE SKEWERS**

½ cup olive oil
Juice of 2 limes

1 tablespoon chopped fresh cilantro, plus more
for garnish
1 tablespoon chopped fresh parsley
1 tablespoon plain yogurt
1 jalapeño, chopped
2 large garlic cloves, chopped
12 jumbo (U10, see page 77) shrimp, peeled
(tails left on) and deveined
4 andouille sausages (or other fully cooked
smoked sausages), cut into 2-inch pieces
2 tablespoons unsweetened shredded coconut,
toasted

There's an amazing powder, sometimes called soungouff ou crevettes, from central Africa. It's made of fermented shrimp shells and chile. You're not going to find it other than in an African market, but if you do, bring some home and use it like a salt. It's so good in this dirty rice.

## MAKE THE RICE

1. Soak the rice in cold water for 30 minutes. Drain and transfer to a medium saucepan. Add the olive oil, almonds, ginger, garlic, garam masala, curry powder, and cardamom and cook over medium heat until the almonds are lightly browned and the spices are very fragrant, about 5 minutes. Add the coconut milk and chicken broth and bring to a simmer. Cook gently for 10 minutes. Turn off the heat and stir in the salt. Cover and let the rice sit for 25 minutes.

## MAKE THE CILANTRO-YOGURT SAUCE

2. Whisk all the ingredients together.

## MAKE THE SKEWERS

3. Preheat a gas grill to medium.

4. Process the olive oil, lime juice, cilantro, parsley, yogurt, jalapeño, and garlic in a food processor to make a smooth paste.

5. Thread the shrimp and sausage pieces on skewers, alternating shrimp and sausage on each skewer. Put the skewers on a rimmed baking sheet and pour the marinade over them, making sure all the pieces are coated. Cover with plastic wrap and let sit for 20 minutes.

6. Grill the shrimp and sausage skewers until the shrimp are bright pink and fully cooked, about 3 minutes per side.

7. To serve, pile the rice onto a serving platter, remove the cardamom pods, and top with the skewers. Drizzle on the cilantro-yogurt sauce and sprinkle with toasted coconut and additional cilantro.

# CHARRED CALAMARI WITH TOMATO, OLIVE & ORZO SALAD

**SERVES 6**

When it comes to European culinary influences, my favorite is Greek. Growing up, I was introduced to the country's food by my soccer buddy Marcos, whose mother would feed us whenever I went to their house. She'd make things like moussaka, tzatziki, baklava, and Greek lentil soup. In this dish calamari is prepared like octopus (given a long, slow simmer before being charred on the grill), then flavored with lemon, olive oil, parsley, and mint. The salad is a Greek classic, my nod to Marcos's mom and her great home cooking.

### FOR THE CALAMARI

1½ pounds medium calamari (bodies and tentacles), cleaned
1 tablespoon olive oil
Juice of 1 lemon
4 garlic cloves, chopped

### FOR THE SALAD

1 cucumber, peeled and chopped
1 cup cherry tomatoes, halved
½ cup kalamata olives, pitted
½ cup green olives, pitted
1 cup cooked orzo
½ cup crumbled feta
3 tablespoons olive oil
Juice of 1 lemon
1 teaspoon paprika
½ teaspoon ground cumin
1 tablespoon chopped fresh dill
1 tablespoon chopped fresh mint
1 tablespoon chopped fresh parsley

*Put 2 garlic cloves on a skewer and grill them while you char the calamari. Chop them up and toss into the salad for a layer of garlicky nuttiness.*

1 tablespoon olive oil

Juice of 1 lemon

2 tablespoons chopped fresh parsley

2 tablespoons chopped fresh mint

½ teaspoon ground cumin

½ teaspoon chile powder

½ teaspoon sweet paprika

½ teaspoon honey

### MAKE THE CALAMARI

1. Put the calamari, oil, lemon juice, and garlic in a bowl and toss well. Cover with plastic wrap and refrigerate for 2 hours.

2. Lift the calamari out of the bowl, leaving any juices behind, and put it in a saucepan. Cover with cold water by at least 2 inches and bring to a boil. Reduce the heat and simmer gently until it is tender, about 2 hours.

### MAKE THE SALAD

3. Toss the cucumber, tomatoes, olives, orzo, feta, olive oil, lemon juice, paprika, and cumin together in a salad bowl. Add the dill, mint, and parsley, toss again, and let sit for 15 minutes at room temperature to let the flavors marry.

### FINISH THE DISH

4. Preheat a gas grill to high.

5. Whisk the olive oil, lemon juice, parsley, mint, cumin, chile powder, paprika, and honey together in a serving bowl.

6. Drain the calamari and pat it dry. Grill until slightly charred on both sides, 3 to 4 minutes. Transfer to a cutting board and cut the bodies into rings (leave the tentacles whole). Add to the vinaigrette, toss, and serve with the salad.

# "BACK-POCKET" SALMON GRILLED ON A PLANK

**SERVES 4**

The standout flavors of this dish—ginger, garlic, soy, and mustard—are ideally suited to salmon. It's one of those combinations that I like to call a "back-pocket recipe" because once you've made it two or three times, you won't even have to open up the cookbook to prepare it. It will always be in your back pocket as an easy, delicious, go-to dish.

Grilling on a wood plank is fun; it's like using a steamer and smoker at the same time. But you can use this recipe whether you have a plank or not. Try searing or broiling or—the lightest method of all—steaming. Serve it with Plátanos Mash (page 288) or End-of-Summer Succotash (page 278).

**1 wood plank for grilling, about 6 x 12 inches (see Note)**
**1 tablespoon chopped fresh dill**
**1 teaspoon chopped garlic**
**1 teaspoon chopped peeled ginger**
**1 tablespoon soy sauce**
**1 tablespoon Dijon mustard**
**1 tablespoon olive oil, plus more for brushing**
**1 (2-pound) salmon fillet, skin on**
**Kosher salt**

Note: You can find wood planks for grilling at some kitchenware and big box stores and online. The most common are cedar, but you can also find hickory, maple, and cherry.

1. Soak the wood in a pot of water for 1 hour so it won't catch fire when it goes onto the grill.

2. Preheat a gas grill to medium.

3. Stir the dill, garlic, ginger, soy sauce, mustard, and olive oil together. Rub this mix all over the salmon. Brush the wood generously on one side with olive oil and sprinkle it with salt. Place the fish skin side down on the oiled side of the plank, then wrap loosely with heavy-duty aluminum foil, leaving the back of the plank exposed.

4. Lay the plank directly on the grate and grill the fish for 15 minutes. Let it rest for 15 minutes before unwrapping and serving.

# RIB EYE ON THE BONE

**SERVES 4 OR MORE**

Rib eye is the Rolls-Royce of steaks. It's bursting with beefy flavor and the marbling ensures it will be juicy. It just needs a little rub—in this case one made with coffee and chocolate—to give it some attitude. A vinaigrette made with grilled jalapeños and scallions spices things up.

   This can be the Big Steak Dinner for Four—or you can slice the steaks and serve them with a lot of other dishes for more guests.

**4 (1-inch-thick) bone-in rib eye steaks**
**Coffee-Chocolate Rub (page 195)**
**2 jalapeños**
**6 garlic cloves, peeled**
**4 scallions**
**8 tablespoons olive oil**
**Juice from 2 lemons**
**2 teaspoons Dijon mustard**
**4 drops Worcestershire sauce**
**2 tablespoons chopped fresh parsley**
**2 teaspoons chopped fresh tarragon**
**Kosher salt and freshly ground black pepper**

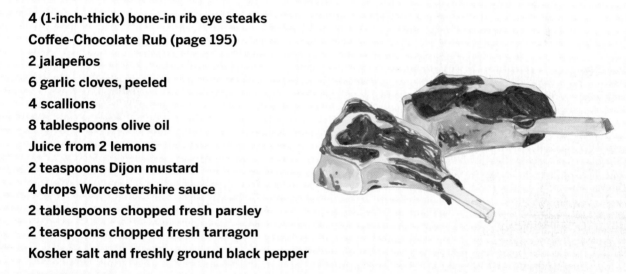

1. Take the steaks out of the refrigerator 30 minutes before you plan to grill them. Preheat a gas grill to medium.
2. Rub the steaks with the coffee-chocolate rub. Brush the steaks, jalapeños, garlic cloves, and scallions with 1 tablespoon of the olive oil. Put the steaks and vegetables on the grill. Grill the vegetables until they're charred all over, about 6 minutes. Grill the steaks to your desired doneness (6 minutes per side for medium-rare). Transfer the steaks to a platter and let them rest for 10 minutes.
3. Rub the charred skin off the jalapeños and pull off the stems. Chop the jalapeños, garlic, and scallions.
4. Whisk the remaining 7 tablespoons oil with the lemon juice, mustard, Worcestershire, parsley, and tarragon. Stir in the chopped vegetables. Taste and season with salt and pepper.
5. Spoon the grilled green vinaigrette onto the platter with the steaks and serve.

Rib Eye on the Bone (page 193)

# COFFEE-CHOCOLATE RUB

The bitter tones from the coffee beans and chocolate in this rub make it ideal for duck as well as beef. Rub it over and under the skin of a duck breast and let it sit in the refrigerator for at least 1 hour before scoring the skin in a diamond pattern and grilling. If you're using it on steak, you can just rub and grill.

Break open 2 or 3 cardamom pods and put the seeds in a spice grinder with 2 tablespoons shaved bittersweet (64% cacao) chocolate, 2 tablespoons ground coffee, and 1 teaspoon freshly grated nutmeg. Grind until powdery. Store the rub in an airtight container for up to 4 weeks. It makes about ¼ cup, which is enough for 2 pounds of meat.

# MAKE-YOUR-OWN STEAK FAJITAS

**SERVES 4 TO 6**

How do you create the feeling of high-end cooking while still keeping it quick and casual? I serve fajitas. With all the garnishes, this meal is bountiful, but it's also relatively quick, because you start by doctoring prepared salsa. The flavors are bold and the fajitas are unpretentious and a little messy. This is what eating with friends is about.

If you're entertaining a big crowd, you could make some Chipotle Chicken Skewers (page 238), too. As for the steaks, I use flat iron steaks, which is a well-marbled shoulder cut, but you can use London broil or skirt steaks as well.

**FOR THE AVOCADO SALSA**

1½ cups store-bought tomatillo salsa

1 large avocado, seeded, peeled, and diced

⅔ cup chopped fresh cilantro

1 small white onion, minced

1 tablespoon fresh lime juice

Kosher salt

**FOR THE FAJITAS**

1 cup store-bought tomatillo salsa

½ cup chopped fresh cilantro

2 tablespoons fresh lime juice

2 teaspoons minced garlic

½ teaspoon kosher salt

½ teaspoon freshly ground black pepper

4 flat iron steaks (about 2 pounds)

2 red bell peppers, cored and cut into eighths

Olive oil, for brushing

Flour tortillas

**FOR SERVING**

1 medium white onion, minced

½ cup coarsely chopped fresh cilantro

2 limes, cut into wedges

*Mash things up by putting out roti (page 175) instead of tortillas. Heat them on the grill, too.*

## MAKE THE AVOCADO SALSA

1. Mix the tomatillo salsa, avocado, cilantro, onion, and lime juice together in a serving bowl. Taste and season with salt. Cover and set aside.

## MAKE THE FAJITAS

2. Put the salsa, cilantro, lime juice, garlic, salt, and pepper into a 1-gallon zip-top bag and massage to combine. Add the steaks, turn to coat, seal the bag, and marinate at room temperature for 30 minutes.

3. Preheat a gas grill to medium-high.

4. Scrape the marinade from the steaks, place on the grate, and cover with aluminum foil. Grill, turning once and replacing the foil, to desired doneness—10 to 14 minutes for medium-rare. Let the steaks rest on a carving board for 10 minutes. While the steaks grill, brush the bell peppers with olive oil and grill until they are crisp-tender, with a good char, about 5 minutes per side.

5. Grill the tortillas for about 45 seconds per side until they are warm and slightly charred. Wrap in aluminum foil or a kitchen towel to keep warm.

## TO SERVE

6. Carve the steaks across the grain and put on a platter with the peppers. Put out the tortillas, avocado salsa, and bowls of onion, cilantro, and lime wedges. You're set for your guests to make their fajitas.

# TANGY PORK CHOPS
## WITH APPLE & ENDIVE

**SERVES 4**

When I was a kid, pork chops were always served with applesauce. This version, with grilled apples and endives, is a more refined version of that familiar and beloved flavor combination. A quick brine ensures juicy chops, and I brush the chops and apples with mustard and maple syrup as they grill. The finish is a tangy glaze made with apple cider vinegar, maple syrup, and mustard. When the whole dish comes together you have salty, sweet, and sour notes that work beautifully together.

½ cup water

1½ tablespoons sugar

Kosher salt

4 (1-inch-thick) pork rib chops

2 Belgian endives, quartered lengthwise, with core attached

Olive oil, for brushing

Freshly ground black pepper

1 tablespoon plus 1 teaspoon Dijon mustard

1 tablespoon plus 1 teaspoon pure maple syrup

¾ cup apple cider vinegar

1 tablespoon unsalted butter

1 tablespoon chopped fresh marjoram or oregano

2 Granny Smith apples, halved and cored

1 tablespoon chopped fresh parsley, for garnish

*There's always talk about people having a sweet tooth, but I've discovered that most of us crave something sour. The combination of bitter and sweet will make you love these chops.*

1. Combine the water, sugar, and 3 tablespoons salt in a 1-gallon zip-top bag and massage it until the salt dissolves. Add the pork chops, seal the bag, and let the chops brine at room temperature for 20 minutes.

2. Preheat a gas grill to medium-high.

3. Brush the endives with olive oil, then season with salt and pepper. Set aside. Stir 1 tablespoon mustard and 1 tablespoon maple syrup together in a small bowl.

4. Boil the vinegar in a small pot until it reduces to ¼ cup, 5 to 7 minutes. Whisk in the butter and the remaining 1 teaspoon mustard and 1 teaspoon maple syrup. Season the glaze to taste.

5. Remove the chops from the brine, blot dry, and rub with the marjoram.

6. Put the pork, endives, and apples on the grill. Grill, brushing the chops and apples several times with the mustard-maple mix. The endives and apples should be slightly softened and charred, about 4 minutes for the endives and 6 minutes for the apples. Transfer to a cutting board. Grill the chops to medium-rare, about 10 minutes (they will feel firm when you prod them with your finger). Let the chops rest for 10 minutes on a serving platter. Cut the apple pieces in half and cut the endives into long slices. Add them to the platter.

7. Reheat the vinegar–maple syrup glaze. Drizzle over the chops, apples, and endives, sprinkle with the parsley, and serve.

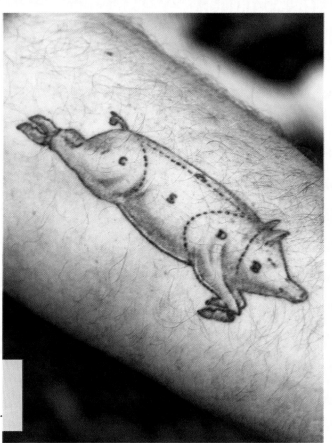

Chefs love their tattoos. I, on the other hand, have none.

# SLOW-GRILLED LAMB PATTIES

**SERVES 4**

For this recipe, I find inspiration in the flavorful food of Morocco. There's bulgur in the mix, which stretches the lamb (as bread crumbs do in meatballs), but it also firms up the patties and gives them some tooth. The slow grilling coaxes out more flavor and keeps the patties juicy. They're good to put out for a five-year-old and a seventy-year-old, and everyone in between. Serve them with Green Bean–Radicchio Salad (page 274).

**2 heaping tablespoons dry bulgur**
**1 cup water**
**1 pound ground lamb**
**1 large egg**
**1 small onion, grated**
**2 garlic cloves, minced**
**2 tablespoons chopped fresh parsley**
**2 tablespoons chopped fresh cilantro**
**1 teaspoon ground cumin**
**1 teaspoon smoked paprika**
**1 teaspoon kosher salt**
**½ teaspoon freshly ground black pepper**
**Olive oil, for brushing**

1. Soak the bulgur in the water for about 30 minutes. Drain.
2. Preheat a gas grill to medium.
3. Put the bulgur in a bowl with the lamb, egg, onion, garlic, parsley, cilantro, cumin, paprika, salt, and pepper. Use your hands to mix well.
4. Form the mixture into 4 oval patties and brush with olive oil. Grill the patties for about 8 minutes on each side for medium-well. Serve hot.

People's Grocery in Oakland, California, operates a local garden to help improve public health, economic development, and food systems.

*Pizza on the Grill with*
*Caesar Salad (page 202)*

# PIZZA ON THE GRILL
## WITH CAESAR SALAD

**SERVES 4**

When I'm home in New York City, more often than not I turn to pizza on the grill. The toppings—mozzarella, oven-dried tomato, olives, roasted peppers, and basil—are traditional, but then I pile on fresh greens tossed in Caesar dressing. It's that hit of greens and garlicky flavor that takes these pizzas over the top.

**FOR THE DOUGH**

1 cup warm water

1 envelope active dry yeast

Pinch of sugar

2 teaspoons kosher salt

2 tablespoons olive oil

2½–3 cups all-purpose flour

2 garlic cloves, minced

1 tablespoon chopped fresh basil

**FOR THE CAESAR DRESSING**

2 large egg yolks

1 tablespoon Dijon mustard

2 garlic cloves, chopped

3 anchovy fillets

½ cup olive oil

Juice of 2 limes

**FOR THE PIZZAS**

1 large fresh tomato, seeded and
   chopped (about 1 cup)

½ cup plus 2 tablespoons olive oil

2 teaspoons freshly ground black
   pepper

**2 teaspoons sugar**

**1 teaspoon minced garlic**

**¼ cup tomato sauce**

**¼ cup sliced black olives**

**¼ cup roasted red peppers**

**2 cups grated mozzarella cheese**

**¼ cup chopped fresh basil**

**1 cup arugula**

**1 cup shredded romaine lettuce**

### MAKE THE DOUGH

1. Put the water in a bowl, stir in the yeast and sugar, and let sit until frothy, about 10 minutes. Add the salt, olive oil, and 2½ cups of the flour and mix until the dough pulls away from the sides of the bowl. Turn out onto a lightly floured surface. Knead until smooth, about 8 minutes, adding up to ½ cup more flour if the dough seems too wet. Put the dough into a well-oiled bowl and cover with a damp cloth. Set aside to rise until doubled, about 1 hour. Turn the dough out onto a work surface and knead in the garlic and basil. Put it back in the bowl, cover with a damp cloth, and let rise until doubled, about 1 hour.

### MAKE THE DRESSING

2. Put the egg yolks, mustard, chopped garlic, and anchovies into a blender. Blend until smooth. With the motor running, pour in the oil in a slow, steady stream, then pour in the lime juice and blend until emulsified, about 1 minute. Scrape the dressing into a bowl, cover, and refrigerate until you need it. It will keep for about 3 days.

### MAKE THE PIZZAS

3. While the dough rises, preheat the oven to 250°F.

4. Put the tomato on a small rimmed baking sheet and toss with 2 tablespoons of the olive oil, the black pepper, and the sugar. Bake until the tomatoes have dried, about 1 hour.

5. Put the remaining ½ cup olive oil in a small bowl. Add the minced garlic and microwave for 30 seconds.

6. Preheat a gas grill to high.

7. Punch down the dough and divide in half. Shape each half into a ball and pat down on a lightly floured surface. Use your fingers to stretch the dough into 10-inch oblongs; it's nice if you leave a slightly thicker rim.

8. Turn half the grill down to medium. Brush 1 piece of dough with the garlic oil and place it, oiled side down, on the high-heat side of the grill. The dough will begin to puff almost immediately. When the bottom crust has lightly browned, use two spatulas to turn the dough over onto the medium-heat side. Working quickly, brush the garlic oil over the crust and then brush with half of the tomato sauce. Scatter with half of the roasted chopped tomatoes, half of the black olives, and half of the roasted red peppers. Sprinkle with 1 cup of the mozzarella and half of the basil. Close the lid and cook the pizza until the cheese melts. Remove the pizza from the grill and set it aside while you prepare the second pizza with the remaining ingredients.

9. Toss the arugula, romaine, and some of the Caesar dressing together. Cut the pizzas in half, pile the salad on top, and serve right away.

Try topping each pizza with a poached egg.

# PEACHES KISSED BY FIRE

**SERVES 4**

This dish is easy, but it looks and tastes fancy—and it's versatile. It is a great addition to a brunch menu. With a big green salad, it's a good light supper. But sometimes I make it on late-summer afternoons when I'm craving a snack. Grilling caramelizes the sugars in the peaches, and the goat cheese and ham bring a nice, tangy contrast. It takes only about 15 minutes to prepare and it's so much more satisfying than a bag of chips.

**4 large peaches, ripe but still firm,
  halved and pitted**
**Olive oil, for brushing**
**Kosher salt and freshly ground black
  pepper**
**1 (3-ounce) log goat cheese,
  crumbled**
**8 thin slices country ham or
  prosciutto**

1. Spray the grill rack with nonstick spray and preheat the gas grill to high.
2. Brush the peach halves with olive oil and season with salt and pepper.
3. Grill the peaches until lightly charred, about 2 minutes per side.
4. Place the peaches on a large plate, cut side up. Top each with crumbled goat cheese, season with more salt and pepper, and drape them with the ham.

# GRILLED SWEET POTATOES
## WITH SPICY KETCHUP

**SERVES 4 TO 6**

What a good thing grilled sweet potatoes are! The edges caramelize and char, the outsides have some chewiness to them, and the insides are creamy and sweet. And when you serve them with some ketchup doctored up with garlic and hot pepper flakes and scallions—wow!

**FOR THE SPICY KETCHUP**

**1 tablespoon unsalted butter**

**1 garlic clove, minced**

**1 cup ketchup**

**¼ teaspoon hot red pepper flakes**

**¼ teaspoon cayenne**

**1 scallion, finely chopped**

**FOR THE SWEET POTATOES**

**¼ cup olive oil, plus more for grilling**

**1 tablespoon chopped fresh rosemary**

**1 tablespoon packed light brown sugar**

**1 teaspoon garlic powder**

**¼ teaspoon cayenne**

**Kosher salt and coarsely ground black pepper**

**2 pounds sweet potatoes, peeled**

**1 teaspoon finely chopped fresh parsley**

**MAKE THE SPICY KETCHUP**

1. Melt the butter in a saucepan over medium-low heat, add the garlic, and cook until fragrant, 1 to 2 minutes. Add the ketchup, red pepper flakes, and cayenne. Cook just until the ketchup begins to bubble, 3 to 4 minutes. Remove from the heat, stir in the scallion, and cool.

## MAKE THE SWEET POTATOES

2. Preheat a gas grill to medium.

3. Mix the olive oil, rosemary, brown sugar, garlic powder, cayenne, and salt and pepper to taste in a large bowl. Cut the sweet potatoes lengthwise into ½-inch-thick slabs. Add the sweet potatoes to the bowl and toss with your hands to coat them well.

4. Brush the grill grate lightly with olive oil. Place the sweet potatoes on the grate and grill until tender and charred, turning occasionally, about 15 minutes total.

5. Cut the sweet potatoes into ½-inch sticks and pile on a platter. Garnish with the parsley and serve with the spicy ketchup.

# HOW DO YOU GRILL THAT?

### ASPARAGUS

Cut off the hard bottom ends of the spears. Coat the asparagus with olive oil and season with salt. Grill over high heat, turning occasionally, until they get a nice char, 5 to 10 minutes.

### BANANAS

Slice the bananas in their skins in half crosswise and then lengthwise, so each banana yields 4 pieces. Drizzle the cut sides of the bananas with honey and sprinkle with cinnamon sugar. Let them sit for 5 minutes.

Grill the bananas, cut side down, over high heat until grill marks appear, about 2 minutes. Turn them with tongs and grill over medium heat until the skin pulls away from the bananas, about 5 minutes.

### CARROTS

Peel the carrots, coat them with oil, and season with a sprinkle of salt and pepper. Grill over medium-high heat for 15 to 20 minutes, depending on size, until tender and charred. Turn them every 5 to 6 minutes. About 2 minutes before they're done, sprinkle them with Berbere (page 297).

### CUCUMBERS

Cut the cucumbers in half lengthwise, cut each half into thirds, and cut each third in half to make 12 spears per cucumber. Toss the cucumber with salt and let drain in a colander for 30 minutes. Blot the spears dry and toss with chopped fresh dill.

Grill on oiled grates over high heat until you have good grill marks, 2 to 3 minutes per side.

### FENNEL

Rinse the fennel well under cold water and dry with a paper towel. Cut off the stalks and the root end, leaving only the white bulb. Cut small bulbs in half through the core; cut large bulbs into 2-inch wedges, leaving a bit of core on each wedge.

Toss the fennel with olive oil, lemon juice, and a sprinkle of salt and pepper. Grill the fennel, cut side down, on oiled grates over high heat until the bulbs are tender and browned, 10 to 15 minutes on each side. (If the bulbs start to burn, move them to the low-heat side of the grill.)

## ONIONS

For best results, cut onions into ½-inch-thick slices—thick slices are less likely to fall apart.

Brush both sides of the onion slices with olive oil and sprinkle with salt and pepper, a favorite seasoning blend, or chopped fresh herbs.

Grill, covered with aluminum foil, on oiled grates over medium heat, turning, until tender and nicely charred, 15 to 20 minutes. Covering the onions will help them cook more evenly through the center.

## POTATOES

Toss fingerlings in olive oil and salt and grill on oiled grates over low heat, turning, until the skins are crisp and the potatoes are tender, 30 to 35 minutes. Let them cool a bit, then toss with chopped fresh chives. Or slice them and toss with some mustard that you've thinned with vinegar.

Wrap russets in aluminum foil and grill over low heat until tender, 40 to 45 minutes. Give them a few minutes to cool, then unwrap and serve with sour cream, crumbled bacon, and grilled garlic.

## ROMAINE LETTUCE

Rinse the lettuce and pat dry. Cut the head in half lengthwise. Drizzle with olive oil, then use a brush to spread the oil evenly over the surface. Grill on oiled grates over medium heat to char and cook through, 4 to 5 minutes a side, turning occasionally. Move the halves to low heat if you need to.

# COOKING WITH KIDS

KIDS WANT TO BE AS CLOSE TO THE ACTION AS POSSIBLE. THAT'S WHAT I wanted when I was in the kitchen with my grandmother, where she would set me to shelling peas or peeling rhubarb or plucking a chicken. Little by little my kitchen skills developed, and she would give me bigger jobs. And then the day came. I was with my father and Uncle Torsten, getting the boats ready for the season. At the end of the day, my father looked at me and said, "Marcus, if you don't cook, we don't eat." That was the first meal I cooked by myself. I was just a kid, years from becoming a chef, but I had started to learn the power of food.

The core of what I do today was passed down to me, and I love to ignite that spark in a new generation. They'll all have to cook for themselves and for others one day. So I give cooking classes for kids in my restaurant every month. One thing I've found is how wide their knowledge of food is. I was cooking grilled chicken and couscous with a lot of vegetables at the YMCA on 135th Street one day. I was adding cheese at the end, and this inner city kid pipes up, "Is that burrata or is that ricotta?" When I was his age, I knew fish and meatballs. And I've learned that kids are the most honest tasters you could have. They don't put a filter on their reactions.

Bring your kids into the kitchen and teach them skills. Chances are you'll learn from them, too. And get kids to understand the "why." Not just the "why we cut vegetables the same size before we cook them." The "why we eat the foods we eat" is deeply important. Teach them their culture, their history.

# MUSIC TO COOK BY

Jesus Children ★ Robert Glasper featuring Lalah Hathaway
  and Malcolm-Jamal Warner

The Buggy Ride ★ Wynton Marsalis

Can You Stand the Rain ★ New Edition

Raspberry Beret ★ Prince

Lovely Day ★ Bill Withers

Butterfly ★ Jamiroquai

Another Again ★ John Legend

Human Nature ★ Michael Jackson

Hard Knock Life ★ Jay-Z

Stories for Boys ★ U2

Happy ★ Pharrell Williams

Everyday Sunshine ★ Fishbone

The Sweetest Taboo ★ Sade

Pour Some Sugar on Me ★ Def Leppard

# BLUEBERRY CRUNCH GRANOLA

**MAKES ABOUT 5 CUPS**

This is one of my go-to breakfast dishes. Yes, I could buy granola, but the beauty of making it at home is that it's cheaper, it's fresher, and I can customize it so it's exactly the way I like it. And when you've got kids, you can let them mix and match so they can create their own personal granola. And then watch them develop a healthy breakfast habit that will stay with them for life.

Spoon it over plain yogurt or serve it in a bowl with milk or almond milk.

**2 cups rolled oats**

**1 cup dried blueberries**

**¾ cup sliced almonds**

**½ cup unsweetened shredded or flaked coconut**

**½ cup raw cashews**

**¼ cup packed brown sugar**

**1½ teaspoons ground allspice**

**4 tablespoons (½ stick) unsalted butter**

**2 tablespoons pure maple syrup**

**1 teaspoon ground cinnamon**

1. Preheat the oven to 300°F.
2. Toss the oats, blueberries, almonds, coconut, cashews, brown sugar, and allspice together in a large bowl.
3. Melt the butter with the maple syrup in a small saucepan over low heat. Pour it into the granola and toss to coat.

4. Spread the granola on a baking sheet. Bake until it is golden brown, stirring occasionally, about 20 minutes. Sprinkle the cinnamon over the granola and stir it in. Eat some of it warm if you want. Otherwise, let it cool and keep in an airtight container for up to 3 weeks.

Granola is a very forgiving mix, so let the kids mix and match:
★ The blueberries can be raisins, or dried cherries, or cranberries, or even cut-up dried apricots, mango, or pineapple.
★ The nuts can be pecans or walnuts or slivered almonds.
★ The kids may want to swap in more sliced almonds for the coconut.
★ The syrup can be agave or brown rice syrup (the syrup I knew when I was growing up was made with sugar beets).
★ The butter can be olive oil.
★ And if the kids like seeds, they can replace some of the nuts with raw pumpkin seeds or sunflower seeds.

# BRINGING KIDS INTO THE KITCHEN MAY MEAN

that dinner takes longer to prepare and the kitchen will be messier, but it's rewarding on so many levels. Here are some tips I can share from the hundreds of cooking classes I've done with kids.

★ Supervise the kids at all times.

★ Use measurements to improve math skills.

★ Impart a mantra: Clean hands. Clean surfaces.

★ Teach them to respect knives. Start by giving young ones table knives and soft things to cut.

★ Set firm guidelines about using the stove, but keep the kids at your side so they can see what's going on.

★ If you grill, get them involved. They get to see fire working in a way that they don't see on the stove. And you can let them start using the grill as a stove, too—have them cook a little sauce over the fire.

★ Introduce new ingredients. Let the kids learn how vegetables react when you apply heat. And start making all-vegetable meals.

★ Let the kids add or change ingredients. Empower them to be part of the process.

★ Have them taste whatever you're cooking together. And taste again after it's been salted.

★ Relax. Does it really matter if one corner of the fish stick isn't coated with bread crumbs?

# RED, WHITE & GREEN SPAGHETTI

**SERVES 4**

There's this thing about kids not eating spinach, but if you stir it into creamy ricotta cheese and then use it to top some whole wheat spaghetti with tomato sauce, they'll love it! And if you have leftovers, you'll get two meals in one (see The-Day-After-Pasta Frittata, page 54).

**2 tablespoons olive oil**
**2 garlic cloves, minced**
**2 cups baby spinach**
**½ cup ripped fresh basil leaves**
**1 pound whole wheat spaghetti**
**2 cups seasoned tomato sauce, such as Newman's**
    **Own Organic Traditional Herb Pasta Sauce**
**1 pound ricotta cheese**
**¼ cup freshly grated Parmesan cheese**
**Kosher salt and freshly ground black pepper**

1. Heat the olive oil in a skillet over medium heat. When it shimmers, add the garlic and spinach and cook, stirring, until the spinach wilts, 1 to 2 minutes. Stir in the basil. Remove from the heat.
2. Bring a large pot of salted water to a boil for the spaghetti. Cook the spaghetti until it's al dente, 8 to 10 minutes.
3. While the pasta cooks, heat the tomato sauce in a small saucepan over low heat.
4. Drain the spaghetti and return it to the pot, off the heat. Add half the tomato sauce and toss well. Keep the pasta warm on the back of the stove.
5. Fold the ricotta and Parmesan cheese into the spinach and season to taste with salt and pepper. Stir in the remaining tomato sauce.
6. Serve the spaghetti in deep bowls and top each portion with a generous dollop of the ricotta and spinach mixture.

Have kids pick and rip the basil leaves and they can stir the ricotta topping together. They can measure the sauce and stir it as it heats, too.

It's also a great opportunity to teach how ingredients change when they're cooked. Let them feel the dried spaghetti, then the cooked spaghetti. And by all means, have them taste the pasta to check if it's done.

# PEANUT NOODLES
## WITH SLAW

**SERVES 4 TO 6**

This dish is as fun to make as it is to eat. And it's good for you: Soba noodles are made with buckwheat flour, and your children may notice that the taste is milder than traditional wheat pastas. But just as important, it tastes good. The sauce is a mix of delicious flavors and textures: creamy peanut butter, soy sauce for salt, agave syrup for sweetness. Think of this dish as a kids' version of the popular Asian dish pad Thai—be prepared for them to request it again and again.

### FOR THE PEANUT VINAIGRETTE

**2 garlic cloves, minced**
**⅓ cup creamy peanut butter**
**⅓ cup rice wine vinegar**
**3 tablespoons agave syrup**
**3 tablespoons soy sauce or tamari**
**1 tablespoon sesame oil**
**1 teaspoon Sriracha sauce**

### FOR THE NOODLES

**1 pound soba noodles (or ramen noodles or spaghetti), cooked until al dente**
**1 cup chopped romaine lettuce leaves**
**1 cucumber, thinly sliced**
**1 carrot, peeled and shaved with a vegetable peeler**

**4 Napa cabbage leaves, finely shredded**
**2 tablespoons ripped fresh cilantro leaves**
**⅓ cup chopped roasted salted peanuts or cashews**

### MAKE THE PEANUT VINAIGRETTE

1. Whisk all the ingredients in a large bowl.

### MAKE THE NOODLES

2. Add the noodles to the vinaigrette and toss until the noodles are evenly coated. Cover with plastic wrap and refrigerate until the noodles are cold, at least 1 hour.
3. Toss in the lettuce, cucumber, carrot, and cabbage. Garnish with the cilantro and peanuts and serve.

Have the kids whisk the vinaigrette and rip up the cilantro.
    And have them wash their hands so they can toss the noodles and sauce together.

# BAKED POTATOES STUFFED WITH STINKY CHEESE & BACON

**SERVES 6**

When I was a kid, we ate a lot of baked potatoes—and I never got tired of them. I used to hover around the oven, waiting for them to come out, piping hot. I can still hear my mother's voice admonishing me, "Marcus, watch out!" as she pulled a tray of steaming goodness from the hot oven. What made baked potatoes so appealing back then remains true today. They are the ultimate blank canvas.

This recipe features one of Mom's favorite combos: bacon, rosemary, and stinky blue cheese—which I loved. But almost anything you have in your crisper, freezer, or pantry—from classic baked beans and cheddar cheese, to an Italian-inspired mix of salami, green olives, and onions, to leftover Bolognese sauce or takeout curry, to garlic butter and steamed shrimp—would work as a stuffing. Even a simple scrambled egg can become a golden crown on top of a baked potato. Use your imagination and, most of all, have fun.

**6 (8-ounce) russet potatoes**

**1 garlic bulb**

**1 tablespoon olive oil, plus more for brushing**

**4 slices bacon, diced**

**1 red onion, finely chopped**

**¼ cup plus 6 tablespoons sour cream**

**¼ cup plus 2 tablespoons crumbled blue cheese**

**4 tablespoons (½ stick) unsalted butter, softened**

**Needles from 4 sprigs fresh rosemary, chopped**

**Kosher salt and freshly ground black pepper**

1. Preheat the oven to 400°F.

2. Prick the potatoes all over with a fork or a skewer. Cut off and discard the top quarter of the garlic bulb and place the bulb on a square of aluminum foil; drizzle it with the olive oil and wrap tightly. Place the potatoes and wrapped garlic directly on an oven rack and bake until the garlic and potatoes are tender (squeeze them), 45 minutes for the garlic and about 1 hour 15 minutes for the potatoes. Let cool. Don't turn off the oven.

3. Cook the bacon in a skillet over medium-high heat until brown and crisp, then add the onion and cook for 1 minute more. Use a slotted spoon to transfer the bacon and onion to a mixing bowl.

4. Cut off the top third of each potato lengthwise. Use a spoon to scrape the flesh into the bowl with the bacon. Scoop the flesh from the bottom part of each potato, leaving a ¼-inch shell intact, and add it to the bowl.

5. Add ¼ cup of the sour cream, ¼ cup of the blue cheese, the butter, and rosemary to the potato flesh. Squeeze the roasted garlic out into the bowl. Use a fork to mash the potatoes and mix them with the other ingredients, then season with salt and pepper. Divide the stuffing among the potato shells.

6. Place the stuffed potatoes on a baking sheet and sprinkle them with salt. Brush the top skins on both sides with olive oil and put them on their own baking sheet. Bake until the stuffed potatoes are lightly browned and the potato skins are crisp, about 25 minutes.

7. Spoon 1 tablespoon of the sour cream and 1 teaspoon of the blue cheese on top of each potato, sprinkle some salt on the potato skins, and serve.

There are so many jobs kids can do with this recipe:
★ Poke the potatoes.
★ Drizzle and wrap the garlic.
★ Pull off the rosemary needles.
★ Mash the potatoes.
★ Fill the potatoes.
★ Put on the toppings.
And they should stand by the oven, waiting for this goodness to appear— like I did.

# VEGETABLE FLATBREAD PIZZAS

**SERVES 4**

Making pizza with your kids is easy. If you start by using any of their favorite vegetables and then add new vegetables each time you make it (cauliflower this time, mushrooms the next), your kids will gradually broaden their palates. They say it takes five or six exposures for the average kid to develop a taste for a new flavor. So keep trying!

**2 cups broccoli florets**
**2 pieces soft flatbread, such as Aladdin Bakers**
**Plain Flat Bread**
**Olive oil**
**6 asparagus spears**
**2 garlic cloves, thinly sliced**
**1 cup seasoned tomato sauce, such as Newman's**
**Own Marinara Pasta Sauce**
**8 cherry tomatoes, cut into thin slices**
**8 ounces fresh mozzarella cheese, sliced**
**2 tablespoons freshly grated Parmesan cheese**
**8 fresh basil leaves**

> Older kids can cut up the broccoli and asparagus as long as you supervise them and their knives.
> Kids of all ages should put the pizzas together.

1. Preheat the oven to 450°F.

2. Bring a pot of salted water to a boil. Add the broccoli, return to a boil, and cook for 1 minute. Drain and set aside.

3. Brush the flatbread with olive oil, put it on a baking sheet, and bake until lightly crisped, 3 to 4 minutes. Set aside.

4. Put the asparagus on a small baking sheet, brush it with olive oil, and roast until lightly charred, about 5 minutes.

5. Cut the asparagus into 1-inch pieces and the broccoli into bite-size pieces. Combine the broccoli, asparagus, and garlic in a bowl.

6. Spread the tomato sauce over the flatbreads. Evenly sprinkle the vegetables on top and then the cherry tomatoes. Top with the slices of mozzarella and the Parmesan cheese.

7. Bake just until the cheese is lightly browned and starting to bubble, 4 to 5 minutes. Tear the basil into pieces and scatter them over the pizzas. Drizzle with a little olive oil, slice into squares, and serve.

# ZUCCHINI FRITTERS

**MAKES 18 FRITTERS**

Think of these fritters—which have, as their heart, zucchini, feta, and arugula—as little veggie burgers without the bun. They're a fast and great way to get vegetables onto a kid's plate because they're hidden in a batter. Sometimes I serve the fritters with my twice-fried chicken (page 69), but a supermarket rotisserie chicken would work just as well. If it's meatless Monday, serve them with the Orange-Fennel Salad on page 273. Leftovers are great; reheat them in the oven—or in a cast iron skillet to get them really crunchy. There's no good reason to eat these with a knife and fork. Your kids—and you—will be much happier eating with your hands.

**FOR THE GARLIC-YOGURT DIP**

**6 tablespoons plain yogurt**

**2 tablespoons mayonnaise**

**Juice of 1 lime**

**2 garlic cloves, minced**

**½ teaspoon Aleppo pepper (see Note, page 47) or hot red pepper flakes**

**Kosher salt and freshly ground white pepper**

**FOR THE ZUCCHINI FRITTERS**

**2½ cups grated zucchini (use the big holes on a box grater)**

**½ teaspoon kosher salt**

**1 large egg**

**1 large egg yolk**

**½ cup all-purpose flour, plus more if necessary**

**½ cup crumbled feta cheese**

**1 cup finely chopped arugula**

**½ cup chopped scallions**

**1 tablespoon plus 2 teaspoons chopped fresh dill**

**2 teaspoons finely chopped fresh parsley**

**½ cup olive oil**

**½ cup corn oil**

The kids can make the dip, grate the zucchini (keep an eye on them and grate the ends of the zucchini yourself so the kids don't get their fingers cut), and start squeezing the zucchini dry. You'll probably have to finish squeezing because your hands are bigger and stronger.

**MAKE THE GARLIC-YOGURT DIP**

1. Stir the yogurt, mayonnaise, lime juice, garlic, and Aleppo pepper together in a small bowl. Give it a taste and season with salt and white pepper. Cover and refrigerate.

**MAKE THE ZUCCHINI FRITTERS**

2. Toss the zucchini and salt together in a large bowl. Let stand for 5 minutes. Dump the zucchini onto a kitchen towel, gather up the ends, and squeeze out as much liquid as possible.

3. Put the zucchini in a bowl. Add the egg, yolk, flour, and feta and mix until combined. Toss in the arugula, scallions, all the dill, and the parsley. If the batter is very wet, add 1 to 2 tablespoons flour until the batter binds well.

4. Heat ¼ cup of the olive oil and ¼ cup of the corn oil in a large skillet over medium heat. When it shimmers, drop the batter by a rounded tablespoonful into the skillet. You should hear an immediate sizzle; if you don't, the oil isn't hot enough, so wait a moment before adding more batter. Flatten the fritters with the back of a fork and fry until they're golden, moving the fritters around the skillet so they fry evenly, about 5 minutes on each side. Drain on paper towels. Fry the rest of the fritters, adding more olive oil and corn oil as needed.

5. Serve with the Garlic-Yogurt Dip.

# SHREDDED TURKEY CHILI

**SERVES 6**

You're never too young to learn the value of leftovers. Here, roasted turkey and black beans are turned into a hearty chili that's relatively mild for a kid's palate but flavorful enough to please any adult. Top the chili with sour cream, avocado, onions, cilantro, and tortilla chips, and you've got a winter feast.

3 tablespoons olive oil

2 red bell peppers, seeded and diced

1 large yellow onion, diced

1 garlic clove, minced

1 tablespoon chile powder

1 tablespoon cumin seeds, crushed

½ teaspoon ground coriander

½ teaspoon cayenne

2 teaspoons kosher salt

2 teaspoons packed brown sugar

4 dashes Tabasco sauce

1 (28-ounce) can whole tomatoes in juice

1 (19-ounce) can black beans, rinsed and drained

½ cup water

2 cups shredded leftover turkey or chicken

Sour cream

Crushed tortilla chips

Diced avocado

Fresh cilantro leaves

Chopped onion

Kids can shred the turkey, rinse the beans, crush the chips, and pick the cilantro leaves.

You could also pour the tomatoes into a large bowl and have the kids break them up with their hands before adding them to the chili.

Let them stir; let them taste. Let them learn how the flavors change as the chili cooks.

1. Heat the olive oil in a heavy, medium pot over medium heat. When it shimmers, add the peppers, onion, and garlic and cook, stirring occasionally, until the onion is golden, 12 to 15 minutes. Add the chile powder, cumin, coriander, cayenne, salt, and brown sugar and cook, stirring, until fragrant, about 1 minute. Add the Tabasco and tomatoes with their juice, breaking the tomatoes up with a spoon. Then add the beans and water and bring to a boil. Reduce the heat and simmer, partly covered, until the chili has thickened, 20 to 25 minutes. Taste and adjust the seasoning if necessary. Turn off the heat.

2. Fold in the turkey and let the chili stand, covered, until the turkey is heated through, 5 minutes. Don't continue stirring as you heat the chili, otherwise the turkey will break up and get stringy.

3. Put out bowls of sour cream, tortilla chips, avocado, cilantro, and onion so everyone can personalize the chili.

# HELGA'S MEATBALLS & GRAVY WITH CARROT-APPLE MASHED POTATOES

**SERVES 4, WITH ABOUT 6 MEATBALLS EACH**

This recipe is both a culinary heirloom (it's my grandmother's recipe for meatballs) and a postcard from Sweden, where meatballs and mashed potatoes are sold in kiosks. As new immigrants arrive in Sweden, hot dog stands may morph to sell kebabs or wok cooking, but the meatball kiosk remains a constant. There's nothing more warming in the freezing winter than standing on a corner, eating hot meatballs and mashed potatoes.

I grill these meatballs (inside, on a grill pan) to give them a deeper flavor and to cut back on the fat, and I've added carrots and apple to the mashed potatoes, which makes them slightly sweet. The gravy recipe is pure Grandmother Helga.

Serve these with Pickled Cucumbers (page 298).

## FOR THE MEATBALLS

2 tablespoons olive oil

1 medium red onion, finely chopped

½ cup dry bread crumbs

¼ cup heavy cream

½ pound ground chuck or sirloin

½ pound ground veal

½ pound ground pork

2 tablespoons honey

1 large egg

Kosher salt and freshly ground
    black pepper

Meatballs were my gateway to cooking. My sisters and I had meatball-rolling competitions—which I usually lost.

By all means have kids mix the meatballs and roll them. Really, who cares if they're not all the same size?

### FOR THE GRAVY

1 cup chicken broth

½ cup heavy cream

¼ cup lingonberry preserves

2 tablespoons juice from Pickled
   Cucumbers (page 298)

Kosher salt and freshly ground black
   pepper

### FOR THE CARROT-APPLE MASHED POTATOES

3 large Yukon Gold potatoes, peeled
   and quartered

2 large carrots, peeled and chopped

1 medium Granny Smith apple,
   peeled, cored, and sliced

2 tablespoons olive oil

1 red onion, thinly sliced

2 garlic cloves, thinly sliced

2 medium shallots, thinly sliced

1 tablespoon balsamic vinegar

1 tablespoon honey

½ cup buttermilk

½ teaspoon horseradish, preferably
   freshly grated

Kosher salt and freshly ground black
   pepper

### MAKE THE MEATBALLS

1. Heat the olive oil in a small skillet over medium heat. When it shimmers, add the onion and cook until softened, about 5 minutes. Remove from the heat and let cool.

2. Combine the bread crumbs and heavy cream in a large bowl, stirring with a fork until all the crumbs are moistened.

3. Add the sautéed onion, beef, veal, pork, honey, egg, and salt and pepper to the bread crumbs and mix well. Wet your hands (it keeps the meatballs from sticking) and shape the mixture into meatballs the size of golf balls, placing them on a plate lightly moistened with water. You should end up with about 24 meatballs.

4. Heat a grill pan over medium-high heat. Grill the meatballs, in batches if necessary, until browned all over and cooked through, about 9 minutes.

My grandmother Helga, in her apron.

### MAKE THE GRAVY

5. Bring the broth, cream, preserves, and pickle juice to a simmer in a large saucepan over medium-high heat.

6. Add the meatballs to the gravy, reduce the heat to medium, and simmer until the gravy thickens slightly and the meatballs are heated through, about 5 minutes. Season with salt and peper to taste. Keep warm.

### MAKE THE CARROT-APPLE MASHED POTATOES

7. Meanwhile, put the potatoes into a large saucepan, cover with salted cold water by at least an inch, and cook until tender, about 20 minutes. Put the carrots and apples in another saucepan, cover with salted cold water by at least an inch, and cook until tender, about 15 minutes.

8. While the potatoes, apples, and carrots cook, heat the olive oil in a medium skillet over medium-high heat. When it shimmers, add the onion, garlic, shallots, vinegar, and honey. Reduce the heat to medium-low and cook, stirring often, until the onion and shallots are tender, about 10 minutes.

9. Drain the potatoes and the carrots and apples and return them to one of the cooking pots. Mash coarsely with a fork or potato masher. Stir in the buttermilk, horseradish, and onion mixture. Season with salt and pepper to taste.

10. To serve, spoon the carrot-apple mashed potatoes onto dinner plates and top with the meatballs and gravy.

# THE BASIC MEATBALLS ARE SWEDISH,

but that doesn't mean you always have to serve "Swedish meatballs." The following variations are a reflection of our changing cultures and populations—and how our different cuisines come together beautifully.

## HELGA'S MEATBALLS & TOMATILLO-AVOCADO SALSA

Start by cooking the meatballs in a large skillet with 3 tablespoons olive oil. Transfer to a serving dish.

Add 2 minced garlic cloves, 1 minced serrano chile (seeded), and 1 finely chopped shallot to the fat in the skillet and sauté over medium-high heat until fragrant, about 2 minutes. Add 2 finely chopped tomatillos and sauté until softened, another 3 minutes.

Scrape all this into a bowl and fold in 1 diced avocado, 1 finely chopped jalapeño pepper (seeded), 1 teaspoon chopped fresh cilantro, the juice of 1 lime, and 4 dashes of Tabasco. Taste, then season with salt and pepper.

Serve the meatballs and salsa with a mash (the carrot-apple-potato on page 229 or the Plátanos Mash on page 288).

## HELGA'S MEATBALLS & LION SAUCE

Next time you make the Doro Wat Tostados (page 157), freeze the extra sauce (*doro*); it makes for a killer accompaniment to my grandmother's meatballs. I think of it as a tribute to Ethiopia's Lion of Judah.

Heat 1 cup leftover *doro wat* sauce in a large saucepan. Add the (grilled or sautéed) meatballs and stir to coat them.

Serve with a spoonful of *ayib* (page 157) or cottage cheese and some mashed potatoes or Ethiopian Chickpea Spread (page 284).

# HANNAH'S SHRIMP TACOS

**MAKES 6**

With its sweet flavors and a snap when you bite into it, shrimp may be the first seafood kids fall in love with. I season them with a little chile powder, then cook them with onion, tomatoes, corn, and avocado to make the sweetest little taco filling. It's light, it's fast, and it's fun.

Don't stick with corn tortillas when you make this. Introduce kids to different kinds of wraps: flour tortillas, any Middle Eastern flatbread, pita, even lefse—those Norwegian potato pancakes—if you can find them.

*Here's the kids' job: Have them put together all the tacos and serve them. Do they want to make a platter? Individual plates? Let them make this meal theirs. And listen to ABBA while you're cooking.*

**12 large (18–20) shrimp, peeled and deveined**
**Kosher salt and freshly ground black pepper**
**¼ teaspoon mild chile powder**
**2 tablespoons olive oil**
**2 garlic cloves, thinly sliced**
**1 medium red onion, finely chopped**
**2 tablespoons corn kernels (frozen are fine)**
**2 ripe tomatoes, diced**
**1 avocado, pitted, peeled, and thinly sliced**
**Juice of 2 limes**
**1 tablespoon chopped fresh cilantro**
**1 tablespoon freshly grated Parmesan cheese**
**½ small head iceberg lettuce, finely shredded**
**6 corn tortillas**

1. Season the shrimp with salt and pepper to taste, then sprinkle with the chile powder.

2. Heat the olive oil in a large skillet over medium-high heat. When it shimmers, add the garlic, onion, and shrimp and sauté, stirring often, for 5 minutes. Add the corn and sauté for another 2 minutes. Turn the heat down to low, fold in the tomatoes and avocado, and cook until warmed through, 2 to 3 minutes.

3. Combine the lime juice, cilantro, and cheese in a mixing bowl. Add the iceberg lettuce and toss well.

4. Heat each tortilla in a dry skillet over medium-high heat until warm, pliable, and browned in spots, 30 seconds to 1 minute.

5. Divide the shrimp filling evenly among the tortillas. Top with the iceberg salad and serve.

Kids today are often much more advanced in their tastes than their parents were. They eat more sushi and tacos; they're exposed to so many more food experiences. The parent who says, "My kid would never eat that," is often wrong. It's usually the parent who's afraid of something new.

# DELISH FISH STICKS
## WITH TARTAR SAUCE

**SERVES 6**

Fish sticks combine three of my favorite things: food that crunches, food that I can eat with my hands, and food that has fish as the main ingredient. Here I use panko to make the fish sticks extra crunchy and Japanese miso and soy to give the halibut layers of rich, satisfying flavor that kids and grown-ups will love. I say thank you to the many sushi restaurants for the gift of inexpensive miso soup and for opening our palates to miso's umami.

### FOR THE TARTAR SAUCE

½ cup mayonnaise
¼ cup finely chopped dill pickles
2½ tablespoons chopped fresh dill
2 tablespoons drained capers
Juice of 1 lemon
Kosher salt and freshly ground black pepper

*Kids can make the tartar sauce and bread the fish. Another chance to talk about hand-washing.*

### FOR THE FISH STICKS

6 tablespoons white miso
3 tablespoons soy sauce
2 tablespoons chopped fresh dill
1 tablespoon chopped fresh chives
2 large eggs
¾ cup all-purpose flour
1¼ cups panko bread crumbs
1½ pounds halibut fillets, cut into 3-x-1-inch strips
3 tablespoons olive oil
1 lemon, cut into wedges

### MAKE THE TARTAR SAUCE

1. Mix all the ingredients together in a small bowl. Season with salt and pepper. Cover with plastic wrap and refrigerate while you prepare the fish.

### MAKE THE FISH STICKS

2. Stir the miso, soy sauce, dill, and chives together in a shallow bowl. Beat the eggs in another shallow bowl. Put the flour on a plate and the panko on another plate.

3. Toss the fish sticks in the soy-miso mixture, then roll them in the flour to coat; shake off the excess flour. Dip in the eggs, allow the excess egg to drip off, then coat the fish sticks in panko. Again, shake off the excess crumbs. Place the fully coated fish sticks on a rack.

4. Heat half the olive oil in a large non-stick skillet over medium heat. When the oil shimmers, add half the fish and cook, turning often, until golden on all sides, about 4 minutes total. Check one; it should be opaque in the center. Drain on paper towels and cover with aluminum foil to keep warm. Add the remaining olive oil to the skillet and fry the rest of the fish.

5. Put the fish sticks on a platter and garnish with the lemon wedges. Serve with the tartar sauce.

# BIRD-BIRD NUGGETS

**SERVES 6**

This is a great way to introduce kids to the world of layered flavors. A simple marinade for the chicken is layer one; a mix of flour, cornmeal, cornstarch, and herbs is layer two; and the super-crisp panko coating is layer three. Serve these with Drizzled Plantains with Avocado Dip (page 290) and you'll see your kids' eyes widen with delight. Who needs ketchup and fries when you can have food this tasty?

**2 garlic cloves, minced**

**Juice of 1 lemon**

**6 dashes Tabasco sauce**

**½ cup plus 2 tablespoons olive oil**

**Kosher salt and freshly ground black pepper**

**1½ pounds boneless, skinless chicken breasts, cut into**
    **3-x-1-inch strips**

**½ cup all-purpose flour**

**½ cup cornmeal**

**½ cup cornstarch**

**1 teaspoon fresh thyme leaves**

**1 teaspoon chopped fresh rosemary**

**2 large eggs, beaten**

**1½ cups panko bread crumbs**

**4 tablespoons (½ stick) unsalted butter, cut into pieces**

Kids can make the marinade in the zip-top bag and then massage the chicken to make sure the marinade covers everything.

    Definitely have the kids do the breading. It's a great opportunity to teach the importance of washing your hands before and after handling food. And it couldn't be more fun for them to roll up their sleeves and get messy on purpose.

1. Put the garlic, lemon juice, Tabasco, 2 tablespoons of the olive oil, and salt and pepper to taste in a 1-gallon zip-top bag. Massage to combine. Add the chicken, seal the bag, and massage to coat the chicken with the marinade. Marinate at room temperature for 30 minutes.

2. Put the flour, cornmeal, cornstarch, thyme, rosemary, and ½ teaspoon salt in a shallow bowl and whisk to combine. Put the eggs in another shallow bowl and the panko in a third shallow bowl.

3. Dust the chicken with the seasoned flour, patting off the excess. Dip the chicken in the eggs, let the excess drip off, then coat the chicken with the panko. Put the pieces on a rack as you bread them.

4. Heat the remaining ½ cup olive oil in a large skillet over high heat. When the oil shimmers, using tongs, add the chicken pieces and cook, without moving them, until golden on the bottom, about 1 minute. Using tongs, turn the pieces over and cook the other side until golden, about 3 minutes. Add the butter, reduce the heat to low, and continue to cook, turning the pieces frequently, until the chicken is completely browned and cooked through, 5 to 10 minutes. Drain on paper towels before serving.

# CHIPOTLE CHICKEN SKEWERS

**SERVES 6 TO 8, WITH 2 TO 3 SKEWERS EACH**

Kids love food on a stick. The chili sauce is store-bought (see? Chefs take shortcuts, too!), the chipotles add some zing (food for kids doesn't have to be bland), and the orange juice cuts a little of the heat. If you're not a cilantro fan, you can swap it out by doubling the basil.

## FOR THE MARINADE

**1 cup fresh orange juice**

**½ cup chili sauce**

**½ cup fresh lime juice (about 6 limes)**

**2 garlic cloves**

**2 chipotle chiles in adobo (or more to taste)**

**1 teaspoon ground cumin**

**1 teaspoon kosher salt**

**½ teaspoon freshly ground black pepper**

**½ teaspoon chile powder**

## FOR THE CHICKEN

**3 pounds boneless, skinless chicken breasts, cut into 1-inch pieces**

**3 medium red onions, cut through the root into sixths**

**18 (6-inch) bamboo skewers, soaked in water for 30 minutes**

**Kosher salt and freshly ground black pepper**

**1 teaspoon sesame seeds, toasted**

**1 tablespoon chopped fresh cilantro**

**1 tablespoon chopped fresh basil**

Have the kids massage the marinade and chicken, put the skewers together, and garnish.

### MAKE THE MARINADE

1. Combine all the ingredients in a food processor and process until smooth. Taste and adjust the salt and pepper if you need to.

### MAKE THE CHICKEN

2. Put the chicken into a 1-gallon zip-top bag, add ½ cup of the marinade, and massage to coat all the chicken. Marinate in the refrigerator for 2 hours. Reserve the rest of the marinade.

3. Preheat the broiler; if using a gas grill, preheat to medium.

4. While the grill or broiler is heating up, slide 1 piece of onion onto each skewer, followed by 3 pieces of chicken. Continue until you've filled all the skewers. Arrange the skewers in a single layer on a large baking sheet. Season lightly with salt and pepper and brush with ¼ cup of the reserved marinade.

5. Broil the chicken skewers, without turning them, until the chicken is cooked through, 8 to 10 minutes. If grilling, they will take 5 to 6 minutes per side. Transfer to a platter and garnish with the sesame seeds, cilantro, and basil.

6. Bring the remaining marinade to a boil in a small saucepan and serve with the skewers.

# SOUPS

WHEN WE'RE NOT FEELING OUR BEST, WE TURN TO SOUP.
When we want to return to our cultural identity, we turn to
soup. It could be ramen or pho or bouillabaisse, a chowder or
chicken soup. Ask any Swede what he ate for dinner at home
on Thursdays. The answer will be universal: pea soup.

One of the things I love about soups is the simplicity of
one-pot cooking and how natural it is to just let them sit. I'm
never afraid to serve soup as a main course, and I know there's
no need to worry if my guests are running twenty minutes late.
It's not like meat, which can dry out, or fish, which will get cold.
Soup will wait—and it only gets better. And if an unexpected
guest shows up, I know I can always stretch it.

For these soups, I've built on my experiences with many
places and many cultures. There's a gazpacho that started in
Spain, a chicken soup inspired by Mexico, a Vietnamese noodle
soup by way of Los Angeles, a chowder from New England. I've
turned to the flavors I love in Thai cooking for my carrot soup.
And I've morphed the pea soup of my childhood from dried
split peas to fresh.

Soups remind me of the difference between hearing a
recording of a song and hearing the singer in person. When
you're there with the singer, improvisations make the song
alive. Improvise with your soups. Add flavors and ingredients
from your heart.

# MUSIC TO COOK BY

Watermelon Man ★ Herbie Hancock

Violet ★ Seal

You Say Tomato, I Say Tomato ★ Ella Fitzgerald
& Louis Armstrong

I Know You Got Soul ★ Eric B. & Rakim

Savoir Faire ★ Chic

Coconut Woman ★ Harry Belafonte

Flor de Lis ★ Djavan

Enen Yaye ★ Aster Aweke

Ojos Verdes ★ Concha Piquer

Eu Vim da Bahia ★ Gilberto Gil

Bread and Butter ★ The Roots

Det Löser Sej ★ Timbuktu

All Your Lovin' ★ Blacknuss

# WATERMELON-TOMATO GAZPACHO

**SERVES 4**

For years now, I've loved salads made with tomato and watermelon, so I decided to take those same flavors and blend them into a gazpacho. I've added jalapeño and harissa to play off the sweetness of the melon and the coolness of the soup. For a less spicy soup, omit the jalapeño.

**2 tablespoons coarsely chopped blanched almonds**
**3 garlic cloves, peeled**
**1 jalapeño, seeded and chopped (optional)**
**½ cup cubed day-old white bread**
**1 teaspoon Harissa (see opposite)**
**3 cups cubed seedless watermelon**
**2½ cups chopped tomatoes**
**3 tablespoons olive oil**
**2 cups water**
**2 tablespoons sherry vinegar**
**1 teaspoon minced fresh cilantro**
**Kosher salt and freshly ground black pepper**

Make extra gazpacho and freeze it for a November treat: Heat it up and serve with sautéed shrimp, or pulse in a food processor to make granita.

1. Toast the almonds, garlic, and half of the jalapeño in a small skillet over medium heat until the garlic is starting to turn golden brown, about 2 minutes. Add the bread and toast for another 2 minutes, then add the harissa and toast for 2 minutes more.

2. Scrape the bread and seasonings into a blender. Add 2 cups of the watermelon, 2 cups of the tomatoes, and 2 tablespoons of the olive oil and blend until smooth. Pour into a pitcher and stir in the water, vinegar, and ½ teaspoon of the cilantro. Taste and season with salt and pepper.

3. For the garnish, toss the remaining jalapeño (if using), 1 cup watermelon, ½ cup tomatoes, and ½ teaspoon cilantro with the remaining 1 tablespoon olive oil. You can serve the soup right away or refrigerate until chilled.

4. To serve, pour the gazpacho into soup bowls and spoon some of the watermelon-tomato garnish on top.

Visit your local farmers' market to learn how to use different fruits and vegetables, like these stunning Black Galaxy tomatoes.

# HARISSA

You can find tubes and jars of this Middle Eastern spice paste in most markets these days, but it's so much better when you make it at home. Mine's perfumed with coriander and caraway and it's not overpoweringly hot—the heat is seductive.

Heat ¾ cup olive oil in a small sauté pan over medium heat. When the oil shimmers, add 2 minced garlic cloves and cook until golden, about 4 minutes. Remove the pan from the heat. Stir in 1 cup mild chile powder (maybe Aleppo pepper), 1 tablespoon ground coriander, 1 teaspoon ground caraway seeds, 1 teaspoon kosher salt, and 2 tablespoons chopped fresh mint. Let cool. Store in an airtight container in the refrigerator for up to 2 weeks.

This makes about 1¼ cups.

# PICKLED TOMATO SOUP
## WITH CORN BREAD CROUTONS

**SERVES 4**

Nothing says summer like fresh, ripe tomatoes. But when tomatoes are out of season and I'm craving bright, fresh flavors, I make this soup. Cider vinegar, ginger, and lemongrass work magic on a can of tomatoes, creating a bright tang—like a pickle. I see this soup as a combination of the sour flavors I learned to love in the past and the tastes of Southeast Asia that I crave today. The corn bread croutons add texture, of course; it's like having a soup and a sandwich in a bowl.

### FOR THE TOMATO SOUP

**3 tablespoons vegetable oil**

**1 stalk lemongrass, minced (see "Prepping Lemongrass," page 45)**

**3 shallots, sliced**

**3 garlic cloves, minced**

**1 (2-inch) piece ginger, peeled and minced**

**1 tablespoon coriander seeds**

**4 cups vegetable broth**

**1 (28-ounce) can tomatoes**

**½ cup apple cider vinegar**

**Kosher salt**

*The combination of tomato soup and grilled cheese is about as American as you can get. This is my remix.*

### FOR THE CROUTONS

**4 (½-inch) slices Market-Fresh Corn Bread (page 285)**

**3 tablespoons unsalted butter, melted**

### MAKE THE TOMATO SOUP

1. Heat the oil in a large saucepan over medium heat. When the oil shimmers, add the lemongrass, shallots, garlic, ginger, and coriander seeds. Cook until the shallots soften, about 3 minutes. Turn the heat to high, add the broth, tomatoes, and vinegar, and bring to a boil. Break the tomatoes up with a spoon. Turn down the heat and simmer for 20 minutes to blend the flavors.

**MAKE THE CROUTONS**

2. While the soup simmers, preheat the oven to 450°F.

3. Cut the corn bread into ¾-inch cubes, spread on a baking sheet, and brush with the melted butter. Bake, tossing 2 or 3 times, until the croutons' edges are crispy and golden brown, 10 to 12 minutes.

**FINISH THE SOUP**

4. Working in batches, carefully puree the soup in a blender and put through a fine strainer. Taste and season with salt.

5. Ladle the soup into bowls and top with the croutons.

# PARSNIP SOUP WITH APPLES & WALNUTS

**SERVES 6**

Tender parsnips, perfumed with cumin and garam masala and blended with cream, make a golden soup that's velvety soft. Topped with a garnish of apples and walnuts, it's truly luxurious and will warm you to your core. Impress your guests and serve it as a first course to lamb or roast pork.

**FOR THE GARNISH**

1 tablespoon olive oil

½ cup walnuts, coarsely chopped

1 garlic clove, minced

Juice of ½ lemon

½ tablespoon walnut oil (see Note)

1 apple, cored and finely diced

1 tablespoon chopped fresh parsley

1 tablespoon chopped fresh tarragon

Kosher salt and freshly ground black pepper

**FOR THE SOUP**

¼ cup olive oil

3 cups peeled and diced parsnips

1 cup peeled and diced Jerusalem artichokes (see Note)

2 garlic cloves, chopped

2 teaspoons garam masala

1 teaspoon ground cumin

½ teaspoon ground turmeric

Kosher salt

2 cups chicken broth

1 cup heavy cream

3 cups water

Juice of ½ lemon

Freshly ground black pepper

Notes: Walnut oil is available in some markets, specialty stores, and online. Store in the refrigerator.

Jerusalem artichokes are often called "sunchokes." If you can't find them, replace them with more parsnips.

## MAKE THE GARNISH

1. Heat the olive oil in a medium skillet over medium heat. Add the walnuts and cook until golden brown, about 4 minutes. Add the garlic and lemon juice and cook until fragrant, about 30 seconds. Drizzle in the walnut oil and remove from the heat. Let cool to room temperature, then stir in the apple, parsley, and tarragon. Season with salt and pepper.

## MAKE THE SOUP

2. Heat the oil in a large pot over medium heat. Add the parsnips, Jerusalem artichokes, garlic, garam masala, cumin, turmeric, and ½ teaspoon salt. Cook until the parsnips start to brown, 3 to 4 minutes. Add the chicken broth, cream, and water, bring to a simmer, and cook until the vegetables are tender, about 25 minutes. Working in batches, carefully puree the soup in a blender. Return to the pot and stir in the lemon juice. Taste and season with salt and pepper.

3. To serve, divide the soup among six bowls. Add a spoonful of the apple-walnut garnish to the middle of each bowl.

# THREE-SHADES-OF-GREEN VEGETABLE BROTH

**SERVES 6**

Like most of us, I eat meat on a regular basis. But I often want to give my body a break from animal protein, so I go vegetarian for a day at least once a week. This green broth, made with spinach, parsley, basil, and avocado, is one of my favorite light meals. The herbs and vegetables give the soup a clean feel that's complemented by creamy bites of avocado and tofu. The soup by itself is satisfying, but you could serve it with an open-faced grilled cheese.

**2 cups packed spinach**
**2 tablespoons fresh parsley leaves**
**2 tablespoons fresh basil leaves**
**¼ cup plus 1 tablespoon olive oil**
**1 red onion, chopped**
**2 garlic cloves, minced**
**2 jalapeños, minced**
**1 tablespoon white miso**
**1 bay leaf**
**5 cups water**
**3 tablespoons couscous**
**Kosher salt and freshly ground black**
  **pepper**
**1 avocado, pitted, peeled, and diced**
**½ cup cubed silken tofu**
**1 scallion, chopped**
**Juice of 1 lime**

Venture outside your own city and you'll find some of the best produce available. Miller Farm is located in the Hudson Valley, about two hours north of Harlem.

1. Put the spinach, parsley, basil, and ¼ cup olive oil into a food processor and process until you have a smooth paste. Set aside.

2. Heat the remaining 1 tablespoon oil in a large saucepan over medium heat. When it shimmers, add the onion, garlic, and jalapeños and cook until the onion softens but doesn't brown, 3 to 4 minutes. Add the miso, bay leaf, and water. Bring to a simmer and cook for 25 minutes.

3. Stir half of the spinach puree into the simmering broth and cook for an additional 15 minutes. Add the couscous, remove from the heat, and let sit for 10 minutes to allow the couscous to fluff. Discard the bay leaf. Taste and season with salt and pepper.

4. Combine the remaining puree with the avocado, tofu, scallion, and lime juice. Fold together so you don't break up the avocado.

5. Divide the avocado-tofu mixture among six bowls and pour the hot broth on top. Season with salt and pepper to taste and serve immediately.

# PUMPKIN SEED SOUP

**SERVES 8**

Pumpkin seeds are very popular in Mexican cooking, most often roasted and salted to make a crunchy and nutty snack. I like turning them into a soup. I start with the Mexican flavors of corn and jalapeño, then add some ginger for a different kind of heat and cardamom, nutmeg, and cinnamon to bring out the natural sweetness of the pumpkin seeds.

## FOR THE SOUP
**2 tablespoons olive oil**

**1¾ cups raw pumpkin seeds**

**1 red onion, thinly sliced**

**1 (3-inch) piece ginger, peeled and chopped**

**3 garlic cloves, finely chopped**

**1 jalapeño, seeded and minced**

**1 teaspoon paprika**

**4 cups water**

**1 cup dry white wine**

**2 cups heavy cream**

**1 teaspoon chopped fresh thyme**

**⅛ teaspoon ground cinnamon**

**⅛ teaspoon freshly grated nutmeg**

**⅛ teaspoon ground cardamom**

**Kosher salt and freshly ground black pepper**

**2 cups fresh corn kernels**

## FOR THE GARNISH
**¼ cup raw pumpkin seeds**

**¼ cup chopped peanuts**

**¼ teaspoon chile powder**

**¼ cup chopped garlic**

**2 teaspoons pumpkin seed oil**
**(see Note)**

*Note:* Pumpkin seed oil is strong, but delicious. You can find it in health food stores and online. You can substitute walnut or hazelnut oil.

## MAKE THE SOUP

1. Heat the oil in a large skillet over medium heat. When the oil shimmers, add the pumpkin seeds, onion, ginger, and garlic and cook, stirring, until the garlic is lightly browned, 2 to 3 minutes. Add the jalapeño, paprika, water, and wine. Bring to a simmer and cook gently for 25 minutes to develop the flavors. Working in batches, carefully puree the soup in a blender or food processor until smooth.

2. Return the puree to the skillet over medium heat. Add the cream, thyme, cinnamon, nutmeg, and cardamom. Season to taste with salt and pepper and simmer for 10 minutes. Press the soup (it will be thick) through a strainer and discard the solids.

3. Meanwhile, cook the corn kernels in boiling water for 2 minutes, drain, and set aside.

## MAKE THE GARNISH

4. Put the pumpkin seeds, peanuts, and chile powder into a skillet over low heat. Cook, stirring occasionally, for 7 minutes. Add the garlic and cook until the pumpkin seeds darken and start to pop, 10 to 12 minutes. Stir in the pumpkin seed oil.

5. Divide the corn among eight bowls and ladle 1 cup of soup into each bowl. Top each bowl with the garnish and serve.

# GREEN PEA SOUP
## WITH SEARED SCALLOPS

**SERVES 4**

There's a natural sweetness in peas, and I highlight that sweetness by pairing this very quick soup with seared scallops and mint. For balance, there's wine and buttermilk. It's a healthy and delicious weeknight supper. Fresh peas are always nice, but using frozen peas not only saves on prep time, it means you can make this soup year-round.

**2 tablespoons olive oil**

**1 medium red onion, thinly sliced**

**2 garlic cloves, chopped**

**1 cup dry white wine**

**2 cups water**

**2 cups green peas (fresh or frozen)**

**Juice of 1 lemon**

**1 cup buttermilk**

**4 dashes Tabasco sauce**

**1 teaspoon honey**

**1 teaspoon chopped fresh mint**

**1 teaspoon chopped fresh dill**

**Kosher salt**

**8 sea scallops**

1. Heat 1 tablespoon of the olive oil in a large saucepan over medium heat. Add the onion and garlic and cook until the onion starts to soften, about 2 minutes. Add the white wine and water and bring to a simmer. Reduce the heat and cook, covered, for 10 minutes. Add the fresh peas and cook until the peas are tender but remain bright green, 3 to 5 minutes. (If you're using frozen peas, just rinse them under hot water for 1 minute and add them; no further cooking needed.)

2. Transfer the peas and all the liquid to a blender, add the lemon juice, buttermilk, Tabasco, and honey, and puree until smooth.

3. Pour the soup back into the saucepan, add the mint and dill, and taste for salt. Keep it warm over medium-low heat.

4. Heat the remaining 1 tablespoon olive oil in a skillet over high heat. When the oil shimmers, add the scallops and sear them for 2 minutes on one side, then 1 minute on the other.

5. Place 2 scallops in each of four soup bowls. Ladle the soup on top of the scallops and serve.

# SALMON IN A SEA OF COCONUT

**SERVES 4**

Growing up on the west coast of Sweden, I was lucky enough to have access to some of the best salmon in the world, which I would catch with my father sometimes. But I think if I was told that I could eat the food of one region only for the rest of my life, it would be the cuisines of Southeast Asia. So this recipe highlights my salmon, but I also turn to coconut milk, fresh ginger, and white miso. Weirdly delicious water chestnuts add a hint of bitterness and crunch and the hearts of palm contribute a meaty chew.

3 tablespoons olive oil

3 ounces shiitake mushrooms, stemmed and sliced (about 1 cup)

2 shallots, sliced

1 teaspoon grated peeled ginger

2 cups fish stock

1 cup coconut milk

1 tablespoon dry white wine

1 tablespoon white miso

4 ounces Chinese egg noodles (fresh or dried)

Juice of 1 lime

4 scallions, sliced

½ cup canned drained water chestnuts, coarsely
    chopped (see Note)

2 canned hearts of palm, well rinsed and sliced
    (see Note)

½ ripe avocado, diced into small pieces

Kosher salt

1 pound skinless salmon fillet, cut into 4 pieces

½ tablespoon wasabi powder (see Note)

1 tablespoon sesame seeds

2 teaspoons chopped fresh mint

2 teaspoons chopped fresh dill

**Notes:** You can find canned water chestnuts and hearts of palm in most grocery stores.

Wasabi powder is in the Asian section of most grocery stores. Check the label to make sure it's wasabi—not horseradish and food coloring.

1. Heat 2 tablespoons of the olive oil in a large pot over medium heat. When the oil shimmers, add the mushrooms, shallots, and ginger and cook until the mushrooms are just tender and starting to brown, about 6 minutes. Add the fish stock, coconut milk, white wine, and miso and bring to a boil. Stir in the noodles, reduce the heat to low, and cook until just tender, 4 to 5 minutes.

2. Stir in the lime juice, scallions, water chestnuts, hearts of palm, and avocado. Season with salt (start with ½ teaspoon salt and add more carefully to keep from overpowering the delicate flavors). Turn off the heat, cover the pot, and keep warm.

3. Sprinkle the skinned side of the salmon with the wasabi and sesame seeds. Heat the remaining 1 tablespoon olive oil in a large skillet over medium-high heat and add the salmon fillets, skin side down. You'll see the salmon change color as it cooks from the bottom. When it is still rare, 3 to 4 minutes, flip the fillets so the heat can kiss the top of the fish. Turn off the heat.

4. Spoon the noodles and soup into four soup bowls, then top each serving with a piece of salmon and sprinkle with the chopped mint and dill.

# I LOVE CARROTS SOUP

**SERVES 4**

Carrots are one of my favorite vegetables. Here, I use the juice to make a hearty soup. This is not your average carrot soup: The kaffir lime leaves, lemongrass, coconut milk, and cardamom make it very aromatic, and the Israeli couscous, almost like tapioca pearls, adds texture. Your kitchen will smell great while you make this. Serve the soup on its own or as a starter to a seafood dinner.

½ cup Israeli couscous
2 tablespoons unsalted butter
3 cups water
1 cup coconut milk
1 teaspoon white miso
2 kaffir lime leaves (see Note)
1 (2-inch) piece ginger, peeled and grated
2 garlic cloves, peeled
1 stalk lemongrass, smashed (see "Prepping
    Lemongrass," page 45)
½ teaspoon ground cardamom
½ teaspoon ground ginger
2 cups carrot juice
½ cup fresh orange juice
Juice of 1 lime
Kosher salt
6 tablespoons diced soft tofu

Note: If you can't find kaffir lime leaves, you can substitute the grated zest of 1 lime and ½ teaspoon minced fresh mint.

1. Bring a pot of salted water to a boil. Add the couscous and cook until almost al dente, 2½ to 4 minutes. Drain, toss with the butter, and spread out in a bowl so it doesn't steam.
2. Combine the water, coconut milk, miso, lime leaves, fresh ginger, garlic, lemongrass, cardamom, and ground ginger in a saucepan over medium-high heat. Bring to a simmer, then reduce the heat to low and cook for 20 minutes. Remove and discard the lime leaves and lemongrass.
3. Place the soup base in a blender or food processor and add the carrot, orange, and lime juices and ½ teaspoon salt. Blend until smooth. Taste and adjust the salt as needed.
4. To serve, evenly divide the couscous and tofu among the bowls and pour the soup on top.

# CORN & CLAM CHOWDER

**SERVES 4**

There's no doubt about it: This soup is a classic that should be in every cook's repertoire. It's smoky (from the bacon), briny (from the clams), and rich (from the cream
and creamed corn). It's also the kind of soup you can make your own. Stir in a teaspoon or two of white miso to up the umami. Add a shot of hot sauce to give it some
heat. Or serve the soup with grilled lobster and make this a real celebration.

**3 slices bacon, chopped**
**1 cup chopped celery**
**1 cup chopped onions**
**2 garlic cloves, minced**
**2 dozen littleneck clams, scrubbed**
**1 cup dry white wine**
**1 cup heavy cream**
**1 cup clam juice**
**1 carrot, peeled and chopped**
**1 (15-ounce) can creamed corn**
**1 pound red-skinned potatoes, peeled and cut into**
 **½-inch dice**
**2 sprigs fresh thyme**
**1 large bay leaf**
**2 tablespoons chopped fresh chives**
**Juice of 2 limes**
**2 slices day-old whole wheat bread, toasted**

1. Put the bacon into a large, wide saucepan over medium-
high heat and sauté until the fat is rendered, 3 to 4 minutes.
Add the celery, onion, and garlic and continue sautéing
until the onion is starting to turn golden, 3 to 4 minutes
(be careful not to burn the bacon). Add the clams and white wine. Cover and cook, shaking the
pan occasionally, until the clams open, about 5 minutes. If they do not open, cook a little longer.
Discard any clams that refuse to open. Use tongs to transfer the clams to a bowl.
2. Add the cream, clam juice, carrot, corn, potatoes, thyme, and bay leaf to the pan. Bring to a

gentle boil over medium-high heat, then lower the heat and simmer for 15 minutes to marry the flavors.

3. Remove the clams from their shells and toss with the chives and lime juice in a small bowl. Pour any liquid in the clam bowl back into the chowder. Discard the thyme and bay leaf.

4. To serve, divide the clams among four bowls and ladle in the chowder. Rip the toasted bread into pieces and top the chowder.

# LITTLE SAIGON BEEF NOODLE SOUP

**SERVES 6 TO 8**

There's a great Vietnamese mall that pops up as you head out of Los Angeles on your way to San Diego—with stall after stall of food vendors. I always stop for a bowl of pho—that aromatic beef and noodle soup. Beef necks are perfect to use when you make the stock. They're meatier than oxtails, but they have lots of collagen so you'll get that great sticky mouthfeel. Simmering the neck bones and aromatics in chicken stock adds even more richness. Where I veer off from classic pho is by adding the crunch of snow peas and carrots to the traditional garnishes of cilantro, mint, and chiles.

If you've never experienced the amazing combination of fish and fragrant beef stock, try it here. Substitute cubed white fish (like halibut or cod) or sliced scallops for the London broil and ladle the steaming broth over the fish.

**3 quarts low-sodium chicken broth**

**1¼ pounds meaty beef neck bones or shank bones**

**8 scallions**

**3 star anise**

**1 (1-inch) piece ginger, peeled**

**Kosher salt and freshly ground black pepper**

**1 pound London broil**

**6 ounces dried rice noodles (see Note)**

**1 cup fresh cilantro leaves**

**1 cup fresh mint leaves**

**3 serrano chiles, sliced thin**

**2 limes, cut into wedges**

**1½ cups snow peas, ends trimmed**

**1 large carrot, peeled and coarsely grated**

**Sriracha or any other hot chile sauce**

Note: You'll find rice noodles in most large grocery stores or in Asian markets.

1. Combine the broth, beef bones, 3 of the scallions, the star anise, and ginger in a stockpot and bring to a boil. Reduce the heat, cover the pot, and simmer gently for 3 hours. Strain the broth, discarding the solids. Season the broth with salt and pepper. (You can make this days or weeks in advance. Use your freezer.)

2. Freeze the London broil for 15 to 20 minutes. Slice it across the grain as thin as possible.

3. Put the rice noodles in a large bowl, cover with hot water, and soak for 3 minutes. Drain, then use scissors to cut the noodles so that they are about 4 inches in length.

4. Slice the remaining 5 scallions and place them on a platter. Arrange the cilantro leaves, mint leaves, sliced chiles, and lime wedges on the platter. Put the condiment platter on the dinner table.

5. Bring the broth to a boil and add the noodles. Cook until they're just barely tender, about 2 minutes. Don't overcook or they will become mushy.

6. Divide the snow peas and grated carrot among soup bowls, then ladle the soup and noodles on top. Lay slices of the London broil on the top of the soup—the noodles will hold them up. Serve at once, letting diners dress their soup to individual taste with the condiments and Sriracha.

Temperature matters with pho. Make sure your broth is hot!

# CRUNCHY YARDBIRD SOUP

**SERVES 4**

My chicken soup has some Italian pasta and cheese, a good dose of Southern heat, and the tortillas and lime of Mexican chicken soup. It's nurturing and a feast of contrasting textures. My friends with young kids tell me that the crunchy tortilla chips make this dish a hit in their home, too.

**6 cups water**
**4 teaspoons Tabasco sauce**
**4 bone-in, skin-on chicken thighs**
**1 red onion, thinly sliced**
**2 garlic cloves, minced**
**1 fresh thyme sprig**
**1 teaspoon paprika**
**1 carrot, peeled and thinly sliced**
**½ cup orzo**
**1 tablespoon olive oil**
**1 tablespoon freshly grated Parmesan cheese**
**½ tablespoon chopped fresh chives**
**2 cups tortilla chips**
**1 lime, quartered**
**Fresh cilantro, for garnish**

*Poor Southerners often refer to chicken as a "yardbird," but it's also my tribute to Charlie Parker.*

1. Put the water, Tabasco, chicken, onion, garlic, thyme, and paprika into a large saucepan over high heat. Bring to a boil, reduce the heat, and simmer until the chicken is just cooked through, about 20 minutes. Remove the chicken and let it cool on a plate. Add the carrot to the pot and simmer gently for 10 minutes, until just tender. Pull the chicken meat from the bones, shred it, and return to the broth. Discard the skin and bones—or freeze them to use in another stock.

2. Cook the orzo in boiling salted water for 6 minutes. Drain and toss with the olive oil, Parmesan, and chives.

3. Crumble the tortilla chips with your hands and divide them evenly among the soup bowls. Divide the orzo among the bowls, then ladle the soup on top. Squeeze lime into each serving and garnish with cilantro.

For an extra step, cut corn tortillas into thin strips and fry them in about 1/2 inch of peanut oil until crisp. Drain on paper towels, toss with Berbere (page 297), and use to top the soup.

If you've got a carcass from a roast chicken in the freezer, get those bones in there. Remove them when you take out the thighs and skim the stock.

# SIDES & CONDIMENTS

I'M NOT SURE THAT "SIDES" IS THE RIGHT NAME OR THE right way to think about the dishes in this chapter. Just like leftovers, this is the good stuff. So maybe it would make more sense to think of them as the happy dishes. Or the seasonal dishes—because they do give us the chance to eat with the seasons. A chicken is going to taste like a chicken whether it's March or October. But think about the flavor of tomatoes and corn in the summer, of collards that have been touched by frost: There's no comparison between them and ordinary supermarket produce. When we eat seasonally, it's more than likely that we are eating of a place, buying from local farmers who have brought their produce to us—as they do at our new farmers' market in Harlem.

When I was growing up, potatoes were *the* side dish. Second to potatoes were the root vegetables—beets in particular; they

would keep for a long time in the cellar. But my mom and grand-mother had working gardens, and we ate from those gardens. My family's cooking traditions changed after my grandparents and father died, but pieces of it remain. My mother keeps gathering berries and foraging for wild mushrooms; my sister maintains the fruit trees; and I make pickles. I start with the 1-2-3 formula I learned from my grandmother Helga: one part vinegar, two parts sugar, and three parts water, with a bay leaf, peppercorns (black and white, for their different flavors), maybe a piece of horse-radish. I brought this formula with me to Aquavit, where I was chef, and used it for all kinds of vege-tables and herring—even plums. I hope you pick up on this tradition. You've got to have pickles.

# MUSIC TO COOK BY

Du ska va President ★ Imperiet

Unfinished Sympathy ★ Massive Attack

Karma Police ★ Radiohead

We Fight/We Love ★ Q-Tip featuring Raphael Saadiq

Pretty Wings ★ Maxwell

Cornbread, Fish & Collard Greens ★ Anthony Hamilton

Ring of Fire ★ Johnny Cash

Green Light ★ John Legend featuring Andre 3000

Music Sounds Better with You ★ Stardust

Soft and Wet ★ Prince

Lost Ones ★ Lauryn Hill

Devils Haircut ★ Beck

# LUXURY IN JANUARY

**MAKES ABOUT 8 CUPS**

Every summer, my grandmother and I would can and pickle fresh fruits and vege-tables. Then all winter long, she would turn to her pantry to supplement our hearty dishes with bright notes of flavor from the fresh produce we'd put away. These toma-toes are built on the same idea. There is nothing like summertime tomatoes, so I roast and freeze them at their peak. I call them Luxury in January because nothing makes me happier than going to my freezer and whipping out a container of juicy tomatoes to serve with pasta, roast chicken, or steak on a brisk, wintry day.

**8 large ripe tomatoes**
**Juice of 1 lemon**
**2 garlic cloves, sliced**
**Leaves from 2 sprigs fresh thyme**
**1 teaspoon Aleppo pepper (see Note) or hot red pepper flakes**
**1 teaspoon sugar**
**1 teaspoon kosher salt**

1. Preheat the oven to 250°F.
2. Cut the tomatoes into 6 wedges each. Toss them in a bowl with the remaining ingredients. Set the tomatoes on a rimmed baking sheet and slow-roast until fragrant and slightly collapsed—but still juicy—1½ to 2 hours. Turn the heat off and let the tomatoes sit in the oven for another 30 minutes.
3. Pack the tomatoes and all the juices in containers and freeze. Thaw when you're ready to use them.

> Note: Aleppo pepper is a distinctive chile from the Middle East, usually sold as crushed flakes or ground powder. It is milder and fruitier than hot red pepper flakes, which can be used as a substitute.

★ Rub wedges of tomato on crusty toast and top with burrata cheese or mozzarella.

★ Put a wedge or two on a piece of corn bread.

★ Use as a pasta sauce, blended or not.

★ Blend and use to build a Bloody Mary.

This salad can be a course on its own,
or serve it alongside fish or chicken.

# ORANGE-FENNEL SALAD

**SERVES 8**

My mother made a simple cousin of this salad: thinly sliced carrots dressed with orange juice. In Sicily, this classic salad would be a pure but simple combination of fennel, orange, and black olives. I omit the olives, and add pecans for a great crunch, and I season the dressing with paprika and fennel seed to heighten the flavor.

If they're in season, add some pomegranate seeds; their tart flavor complements the fennel perfectly and they're packed with healthy antioxidants. Look for different winter oranges, too. Cara Cara, maybe, or blood oranges—which are a very Sicilian ingredient—are beautiful in the salad.

**2 fennel bulbs, cored and thinly sliced**
**2 garlic cloves, thinly sliced**
**Segments and juice (see page 85) of 2 oranges**
**3 tablespoons olive oil**
**2 teaspoons balsamic vinegar**
**½ teaspoon garlic powder**
**½ teaspoon paprika**
**½ teaspoon ground fennel seed**
**½ cup chopped pecans**
**1 bunch frisée, chopped**

Put the fennel, garlic, orange segments and juice, olive oil, vinegar, garlic powder, paprika, fennel seed, and pecans in a salad bowl. Toss well. Add the frisée and toss again.

# GREEN BEAN– RADICCHIO SALAD

**SERVES 6**

I think about contrasts with salad. Fresh green beans are almost sweet, so I balance them with a hint of bitterness from radicchio leaves. The anise hint of tarragon provides a counterpoint to the slight tanginess of ricotta salata. Soft tofu offsets the crunch of the vegetables: Think of it as a soft poached egg on top of your salad.

## FOR THE DRESSING

**1 tablespoon minced shallot**
**1 garlic clove, minced**
**4½ teaspoons sherry vinegar**
**1 teaspoon Dijon mustard**
**1 teaspoon honey**
**Juice of ½ lime**
**¼ cup extra-virgin olive oil**
**1 tablespoon walnut oil (see Note)**
**Kosher salt and freshly ground black pepper**

## FOR THE SALAD

**½ pound green beans, trimmed**
**½ pound yellow wax beans, trimmed**
**4 cups packed torn radicchio leaves**
**4 ounces tofu, cubed**
**¼ cup almonds, toasted and chopped**
**2 teaspoons chopped fresh tarragon**
**2 ounces ricotta salata or other semi-firm white cheese**

The tofu can be soft or firm. Fry it, if you want. Be playful Buy some chicharrónes, crush them, and add for even more crunch.

### MAKE THE DRESSING

1. Whisk the shallot, garlic, vinegar, mustard, honey, and lime juice together in a small bowl. Gradually whisk in the olive oil, then the walnut oil. Season the dressing with salt and pepper. You can make this well in advance. Keep it covered in the refrigerator, but bring it back to room temperature and whisk again before dressing the salad.

### MAKE THE SALAD

2. Cook the green beans in a large pot of boiling salted water until they are just tender, 2 to 3 minutes. Use a slotted spoon or a skimmer to transfer the beans to a colander and immediately rinse with cold water. Cook the wax beans in the same pot of boiling salted water until just tender, 3 to 4 minutes. Transfer them to the colander and immediately rinse with cold water. Drain well.

3. Put the beans and radicchio in a large bowl and toss with the dressing. Transfer the salad to a serving platter. Scatter the tofu, almonds, and tarragon over the salad and use a vegetable peeler to make shavings of the cheese over all.

# RAW KALE SALAD
## WITH ROOT VEGETABLES

**SERVES 4 TO 6**

Meaty kale is much more robust than spinach, so a kale salad is very satisfying without being heavy. Massaging the kale helps it to break down a little: Your hands really are your most important tool here.

I can make a meal of this salad by itself, but it's incredible with the Dill-Spiced Salmon on page 30. Or pair it with lamb chops or fried chicken. And unlike spinach—which wilts away—this salad's still exciting and fulfilling the next day.

### FOR THE DRESSING

**1 tablespoon grated lemon zest**

**2 tablespoons fresh lemon juice**

**1 tablespoon olive oil**

**1 tablespoon soy sauce**

**2 teaspoons agave nectar**

**Kosher salt and freshly ground black pepper (optional)**

### FOR THE SALAD

**2 (12-ounce) bunches kale, stems removed and leaves cut into thin strips**

**2 tablespoons olive oil**

**1 tablespoon apple cider vinegar**

**1½ teaspoons salt**

**1 cup pecan halves**

**1 Granny Smith apple, cored and very thinly sliced**

**¼ cup pure maple syrup**

**2 tablespoons canola oil**

**¼ teaspoon cayenne**

1 medium turnip, peeled and grated (1 cup)
½ medium rutabaga, peeled and grated (1 cup)
1 medium carrot, peeled and grated (½ cup)
2 scallions, thinly sliced on the diagonal

### MAKE THE DRESSING

1. Whisk the lemon zest and juice, olive oil, soy sauce, and agave nectar together in a bowl. Give it a taste and season with salt and pepper, if desired.

### MAKE THE SALAD

2. Place the kale in a large bowl and add the olive oil, vinegar, and 1 teaspoon of the salt. Gently massage the oil and vinegar into the kale with your hands until the kale starts to wilt, 2 to 3 minutes. Let it rest for 30 minutes at room temperature.

3. Preheat the oven to 375°F. Line a baking sheet with parchment paper.

4. Toss the pecans, apple, maple syrup, canola oil, remaining ½ teaspoon salt, and the cayenne in a medium bowl. Spread out in a single layer on the baking sheet. Bake until the pecans are brown and fragrant, 8 to 10 minutes, stirring frequently. Cool in the pan.

5. Add the turnip, rutabaga, carrot, and scallions to the kale. Toss with the dressing, garnish with the pecans and apple, and serve.

# END-OF-SUMMER SUCCOTASH

**SERVES 6 TO 8**

My summertime succotash is a little twist on tradition. I've kept the corn and lima beans, while adding peanuts for crunch (peanuts speak of the South to me). Cilantro, basil, and parsley add fresh, light flavors. The garlic and poblano chile give a little kick. I love to serve this with fish or pulled pork, and since there are usually leftovers, I'll warm up a little bowl for a great late-afternoon snack.

**2 tablespoons olive oil**
**2 tablespoons roasted salted peanuts**
**2 medium red onions, chopped**
**1 large garlic clove, minced**
**2½ cups fresh corn kernels**
**2½ cups fresh lima beans**
**2 medium tomatoes, chopped**
**1 poblano chile, seeded and chopped**
**2 tablespoons unsalted butter**
**Juice of 1 lime**
**3 tablespoons thinly sliced fresh basil**
**2 tablespoons chopped fresh parsley**
**2 tablespoons chopped fresh cilantro**
**Kosher salt and freshly ground black pepper**

1. Heat the olive oil in a large skillet over medium heat. Add the peanuts, onions, and garlic and cook until the onions are translucent, about 5 minutes.
2. Add the corn, lima beans, tomatoes, poblano, and butter to the skillet and simmer until the corn and lima beans are tender, about 15 minutes.
3. Add the lime juice and herbs and season to taste with salt and pepper. Serve warm or at room temperature.

Alluette Jones-Smalls owns Alluette's Café, a vegetarian restaurant in Charleston, South Carolina, which serves truly amazing Southern food. She calls it holistic soul food—I just call it delicious.

# HOT BRUSSELS SPROUTS SLAW

**SERVES 4 TO 6**

I didn't know about slaw until I moved to the U.S.—I hadn't even heard the word. But I soon found out about the crunch it adds to a plate and the tang that reminds me of the pickles that I've loved since I was a boy. So I've started to play with slaw. Here I shred Brussels sprouts—they're little cabbages, aren't they?—cook them in bacon fat and butter to give them layers of flavor, sweeten them up with apples, and add zing with vinegar and ginger.

It's a gateway dish. Serve this to people who say they don't like Brussels sprouts and you'll find them wanting more and more and more.

**¾ pound thick-cut bacon, cut into ½-inch pieces**
**4 tablespoons (½ stick) unsalted butter**
**2 pounds Brussels sprouts, thinly sliced in a food processor**
**Kosher salt and freshly ground black pepper**
**2 Granny Smith apples, peeled, cored, coarsely grated, and squeezed dry**
**1 tablespoon apple cider vinegar**
**1 teaspoon minced peeled fresh ginger**
**1 teaspoon fresh thyme leaves**

1. Cook the bacon in a large skillet over medium-high heat, stirring occasionally, until crisp, about 6 minutes. Drain on paper towels. Pour the bacon fat into a bowl.
2. Turn the heat under the skillet up to high and add 2 tablespoons of the butter and 2 tablespoons of the bacon fat. When the butter stops sizzling, add half the Brussels sprouts. Cook, stirring often, until softened—with some of the sprouts browned and others still bright green—about 8 minutes. Season with salt and pepper and scrape out into a bowl. Cook the rest of the Brussels sprouts in the remaining 2 tablespoons butter and 2 tablespoons bacon fat. Return the first batch of sprouts to the skillet, add the apples, vinegar, ginger, and thyme, and cook, stirring, until the apples are heated through, 1 to 2 minutes.
3. Pile the slaw onto a platter, scatter the bacon on top, and serve.

# SMOKY COLLARDS & KALE, FOR EDITH & FANNY

**SERVES 6 TO 8**

Old-time Southern collards are cooked for a real long time with a ham hock or two and a lot of water so you'll have plenty of "pot likker." I'm not an old-time Southern chef. But I do like smoky flavor, so I start my greens with smoked bacon and add a little bit of liquid smoke at the end. Combining collards and kale gives the dish more complexity than you'd get from just one green. I can't resist adding a twist. Here, it's a little bite from fresh ginger.

Look for kale with small leaves. If you can find Red Russian kale, use it; the color bleeds, so the juices will have a beautiful jewel tone.

6 slices thick-cut bacon

2 garlic cloves, halved

2 shallots, thinly sliced

1 (1-inch) piece ginger, peeled and chopped

2 tablespoons dry white wine

¾ cup vegetable stock

4 cups very thinly sliced stemmed collard greens

Kosher salt

4 cups very thinly sliced stemmed kale

½ tablespoon liquid smoke

Freshly ground black pepper

Edith Fossett and Fanny Hern were slaves in Thomas Jefferson's household, and at the ages of fifteen and eighteen, respectively, they were brought into the White House kitchen to prepare French food under the guidance of Jefferson's chef. They remained working as Jefferson's cooks until his death in 1826. Little is known about these two women, but they must have been incredibly skilled and experienced. Historian Leni Sorensen says, "They were at the absolute top of the chef's game." But there's no doubt that they would have grown up eating what the other slaves ate—corn, field peas, collards. I dedicate this recipe to their memory.

1. Cook the bacon in a large skillet until crisp. Drain on paper towels and crumble into small pieces.

2. Pour out all but 3 tablespoons of the bacon fat. Set the skillet over medium-high heat and add the garlic, shallots, and ginger. Sauté until the garlic is lightly browned, 1 to 2 minutes. Add the wine and stock and bring to a boil, scraping the bottom of the skillet to dissolve any browned bits.

3. Stir in the collards and season with salt. Cover, reduce the heat to medium-low, and cook for 15 minutes. Add the kale, cover, and cook until the greens are tender and the liquid is almost gone, about 20 minutes. If the liquid is cooking away too quickly, turn down the heat. Stir in the liquid smoke and bacon and season with salt and pepper.

Add some chopped apples and a simple vinaigrette to any leftovers and you've got a great salad.

You could also use these greens to fill Swedish Potato Dumplings (page 292).

Deep in the South Side of Chicago, the Original Soul Vegetarian has been serving what they call food as medicine for over thirty years. They're proving that even the hood needs good!

# SHIRO (ETHIOPIAN CHICKPEA SPREAD)

**MAKES ABOUT 3 CUPS**

I seek out vegetarian dishes and this is one I love. You could consider *shiro* the mashed potatoes of Ethiopia; chickpea flour is something everyone can afford and it's nourishing. But nourishing doesn't come close to describing the flavors you get from the caramelized onion puree, the tomatoes, the berbere. It's rich and earthy and satisfying. Serve it as a side dish or add some *shiro* to Berbere Roasted Carrots & Fennel with Oranges (page 296) or just to some cooked broccoli and you have a perfect light and healthy lunch.

**2 medium onions, chopped**
**2 garlic cloves, chopped**
**4 tablespoons olive oil**
**1 teaspoon tomato paste**
**1 tablespoon Berbere (page 297)**
**1 cup canned crushed tomatoes**
**½ cup chickpea flour (see Note)**
**1 cup tomato juice**
**1½ cups water**
**2 teaspoons Spiced Butter (page 160)**
**Kosher salt and freshly ground black pepper**

Flour your hands and roll cold shiro into balls. Deep-fry them and drain on paper towels. Then sprinkle them with salt and berbere and serve with a yogurt dip.

Note: Chickpea flour is also called garbanzo bean flour or gram flour. You'll find it in large grocery stores, health food stores, and online.

1. Put the onions and garlic into a blender or food processor and puree.

2. Heat 1 tablespoon of the olive oil in a skillet over medium-high heat. Add the onion puree and cook, stirring frequently, until the liquid evaporates and the onions start to turn a light brown, about 10 minutes. Stir in the tomato paste and cook, stirring, until the paste turns brick red, about 1 minute. Add the remaining 3 tablespoons oil and berbere and cook, stirring, for 1 to 2 minutes, so the flavors meld. Stir in the crushed tomatoes.

3. Sprinkle in the chickpea flour, stirring briskly to avoid lumps; this will thicken quickly. Whisk in the tomato juice and 1 cup of the water. Reduce the heat to low and simmer for 30 minutes, stirring occasionally. Whisk in the remaining ½ cup water and simmer for 15 minutes. The *shiro* should have the consistency of thick buttermilk; it will thicken as it stands and cools. Stir in the spiced butter, taste, season with salt and pepper, and serve.

# MARKET-FRESH CORN BREAD

**MAKES 1 LOAF**

I make my corn bread in a loaf pan so I can have slices, not wedges. They're much easier to toast that way. The bread is packed with cheese and corn kernels and scallions; it's moist and tangy—there's buttermilk in it. And since I grew up in Sweden, where breads often have spices in them, I perfume my corn bread with cardamom and ginger. It's great with honey butter.

8 tablespoons (1 stick) unsalted butter

⅛ teaspoon ground ginger

⅛ teaspoon ground cardamom

⅛ teaspoon chile powder

⅛ teaspoon paprika

1 tablespoon sugar

1½ cups yellow cornmeal

½ cup all-purpose flour

2 teaspoons baking powder

1 teaspoon baking soda

1 teaspoon kosher salt

2 large eggs

1½ cups buttermilk

1 cup grated sharp cheddar cheese

1 cup fresh corn kernels, including the pulp scraped from the cobs (cut from about 1 large or 2 small ears of corn)

3 scallions, thinly sliced (optional)

> You can't really put a slice of this bread into a toaster, but you can butter it lightly and toast it on a griddle or in a cast iron pan, coaxing out more flavors and getting the edges nice and crisp.

1. Preheat the oven to 425°F and generously butter a 9-x-5-inch loaf pan.

2. Put the butter, ginger, cardamom, chile powder, paprika, and sugar into a small pot over medium heat and cook until the butter is melted and the spices are fragrant, 3 to 4 minutes.

3. Whisk the cornmeal, flour, baking powder, baking soda, and salt together in a large bowl. In a separate bowl, whisk the eggs, buttermilk, and spicy butter together. Pour the wet ingredients into the dry and stir until all the dry ingredients are moistened. Stir in the cheddar and corn, then fold in the scallions, if using.

4. Scrape the batter into the loaf pan. Set the pan on a baking sheet, slide it into the oven, and bake until a skewer stuck in the center comes out clean, 50 to 60 minutes. Turn the loaf upside down onto a rack and let cool for 20 minutes. Then lift off the pan. This bread is best served warm or toasted.

# HONEY BUTTER

This is the perfect accompaniment to Market-Fresh Corn Bread, but it's great spread on a piece of whole wheat toast, too. Make this in advance, so the sage will have time to work its magic.

Beat 2 tablespoons honey, 12 sage leaves (rip them up), and ½ teaspoon kosher salt into 1 stick of softened unsalted butter. Cover and chill for at least 1 hour, and take it out of the refrigerator 15 minutes before serving. This makes about ½ cup.

# PLÁTANOS MASH

**SERVES 6**

The Dominican community up in Manhattan's Washington Heights calls this dish *mofongo*. Latin cuisine never ceases to inspire me, and one of my favorite ingredients to cook with is the plantain—the starchy member of the banana family that's served as a vegetable. Unripe *plátanos* taste like a cross between a potato and a parsnip, but ripe ones have a hint of sweetness, almost like a sweet potato. In fact, here I pair them with sweet potatoes to make a fragrant, creamy mash that's golden with turmeric. They're a little healthier than Mom's mashed potatoes, too, since coconut milk takes the place of lots of butter.

**6 ripe plantains, peeled and cut into chunks (see Note)**
**1 pound sweet potatoes, peeled and cut into chunks**
**4 garlic cloves, peeled**
**1 cup coconut milk**
**1 cup whole milk**
**1 teaspoon ground turmeric**
**Kosher salt and freshly ground black pepper**
**Freshly grated nutmeg**

1. Combine the plantains, sweet potatoes, garlic, coconut milk, milk, and turmeric in a saucepan. Add enough water to barely cover and season with salt and pepper. Bring to a boil over high heat, then cover, reduce the heat, and simmer until the plantains and potatoes are tender, about 40 minutes. Set a colander over a bowl and drain the plantains and sweet potatoes. You want to keep the cooking liquid.

2. Return the plantains and sweet potatoes to the pot and mash them with a fork, potato masher, or heavy whisk. Beat in as much of the cooking liquid as you need to make the mash creamy. Add the nutmeg, taste, and adjust the seasoning. Serve hot.

Note: Ripe plantains may be yellowish brown or almost black, but they'll have some give when you squeeze them. And that's what you want for this dish. The skin is thicker and tougher than a banana's, so you have to slit it with a paring knife to peel it.

# DRIZZLED PLANTAINS
## WITH AVOCADO DIP

**SERVES 4**

Green plantains make very tasty "fries." They're meatier than potatoes and have a more complex flavor. These are really good with chicken nuggets (see page 236) or roast chicken, served with an avocado-peanut dip as a creamy alternative to ketchup. They're a great hors d'oeuvre, too. Top them with some Serrano ham and manchego cheese, if you want to go Spanish, or with some stewed pork.

### FOR THE AVOCADO DIP
**2 tablespoons olive oil**
**2 garlic cloves, chopped**
**1 tablespoon roasted peanuts**
**1 avocado, diced**
**¼ cup plain yogurt**
**2 tablespoons fresh lime juice**
**Kosher salt**

### FOR THE PLANTAINS
**2 cups water**
**3 garlic cloves, smashed**
**Kosher salt**
**1 teaspoon chile powder**
**1 tablespoon pure maple syrup**
**Peanut oil, for frying**
**2 green plantains**

When people think of Napa, they usually think of high-end wine production and gorgeous scenery. The people who work on the vineyards deserve as much attention. They bring their own food and take time to catch up and play cards together.

## MAKE THE AVOCADO DIP

1. Heat the oil in a small skillet over medium-high heat. When it shimmers, add the garlic and peanuts and sauté until the garlic is golden, 1 to 2 minutes. Scrape into a blender. Add the avocado, yogurt, and lime juice and blend until smooth. Scrape into a bowl, season with salt, and cover with plastic.

## MAKE THE PLANTAINS

2. Combine the water, garlic, and 2 teaspoons salt in a medium bowl and set aside. Mix the chile powder and maple syrup in a small bowl and set aside. Line a baking sheet with parchment.
3. Heat about 1 inch of peanut oil in a large skillet to 325°F.
4. Peel the plantains and slice into ½-inch-thick rounds. Fry the plantains in batches until golden yellow, 1 to 1½ minutes per side. As the plantains finish cooking, transfer them with tongs to the baking sheet. Stand the plantains on edge and give them a nice, solid push with the back of a wooden spoon to crush them to half their diameter. Place the plantains in the salted garlic water and let them soak for 1 minute. Remove and pat very dry with a kitchen towel.
5. Bring the oil back up to 325°F. Fry the plantains until golden brown, 2 to 4 minutes per side. Remove with a slotted spoon or spider and drain on paper towels. Arrange on a platter, sprinkle with salt, and drizzle with the chile syrup. Serve hot, with the avocado dip.

# SWEDISH POTATO DUMPLINGS (KROPPKAKOR)

**SERVES 4**

My grandmother Helga would make her potato dumplings at least once a month, and she'd usually use the good stuff—a little bit of stew from the night before, the few slices of roast pork that were left—to fill them. Sometimes, though, she would stuff them with wild mushrooms that my father had foraged. I fill mine with chicken and bacon, parsley, thyme, and a hint of ginger.

Served with lobster, these dumplings seem luxurious; served with a roast chicken, they're a rustic side. And they're always delicious.

**5 (8-ounce) russet potatoes, scrubbed**

**FOR THE STUFFING**

**1 tablespoon canola oil**

**1 red onion, chopped**

**2 garlic cloves, chopped**

**½ pound (unsmoked) bacon, chopped**

**1 boneless, skinless chicken thighs, ground in a
   food processor**

**1 (½-inch) piece ginger, peeled and chopped**

**1 teaspoon soy sauce**

**Leaves from 1 sprig fresh thyme**

**2 teaspoons chopped fresh parsley**

**Kosher salt and freshly ground black pepper**

**FOR THE DUMPLINGS**

**¾ cup all-purpose flour, plus more for dusting**

**1 large egg**

**1 large egg yolk**

**1 teaspoon kosher salt**

**½ teaspoon freshly ground black pepper**

**Olive oil, for sautéing**

*Helga would brown her kroppkakor in the grease she always had on hand. If you're making these to serve with roast chicken, brown them in the chicken fat from the roasting pan.*

*You can also serve these with just some melted Spiced Butter (page 160).*

1. Preheat the oven to 375°F.

2. Prick the potatoes all over with a fork and bake them directly on an oven rack until tender, about 1 hour. Remove the potatoes from the oven and let rest for 5 minutes.

### MAKE THE STUFFING

3. While the potatoes bake, heat the oil in a large skillet over medium heat. Add the onion, garlic, and bacon and cook until the onion is soft and the bacon is crisp, about 7 minutes. Add the ground chicken, ginger, and soy sauce and cook, stirring often to break up the chicken into small bits, until the chicken is cooked, 4 to 6 minutes. Stir in the thyme and parsley, season with salt and pepper, and cool.

### MAKE THE DUMPLINGS

4. Cut the potatoes in half and scoop the flesh out into bowl. Mash with a fork or potato masher or put through a ricer. Add the flour, egg, egg yolk, salt, and pepper. Knead lightly until you have a smooth, soft dough. Be gentle; you don't want to activate the gluten in the flour, which would make the dumplings tough and heavy.

5. Flour your hands and pick up a piece of dough. Roll it into a round the size of a golf ball. Flatten it into one palm, add a bit of the stuffing, pinch the dough over the stuffing, and roll the ball round again, making sure no stuffing escapes. (You may need to patch the ball with a little more dough.) Repeat until either the dough or stuffing runs out. As you finish them, put the dumplings on a

baking sheet lined with lightly floured parchment and cover with a damp towel.

6. Bring a large pot of salted water to a boil. Add the dumplings, but don't overcrowd them. When they rise to the top, simmer for 4 minutes—keep an eye on the heat; you want the dumplings to *simmer*, not boil. Use a slotted spoon or skimmer to transfer them to a towel-lined plate and pat dry. Repeat with any remaining dumplings.

7. Heat a skillet over medium-high heat. Add a slick of olive oil and sauté the dumplings until golden brown, about 4 minutes. Serve hot.

# PICKLED CABBAGE

**MAKES ABOUT 10 CUPS**

You can whip this pickle up in a matter of minutes on a Sunday afternoon and reap great rewards. It keeps for weeks in the fridge, and you can serve it with almost any casual dish—hot dogs and burgers, rotisserie chicken, a fried fish—any time you want vibrant red cabbage pickled with not just vinegar but lime juice, too, for layers of flavor. And then there's the little bit of heat that sneaks in from the Scotch bonnet pepper. The more I talk about it, the more my mouth waters! I always have jars of this stuff in my fridge—small jars; they keep better that way.

**2 cups apple cider vinegar**
**⅔ cup fresh lime juice**
**¾ cup water**
**¾ cup sugar**
**1 bay leaf**
**1 garlic clove, peeled**
**1 Scotch bonnet or habanero pepper, one side slit open with the tip of a knife**
**6 sprigs fresh thyme**
**1 head red cabbage, cored and thinly sliced**

1. Bring the vinegar, lime juice, water, sugar, bay leaf, garlic, pepper, and thyme to a boil in a medium saucepan.
2. Put the cabbage in a large, heatproof bowl and pour the boiling pickling solution over it. Cover with plastic and set a plate on top to keep the cabbage submerged. Let sit for 2 hours. Pack into 1-pint jars and refrigerate for at least 3 hours before serving. The cabbage will keep for up to 1 month.

Do you pack the hot pepper in one of the jars or not? I do. There's always someone who will say, "Hey, that's for me!"

# BERBERE ROASTED CARROTS & FENNEL WITH ORANGES

**SERVES 4**

This side starts as something very familiar—roasted vegetables. But the berbere makes the sweet carrots and fennel taste earthier and the orange gives the dish a sprightly edge. Two little changes, but so much complexity.

**1 pound carrots, peeled and cut into 1-inch chunks**
**4 fennel bulbs, cored and cut horizontally into ⅓-inch slices, fronds reserved**
**2 tablespoons olive oil**
**1 teaspoon Berbere (opposite)**
**½ teaspoon kosher salt**
**¼ teaspoon freshly ground black pepper**
**Segments and juice (see page 85) of 2 oranges**
**¼ cup chopped fresh mint**

1. Preheat the oven to 400°F. Line a rimmed baking sheet with aluminum foil or parchment.
2. Toss the carrots and fennel with the olive oil, berbere, salt, and pepper; make sure the vegetables are well coated. Spread them out on the baking sheet and roast for 20 minutes. Turn the vegetables and roast until you can pierce them easily with a knife, 5 to 10 minutes more.

3. Transfer the vegetables to a serving bowl and let cool to room temperature. Right before serving, toss in the orange segments, juice, and chopped mint. Garnish with the fennel fronds.

# BERBERE

When you drive through Ethiopia, you will see women on the roadsides selling chiles, ginger, and garlic. Others sell spices—coriander, fenugreek, allspice, cardamom. These are some of the ingredients you need to make berbere, the spice mix that permeates every aspect of Ethiopian food. It is a deep red, the color of red clay. It's not a fiery mix. Cooked long and slow, berbere is earthy; added later, it can be lively and bright. When I discovered it, I couldn't wait to begin playing with it. I hope you will, too.

Put 2 teaspoons coriander seeds, 1 teaspoon fenugreek seeds, ½ teaspoon black peppercorns, 3 or 4 allspice berries, 6 cardamom pods, and 4 cloves into a small skillet over medium heat. Toast, swirling the skillet, until fragrant, about 4 minutes. Pour the seeds into a spice grinder and cool. Add ½ cup dried onion flakes and 5 stemmed and seeded chiles de árbol. Grind to a fine powder.

Transfer the spice powder to a bowl and whisk in 3 tablespoons smoked paprika, 2 teaspoons kosher salt, ½ teaspoon freshly grated nutmeg, ½ teaspoon ground ginger, and ½ teaspoon ground cinnamon. This makes about ¾ cup. Store in a sealed jar, out of the light, for up to 6 months.

# THE PICKLED CUCUMBERS I BRING EVERYWHERE

**MAKES ABOUT 1½ CUPS**

No matter what we were eating in Göteborg, there were jars of pickles on the table. If Mom had made spaghetti for dinner, we might not eat them but they'd still be there. Every cook in Sweden will tell you that their pickle is the best, but this one really is. It's a great pickle that will be ready to eat in just 3 hours. And this recipe gives you a perfect starting point for improvisation. Try using this pickling solution with thinly sliced carrots or Japanese turnips or cauliflower cut into tiny florets. Make it yours.

**1 English cucumber (see Note)**
**1 tablespoon kosher salt**
**1½ cups water**
**½ cup white wine vinegar**
**1 cup sugar**
**1 bay leaf**
**2 allspice berries**

Note: **English cucumbers are the very long ones. They don't have a lot of seeds and in supermarkets they usually come sealed in plastic.**

1. Slice the cucumber as thinly as possible—ideally using a mandoline or Japanese V-slicer. Put the cucumber in a colander set over a plate or in the sink, toss with the salt, and let stand for about 30 minutes.
2. Meanwhile, combine the water, vinegar, sugar, bay leaf, and allspice in a medium saucepan and bring to a boil. Remove from the heat and let cool.
3. Rinse the salt off the cucumber, turn it out onto a kitchen towel, and squeeze out as much liquid as possible. Put the cucumber in a 1-quart Mason jar and pour in the pickling solution. Push the cucumber down to make sure it's completely covered, then put the lid on the jar. Refrigerate for at least 3 hours before serving. The pickled cucumber will keep in the refrigerator for at least 2 weeks.

# PICKLED BEETS

You've got to have pickled beets in your repertory.

Put 4 scrubbed beets in a saucepan, cover them with water by at least an inch, and add some salt and 1 tablespoon red wine vinegar. Bring to a boil, then reduce the heat and simmer until you can pierce the beets easily with a skewer or knife, 45 minutes to 1 hour. Drain.

When the beets are cool enough to handle, peel and slice them and put in a Mason jar. Make the pickling solution from the pickled cucumbers and pour the boiling solution over the beets. Push down to make sure the beets are covered. Let cool to room temperature, cover the jar, and refrigerate for at least 3 hours before serving. They'll keep in the fridge for at least 2 weeks.

If you've got them, substitute curry leaves and kaffir lime leaves for the bay and allspice to take the cucumbers on a trip to Southeast Asia.

# APPLE-SAFFRON JAM

**MAKES ABOUT 3 CUPS**

I grew up making this classic Swedish jam with my grandmother Helga. It's fragrant with the spices that Sweden has known since the days of the Spice Route. My grandmother didn't have garam masala, but all the spices that would go into it were in her cupboard. I caramelize the apples on top of the stove, then stew them, which gives the jam a deep, complex flavor. It's one of the easiest jams I can think of, and it's great on sandwiches, on duck and turkey and venison, and yes, even on toast.

**1 teaspoon garam masala**

**2 star anise**

**2 (2-inch) cinnamon sticks, broken into pieces**

**2 cloves**

**6 Granny Smith apples, peeled, cored, and cut into large chunks**

**½ cup sugar**

**1 cup water**

**Grated zest of 1 lime**

**6 tablespoons fresh lime juice**

**4 fresh mint leaves**

**Big pinch of saffron threads**

1. Toast the garam masala, star anise, cinnamon, and cloves in a small, dry skillet over medium heat, stirring, until fragrant, 30 seconds to 1 minute. Transfer the spices to a spice grinder, let them cool slightly, then grind to a powder.

2. Put the apples into a large bowl, add the sugar and spices, and toss. Make sure all the apples are coated.

3. Transfer the apples to a wide, deep pot over medium-high heat and cook, stirring often, until the apples caramelize, about 10 minutes. Add the water, lime zest and juice, mint, and saffron and bring to a simmer. Reduce the heat, cover with a round of parchment, and simmer until the apples are very tender and most of the liquid is gone, about 35 minutes.

4. Scrape the jam into a food processor and pulse until it's chunky and jam-like. Pack into jars, cool to room temperature, then screw on the lids and refrigerate. The jam keeps for 3 weeks.

The Reading Terminal Market in Philadelphia captures a snapshot of how a city likes to eat. Whenever I'm there, I stroll through it, taking in all the sights, from the Italian salumerias to the cheesemongers and vendors celebrating their Pennsylvania Dutch roots, like this girl we met at one of the stands.

# PURPLE MUSTARD

**MAKES ABOUT 2 CUPS**

Most people think mustard is one of those condiments that you only buy, but mustard is surprisingly easy to make at home, and you can vary the flavors and potency to suit yourself. I start this recipe by reducing red wine and Madeira, which adds an elusive sweetness as well as a lush purple color to the mustard. It's beautiful—to the eye and to the tongue—with a plate of roasted vegetables or chicken. And with gravlax.

**2 cups dry red wine**
**1 cup Madeira or port**
**2 shallots, finely chopped**
**2 tablespoons black mustard seeds (see Note)**
**4 white peppercorns**
**Leaves from 2 sprigs fresh tarragon**
**1 cup Dijon mustard**
**1 teaspoon Colman's dry mustard**
**¼ teaspoon wasabi paste**

1. Combine the red wine, Madeira, shallots, mustard seeds, peppercorns, and half of the tarragon in a medium saucepan. Bring to a boil over medium-high heat and boil until the liquids are reduced to ½ cup, about 10 minutes.

2. Transfer the reduction to a blender. Add the Dijon mustard, mustard powder, and wasabi paste and blend until smooth. Chop the remaining tarragon and fold into the mustard. Store in a tightly sealed jar in the refrigerator for up to 2 months.

Note: Check spice shops, health food stores, and Indian markets for black mustard seeds. If you can't find them, you can substitute yellow mustard seeds, which will give you a slightly sharper mustard.

# ADDIS DIP (AWAZE)

**MAKES 1 CUP**

In Ethiopia, we serve *awaze*, which is really just a berbere dip, with meats and bread. Traditionally it's made with the honey wine called *tej,* but I think whiskey gives it greater depth of flavor, so I use Jack Daniel's. This is so good with everything, from a spread on toasted bread to a drop in a soup. Or rub it on a chicken and sear. You'll be surprised at how many times you use it.

It makes a great marinade, too.

**6 tablespoons Berbere (page 297)**
**½ cup olive oil**
**3 tablespoons Jack Daniel's Black**
**Label (or a good bourbon)**
**Juice of 3 lemons**

Whisk all the ingredients together in a small bowl.

*Because of the alcohol and spices in this dip, it will keep for up to 2 months in the refrigerator.*

# SOMETHING SWEET

OKAY, HERE'S MY BIG SECRET. I SOMETIMES EAT DESSERT BEFORE DINNER—especially when I'm traveling. When I'm out on the road, it's not unusual for me to find an amazing gelato place and have some pear sorbet with chile flakes; *then* I'll go looking for that bowl of noodles or a great burger. But most of the time I think that meals should end with something sweet. It tells your tongue that the meal's over.

I like desserts with a sense of humor, desserts that are fun. Like a yogurt pop made in a mini paper cup. And I think a dessert should look the way it's described—so you can see that my Sweet & Salty Mud Pie is as dark as the mud of the Mississippi Delta and topped with salty potato chip crumbles.

Desserts can take you back to your child-hood, too. When I made the peanut topping for my black-bottom pie, I was thinking of the Snickers bars that I ate all the time because I was certain they gave me the energy I needed to play soccer. Cakes are a big deal in Sweden, something only for a big celebration, but cookies were for every day and I ate a lot of them. I still do.

*Picking blueberries as a child taught me about seasonality and taste. If you picked them too early, they were tart. Picked at their prime, the berries were super-sweet and would turn my fingers and lips blue.*

When I make a big batch of cookies, I make sure I've got a supply of Chinese takeout boxes from a party store. That way people can help themselves to a stash. I love the idea of my guests taking boxes of sweet flavors, and I hope sweet memories, back home.

# MUSIC TO COOK BY

Breakfast Can Wait ★ Prince

I Wish I Knew How It Would Feel to Be Free
★ Nina Simone

Candy ★ Cameo

Tea for Two ★ Sarah Vaughan

Sweet Dreams (Are Made of This) ★ Eurythmics

Brown Sugar ★ D'Angelo

Outstanding ★ The Gap Band

The Sweetest Thing ★ U2

Wonderwall ★ Ryan Adams

As We Enter ★ Nas and Damian "Jr. Gong" Marley

Send It On ★ D'Angelo

Mighty Healthy ★ Ghostface Killah

Summertime / Sometimes I Feel Like a Motherless Child
★ Mahalia Jackson

# HOT WAFFLES WITH BLUEBERRY WHIPPED CREAM

**SERVES 8 TO 10**

When I was a kid, waffles were an obsession. I used to sit on a stool in the kitchen—wearing my batter-streaked, blue plastic apron—while I waited impatiently for them to cook. This was before the days of Teflon waffle makers, so if the iron wasn't hot enough, the batter stuck. When I looked like I was about to peek, my mom would yell, "Marcus, stay away from the waffle iron!" She needn't have worried; I was actually afraid of it.

I learned a lot about cooking during those years and I also learned about how things grow. My sister and I would go out with our grand-mother or our parents to pick blueberries and other fruit. I still eat the waffles with berries, but I now make delicious blueberry whipped cream to be served on top of, or next to, the waffles.

**FOR THE BLUEBERRY WHIPPED CREAM**

½ cup blueberries

½ teaspoon chopped fresh mint

1 cup heavy cream

2 teaspoons brown sugar

**FOR THE WAFFLES**

2 cups cake flour

2 teaspoons baking powder

½ teaspoon kosher salt

4 large eggs, separated

2 tablespoons granulated sugar

2 cups milk

4 tablespoons (½ stick) unsalted butter, melted

½ teaspoon vanilla extract

Confectioners' sugar

*Waffles fascinated me when I was a kid. Nothing else we ate had a pattern.*

## MAKE THE BLUEBERRY WHIPPED CREAM

1. Crush the blueberries and mint in a small bowl with a pestle, wooden spoon, or fork.

2. Beat the cream and brown sugar to soft peaks with an electric mixer. Fold in the blueberries, cover, and refrigerate.

## MAKE THE WAFFLES

3. Preheat a waffle iron according to the manufacturer's instructions.

4. Whisk the flour, baking powder, and salt in a large bowl to combine.

5. Beat the egg yolks and granulated sugar with an electric mixer until the yolks turn pale yellow and fluffy. Add the milk, melted butter, and vanilla extract and whisk to combine. Whisk the wet ingredients into the dry until just blended. Don't overmix.

6. Beat the egg whites in a clean bowl with an electric mixer with clean, dry beaters until soft peaks form. Gently fold the egg whites into the waffle batter. Again, don't overmix.

7. Spray the waffle iron with nonstick cooking spray and pour enough batter into the iron to just cover the waffle grid. Close and cook until golden brown, 2 to 3 minutes. Repeat with the remaining batter.

8. To serve, top the waffles with sifted confectioners' sugar and a dollop of the blueberry whipped cream.

# LIPSTICK COBBLER

**SERVES 10 TO 12**

This cobbler gets its name from the bright red fruits I use. The jewel tones of cherries, strawberries, and raspberries become even more intense after baking. And unlike other cobblers, the biscuits get baked first. Some are split and set under the fruit, where they soak up the sweet juices; the rest are crumbled over the fruit, for a cardamom-scented crumb topping.

   Make it in a baking dish or in 10 to 12 individual ramekins.

**FOR THE BUTTERMILK BISCUITS**

2 cups all-purpose flour

¼ cup packed light brown sugar

3 tablespoons granulated sugar

½ teaspoon baking powder

½ teaspoon baking soda

½ teaspoon kosher salt

½ teaspoon ground cardamom

½ teaspoon ground cinnamon

6 tablespoons (¾ stick) cold
   unsalted butter, cut into
   small cubes

1 cup buttermilk

**FOR THE FRUIT**

1 vanilla bean

½ cup honey

Grated zest of 1 lemon

2 tablespoons cornstarch

½ cup dry red wine

2 cups dried sour cherries

2 cups raspberries

2 cups strawberries, hulled and cut in half

¾ cup packed light brown sugar

*Rinse the vanilla pod, let it dry, and bury it in a jar of sugar. It will perfume the sugar.*

*Or put the vanilla pod into a small bottle and cover it with bourbon or vodka. Let it sit for a couple of weeks, and you've made your own vanilla extract. Add more vanilla pods when you have them.*

## MAKE THE BISCUITS

1. Preheat the oven to 400°F. Line a baking sheet with parchment.

2. Whisk the flour, brown sugar, granulated sugar, baking powder, baking soda, salt, cardamom, and cinnamon together in a large bowl. Cut in the butter with your fingers or a pastry blender until the mixture resembles coarse meal. Add the buttermilk and stir with a fork just until a dough forms.

3. Divide the dough into 10 pieces and shape each into a 2-inch round. Set the biscuits on the baking sheet and bake until golden, about 15 minutes. Cool.

## MAKE THE FRUIT

4. Split the vanilla bean and scrape out the seeds with the back of a paring knife. Save the pod and put the seeds in a small bowl with the honey, lemon zest, and cornstarch. Stir and set aside.

5. Bring the red wine to a boil in a medium saucepan over medium heat. Whisk in the honey mixture, add the vanilla pod, and reduce the heat to low. Cook, stirring continuously, until slightly thickened, about 2 minutes. Stir in the cherries, raspberries, strawberries, and ½ cup of the brown sugar and cook until the sugar dissolves, another 3 minutes. Remove the saucepan from the heat and take the vanilla pod out of the pot.

6. Butter a 9-x-13-inch baking dish. Cut 5 of the biscuits in half and arrange the halves, cut side up, in the dish. Spoon the berry filling over the biscuits. Crumble the remaining 5 biscuits over the top of the berry filling. Sprinkle with the remaining ¼ cup brown sugar. Bake the cobbler until bubbling, about 15 minutes. Cool on a rack.

7. Serve warm or at room temperature.

# BLACK BOTTOM—PEANUT PIE

**MAKES ONE 10-INCH PIE**

A classic Southern black-bottom pie has a rich chocolate ganache topped with meringue. I make mine more decadent. Yes, it still has the black bottom, but the topping is a gooey, salty hit of peanuts. Inspiration comes from my favorite childhood snack—the Snickers candy bar. When I was a kid, I would treat myself to a Snickers bar on the way to soccer practice. I was convinced that the combination of chocolate and peanuts gave me the energy I needed to play for hours. I don't eat many candy bars these days, but I still love that combination of flavors.

## FOR THE CRUST

**8 tablespoons (1 stick) unsalted butter**

**1 (11-ounce) box vanilla wafer cookies, such as Nilla wafers**

**2 vanilla beans, split lengthwise**

**½ cup sugar**

## FOR THE PEANUT TOPPING

**1 cup sugar**

**6 tablespoons (¾ stick) unsalted butter, melted**

**3 large eggs**

**½ cup light corn syrup**

**4 teaspoons molasses**

**10 ounces (about 2 cups) unsalted roasted peanuts**

**¾ teaspoon fine sea salt**

## FOR THE GANACHE

**8 ounces bittersweet chocolate (64% cacao), finely chopped**

**1½ cups heavy cream**

## MAKE THE CRUST

1. Preheat the oven to 350°F.

2. Melt the butter in a small saucepan over low heat and cook, stirring occasionally, until the milk solids brown and the butter smells deliciously nutty, about 10 minutes; be careful not to let it burn. Take it off the heat immediately.

3. Pulse the vanilla wafers in a food processor to make coarse crumbs. Scrape the vanilla seeds into the processor, add the sugar and melted butter, and pulse until all the crumbs are moistened. Press the crumbs evenly on the bottom and up the sides of a 10-inch pie plate. Bake until lightly browned, 12 to 15 minutes. Cool on a rack.

4. Turn the oven up to 375°F.

### MAKE THE PEANUT TOPPING

5. Beat the sugar and butter in a large bowl with an electric mixer until fluffy. Beat in the eggs, one by one, then beat in the corn syrup and molasses. Stir in the peanuts and salt.

### MAKE THE GANACHE

6. Place the chocolate in a medium, heatproof bowl. Bring the cream to a boil in a small saucepan over medium heat, then pour over the chocolate. Gently whisk until the chocolate is melted and the ganache is smooth.

7. Pour the ganache into the cooled pie shell and let it set for 10 minutes. Spoon the peanut topping on the ganache. Use an offset spatula or a table knife to spread the filling evenly over the ganache, covering it completely.

8. Bake the pie for 10 minutes, then lower the heat to 325°F and bake until the crust is browned and the topping is set, about 45 minutes.

9. Cool on a rack for at least 1 hour before serving.

# SWEET & SALTY MUD PIE

**MAKES ONE 10-INCH PIE**

This Southern classic (so named because it's as dark as Mississippi mud) is one of my wife's favorite recipes, so it's in heavy rotation chez Samuelsson. I love its simplicity, but I've added just a few of my own touches. Chocolate wafer cookies make a light and crunchy crust. Garam masala adds a layer of complexity to the filling (for a twist, try substituting 1 teaspoon of Chinese five-spice). And I crumble potato chips for a salty topping.

**FOR THE CRUST**

**8 tablespoons (1 stick) unsalted butter**
**1 (9-ounce) box chocolate wafer cookies (such as Famous Chocolate Wafers)**
**½ cup sugar**

**FOR THE FILLING**

**2 tablespoons water**
**1 (¼-ounce) envelope unflavored gelatin**
**2 vanilla beans, split lengthwise**
**3 cups heavy cream**
**½ cup milk**
**1 cup sugar**
**9 ounces semisweet chocolate (56% cacao), finely chopped**
**1 pound cream cheese, softened**
**2 teaspoons garam masala**
**2–3 salted potato chips**

**MAKE THE CRUST**

1. Melt the butter in a small saucepan over low heat and cook, stirring occasionally, until the milk solids brown and the butter smells deliciously nutty, about 10 minutes; be careful not to let it burn. Take it off the heat immediately.

2. Pulse the chocolate wafers in a food processor to make coarse crumbs. Add the sugar and melted butter and pulse until all the crumbs are moistened. Press the crumbs evenly on the bottom and up the sides of a 10-inch pie plate. Chill the crust in the refrigerator for at least 1 hour.

**MAKE THE FILLING**

3. Put the water into a small bowl and sprinkle in the gelatin. Let sit so the gelatin will soften.

4. Scrape the vanilla seeds into a medium saucepan, add the bean pods, 2 cups of the cream, the milk, and sugar. Bring to a boil over medium-high heat. Remove from the heat and take out the vanilla pods.

5. Add the softened gelatin to the hot milk mixture and gently whisk for 1 minute to dissolve.

6. Put the chocolate in a medium, heatproof bowl. Bring the remaining 1 cup heavy cream to a boil in a small saucepan over medium heat, then pour over the chocolate. Whisk gently until the chocolate is melted and the ganache is smooth.

7. Beat the cream cheese and garam masala in a large bowl with an electric mixer until fluffy. Add the chocolate ganache and beat until it is fully incorporated. Add the milk mixture and beat on low speed until the filling is fully combined.

8. Scrape the filling into the chilled crust and crumble the potato chips over the top. Refrigerate until the filling is firm, at least 2 hours, before serving.

# CHEDDAR-CRUSTED APPLE PIE

**MAKES ONE 10-INCH PIE**

My mom tossed apples or pears with spices and made cakes for us. When I was an apprentice chef I discovered tarte Tatin—which I *love*. But it wasn't until I came to the United States that I learned about pie. As I travel around the country, I try to stop in to diners for that American classic: apple pie topped with a slice of cheddar cheese. For my pie, I toss the apples with cinnamon, cloves, ginger, and cardamom—the spices Mom would put in her cakes—and put the cheddar into the pastry, for a salty, flaky contrast to the sweet fruit.

### FOR THE CRUST

**2 cups all-purpose flour, plus more for dusting**

**½ teaspoon kosher salt**

**1 cup coarsely grated sharp cheddar cheese**

**8 tablespoons (1 stick) cold unsalted butter, cut into ½-inch pieces**

**4–5 tablespoons ice water**

### FOR THE FILLING

**1 cup packed light brown sugar**

**3 tablespoons all-purpose flour**

**4 teaspoons cornstarch**

**4 teaspoons ground cinnamon**

**½ teaspoon ground ginger**

**½ teaspoon ground cardamom**

**½ teaspoon kosher salt**

**Pinch of ground cloves**

**Grated zest of 1½ lemons**

**2 pounds Granny Smith apples, peeled, cored, and cut into ½-inch-thick slices**

**3 tablespoons unsalted butter, diced**

## MAKE THE CRUST

1. Pulse the flour, salt, and cheese in a food processor to combine. Add the butter and pulse until the mixture resembles coarse meal. Turn out into a large bowl and sprinkle with 4 tablespoons ice water. Use a fork to blend the dough together. Squeeze a small handful of the dough—if it doesn't hold together, add more ice water until it does.

2. Turn the dough out onto a lightly floured surface and shape into a smooth disk. Wrap the dough in plastic and refrigerate for at least 1 hour. (You can make the dough up to 3 days ahead.)

## MAKE THE FILLING

3. Mix the brown sugar, flour, cornstarch, cinnamon, ginger, cardamom, salt, cloves, and lemon zest together in a large bowl. Add the apples and toss to coat them with the dry ingredients.

4. Preheat the oven to 400°F.

5. Roll the dough out on a lightly floured surface into a 16-inch circle. Keep lifting and turning the dough as you roll to make sure it doesn't stick, dusting the surface with a bit more flour if you need to. Roll the dough loosely onto your rolling pin and unroll it over a 10-inch pie plate. Lift the edges of the crust as you fit it into the pie plate so you don't stretch it. You'll have a lot of overhang.

6. Spoon the filling into the crust and dot it with the butter. Fold the overhanging crust over the filling.

7. Bake for 15 minutes. Lay a piece of aluminum foil over the pie, reduce the temperature to 350°F, and bake until the apples are tender and the crust is golden, 50 to 60 minutes. Let the pie cool for at least 2 hours before serving.

*Serve it à la mode, with vanilla ice cream or whipped cream.*

# GARAM MASALA—PUMPKIN TART

**MAKES ONE 10-INCH TART**

I got the idea for this tart when I was working on the menu for President Obama's first state dinner. The dinner honored the prime minister of India, and I wanted to serve dishes that had an elegant Indian influence. So I flavored what I consider a very American pumpkin pie with a staple of Indian cuisine: garam masala. It hit all the right notes.

You could go rustic and make this tart in a cast iron skillet, but do serve it with Buttermilk Sorbet (page 338).

**FOR THE CRUST**

1¼ cups all-purpose flour, plus more for dusting

½ teaspoon kosher salt

Grated zest of 1 lemon

8 tablespoons (1 stick) cold unsalted butter, cut into ½-inch pieces

2–3 tablespoons ice water

**FOR THE FILLING**

4 large eggs

1 cup packed light brown sugar

2 teaspoons garam masala

½ teaspoon kosher salt

1 (15-ounce) can pumpkin puree

1 cup half and half

2 tablespoons pure maple syrup

Grated zest of 2 lemons

Juice of 1 lemon

1 (1-inch) piece ginger, peeled and minced

1 teaspoon vanilla extract

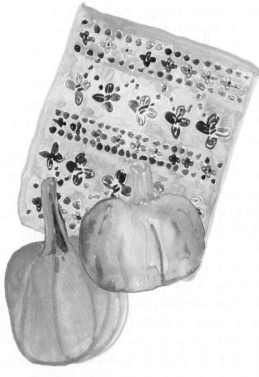

## MAKE THE CRUST

1. Pulse the flour, salt, and lemon zest in a food processor once or twice to combine. Add the butter and pulse until the mixture resembles coarse meal. Add the 2 tablespoons of ice water, pulsing just until the dough starts to come together into a ball. If necessary, add a little more ice water, about 1 teaspoon at a time.

2. Turn the dough out onto a lightly floured surface and shape into a smooth disk. Wrap the dough in plastic and refrigerate for at least 1 hour. (You can make the dough up to 3 days ahead.)

3. Roll the dough out on a lightly floured surface into a 12½-inch circle. Keep lifting and turning the dough as you roll to make sure it doesn't stick, dusting the surface with a bit more flour if you need to. Roll the dough loosely onto your rolling pin and unroll it over a 10-inch tart pan with a removable bottom. Fit the dough into the pan without stretching it and press the dough firmly against the sides of the pan. Roll your rolling pin over the top of the pan to trim the excess dough. Refrigerate for 30 minutes.

4. Preheat the oven to 375°F.

5. Line the crust with foil, pushing it into the seam and tight to the edges, and fill with dried beans, rice, or pie weights. Bake for 8 minutes. Remove the foil and weights and leave the crust on a rack while you make the filling.

## MAKE THE FILLING

6. Lower the oven temperature to 350°F.

7. Beat the eggs well in a bowl. Add the remaining ingredients and whisk until thoroughly blended.

8. Set the tart pan on a baking sheet and pour in the filling. Bake until the filling is almost set—it should still jiggle a bit in the center. Cool on a rack for 30 minutes before removing the outside of the tart pan (leave the tart on the base of the pan). Serve at room temperature.

# OATMEAL-CHERRY COOKIES

**MAKES 5 DOZEN COOKIES**

You may think you know oatmeal cookies, but add dried cherries instead of raisins and perfume them with garam masala and you find that you've upped the sophistication of this comforting cookie. I love them warm from the oven, but sometimes I melt a little chocolate and serve it with the cookies as an elegant fondue. You can also pulse left-over cookies in a food processor and turn them into granola.

**3 cups rolled oats**
**1½ cups all-purpose flour**
**2 teaspoons garam masala**
**1 teaspoon baking soda**
**½ teaspoon kosher salt**
**16 tablespoons (2 sticks) unsalted butter, softened**
**½ cup granulated sugar**
**1 cup packed light brown sugar**
**1 teaspoon vanilla extract**
**2 large eggs**
**1 cup dried cherries, chopped**

*You can freeze cookies in an airtight container for up to 2 months.*

1. Preheat the oven to 350°F, with racks in the middle and upper third. Line two baking sheets with parchment.
2. Stir the oats, flour, garam masala, baking soda, and salt together in a bowl.
3. Beat the butter, both sugars, and vanilla extract in a large bowl with an electric mixer until light and fluffy. Beat in the eggs, one at a time, beating well after each addition and scraping down the sides of the bowl. Stir in the dry ingredients, then stir in the cherries.
4. Drop rounded tablespoons of dough onto the baking sheets, spacing the cookies 2 inches apart.
5. Bake until the tops look set, 10 to 12 minutes, switching the pans from top to bottom and front to back halfway through. Let the cookies cool on the baking sheets for 2 minutes, then transfer to a rack to cool completely. Let the baking sheets cool, line with fresh parchment, and bake the rest of the cookies. Store in an airtight container for up to 5 days.

Mormor's Spice Cookies (page 327), Coconut Macaroons (page 328), Oatmeal-Cherry Cookies (page 323), and Spiced Chocolate-Chip Cookies (page 326)

# SPICED CHOCOLATE-CHIP COOKIES

**MAKES 5 DOZEN COOKIES**

I spice my chocolate-chip cookies with cinnamon, cardamom, and Aleppo pepper.

**2¼ cups all-purpose flour**
**1 teaspoon baking soda**
**1 teaspoon kosher salt**
**¼ teaspoon Aleppo pepper (see Note, page 270) or cayenne**
**¼ teaspoon ground cardamom**
**¼ teaspoon ground cinnamon**
**8 tablespoons (1 stick) unsalted butter, softened**
**¾ cup granulated sugar**
**1 cup packed light brown sugar**
**2 teaspoons vanilla extract**
**3 large eggs**
**2 cups bittersweet chocolate chips (60% cacao)**

1. Preheat the oven to 375°F, with racks in the middle and upper third. Line two baking sheets with parchment.

2. Whisk the flour, baking soda, salt, Aleppo pepper, cardamom, and cinnamon in a bowl.

3. Beat the butter, both sugars, and vanilla extract with an electric mixer in a large bowl until light and fluffy. Add the eggs, one at a time, beating well after each addition and scraping down the sides of the bowl. Stir in the dry ingredients, then the chocolate chips.

4. Drop rounded tablespoons of the dough onto the baking sheets, spacing the cookies 2 inches apart.

5. Bake the cookies until they're golden brown, 9 to 11 minutes, switching the pans from top to bottom and front to back halfway through. Cool the cookies on the baking sheets for 2 minutes, then transfer to racks to cool completely. Let the baking sheets cool, line with fresh parchment, and bake the rest of the cookies. Store in an airtight container for up to 5 days.

# MORMOR'S SPICE COOKIES

**MAKES 5 DOZEN COOKIES**

My grandmother never left Sweden, but her spice rack looked like it belonged to a culinary jet-setter. Making these cookies takes me back to her kitchen in Sweden.

**1½ teaspoons ground cinnamon**
**1 teaspoon ground ginger**
**½ teaspoon ground cardamom**
**¼ teaspoon ground cloves**
**3½ cups sifted all-purpose flour**
**1 tablespoon baking soda**
**1 teaspoon kosher salt**
**½ teaspoon freshly ground white pepper**
**10 tablespoons (1¼ sticks) unsalted butter, softened**
**1 cup granulated sugar**
**½ cup packed light brown sugar**
**2 large eggs**
**¾ cup molasses**

*In Swedish Mormor means grandmother and Morfar means grandfather, and their kitchen was one of my favorite places to hang out as a kid.*

*Morfar, Mom as a young girl, and Mormor*

1. Preheat the oven to 350°F, with racks in the middle and upper third. Line two baking sheets with parchment.
2. Combine the cinnamon, ginger, cardamom, and cloves in a small skillet over medium heat and toast, stirring with a wooden spoon, until fragrant, 2 to 3 minutes.
3. Immediately scrape the spices into a bowl. Add the flour, baking soda, salt, and white pepper and whisk to combine.
4. Beat the butter and both sugars with an electric mixer in a large bowl until light and fluffy. Add the eggs, one at a time, beating well after each addition and scraping down the sides of the bowl. Beat in the molasses. Stir in the dry ingredients.
5. Drop rounded tablespoons of the dough onto the baking sheets, spacing the cookies 2 inches apart. Bake until the tops feel firm when lightly touched, 10 to 12 minutes, switching the pans from top to bottom and front to back halfway through. Cool on the baking sheets for about 2 minutes, then transfer the cookies to a rack to cool completely. Let the baking sheets cool, line with fresh parchment, and bake the rest of the cookies. Store in an airtight container for up to 5 days.

# COCONUT MACAROONS

**MAKES 2 DOZEN COOKIES**

Sweet, chewy, and dipped into an intense chocolate ganache, these American-style macaroons could not be easier. Often I'll make the coconut dough a day or two ahead and refrigerate it, then bake the macaroons just before my friends arrive.

**FOR THE MACAROONS**

**2 large eggs**
**½ cup sugar**
**¼ teaspoon kosher salt**
**3 cups unsweetened shredded coconut**

**FOR THE GANACHE**

**½ cup heavy cream**
**4 ounces bittersweet chocolate (74% cacao), finely chopped**

**MAKE THE MACAROONS**

1. Preheat the oven to 350°F, with racks in the middle and upper third. Line two baking sheets with parchment.
2. Crack the eggs into a large bowl and beat them lightly. Add the sugar, salt, and coconut and stir to combine.
3. Scoop out tablespoon-sized mounds of the coconut dough and place them on the baking sheets.
4. Bake until set and lightly browned, 20 to 30 minutes, switching the pans from top to bottom and front to back halfway through. Cool completely on a rack.

**MAKE THE GANACHE**

5. While the macaroons cool, bring the cream to a boil in a small saucepan over medium-high heat. Put the chocolate in a heatproof bowl. Immediately pour the cream over the chopped chocolate and whisk gently until the chocolate is melted and the ganache is smooth. Cool the ganache to room temperature.
6. Dip the bases of the macaroons in the ganache and place them on the parchment-lined baking sheet. Serve the macaroons once the chocolate is set. In warm weather, you may have to put the macaroons in the refrigerator for 10 minutes to firm up the chocolate.

My Swedish
Princess Cake
(page 330)

# MY SWEDISH PRINCESS CAKE

**MAKES ONE 9-INCH CAKE**

You'll find this cake—a sponge cake filled with jam, pastry cream, and a mountain of whipped cream and enrobed in marzipan, that is named for the princess daughters of Prince Carl of Sweden and Norway, who loved it—at every celebration in Sweden. The color of the almond-paste robe will vary. It will be yellow for a wedding, creamy white for a fiftieth anniversary; here, it's the traditional green, for Christmas. It is usually topped with a pink marzipan rose.

### FOR THE SPONGE CAKE

1½ cups all-purpose flour
1¼ teaspoons baking powder
3 large eggs
¾ cup sugar

### FOR THE PASTRY CREAM

1 cup milk
1 cup heavy cream
2 vanilla beans, split lengthwise
4 large egg yolks
1 cup sugar
½ cup cornstarch

### FOR THE WHIPPED CREAM

1 tablespoon water
½ teaspoon unflavored gelatin
1 cup heavy cream
1 tablespoon confectioners' sugar

### FOR ASSEMBLY

½ cup strained raspberry jam
3 (7-ounce) logs almond paste
½ cup confectioners' sugar, plus more for dusting
1 large egg white, lightly beaten
Green food coloring

*If the idea of marzipan intimidates you, just top the cake with some fresh blueberries, raspberries, or strawberries.*

## MAKE THE SPONGE CAKE

1. Preheat the oven to 350°F. Butter a 3-x-9-inch round cake pan and line the bottom with parchment.

2. Whisk the flour and baking powder together.

3. Beat the eggs and sugar with an electric mixer on high speed until almost white and tripled in volume, about 15 minutes. Add the dry ingredients in thirds, folding them into the eggs.

4. Pour the batter into the pan and bake until the cake is golden brown, springy to the touch, and starting to pull away from the sides of the pan, 30 to 35 minutes. Turn upside down and cool completely on a rack.

## MAKE THE PASTRY CREAM

5. Put the milk and cream into a saucepan. Scrape the seeds out of the vanilla beans and add the seeds and pods to the pan. Bring to a boil over medium-high heat.

6. Whisk the egg yolks, sugar, and cornstarch in a large bowl until smooth. Slowly whisk in about 1 cup of the boiling milk to temper the yolks, then return to the pan and cook, whisking constantly, until the cream thickens and comes to a boil. Remove the vanilla pods. Transfer the cream to a bowl and cool completely.

## MAKE THE WHIPPED CREAM

7. Put the water in a custard cup and sprinkle the gelatin over it. Let sit for 5 minutes. Microwave for 15 seconds and stir to dissolve the gelatin. If it's not liquid, microwave for 10 seconds longer. Let cool until tepid but still liquid.

8. Put the cream, confectioners' sugar, and gelatin into a bowl and beat with an electric mixer until you have stiff peaks. Cover and refrigerate.

## ASSEMBLE THE CAKE

9. Turn the cake out of the pan and remove the parchment. Cut the cake into 3 layers.

10. Put 1 layer on a cake plate. Spread with the raspberry jam (don't go all the way to the edge) and top with the second layer. Spread the pastry cream evenly over the second layer (don't go all the way to the edge). Top with the third layer. Refrigerate until the pastry cream is firm, at least 1 hour.

11. Pile the whipped cream on the top layer and use an offset spatula to even it out. Refrigerate while you prepare the almond coating.

12. Mix the almond paste, confectioners' sugar, egg white, and a few drops of food coloring (you want to make a mint-green paste) in a stand mixer, fitted with the paddle, until smooth.

13. Shape the almond paste into a flat disk on a surface dusted with confectioners' sugar. Roll into

a round slightly less than ⅛ inch thick. Keep the surface and rolling pin dusted with confectioners' sugar and roll the paste between two pieces of parchment if you need to.

14. Gently drape the almond paste over the cake, making it as smooth as possible. Trim the excess to about ⅓ inch and use a small offset spatula to carefully tuck it under the bottom layer.

15. Refrigerate the cake until you're ready to serve. Dust with confectioners' sugar and cut with a serrated knife.

# AMBROSIA VIA SINGAPORE

**SERVES 6**

This is my version of the classic fruit salad known as ambrosia, which many Southerners serve on Christmas. It highlights two of my favorite fruits: mangoes and goji berries. These shriveled berries from Southeast Asia—which look a lot like red raisins—are high in antioxidants and carotenoids and are said to promote longevity—they're a superfood. The dressing for this fruit salad—reduced coconut milk—is inspired by my trips to Singapore.

**¾ cup coconut milk**
**3 tablespoons sugar**
**2 cups unsweetened coconut (big flakes, if you can find them)**
**Segments and juice (see page 85) of 6 oranges**
**2 mangoes, peeled and cubed**
**2 tablespoons dried goji berries (see Note)**
**Juice of 1 lime**
**Fresh mint leaves, for garnish**

1. Bring the coconut milk and sugar to a boil in a small saucepan over medium-high heat. Lower the heat and simmer until it's reduced to ½ cup, about 5 minutes. Cool to room temperature.
2. Toast the coconut flakes in a large skillet over medium heat, stirring often, until the edges are golden brown, 3 to 4 minutes. Transfer to a large bowl.
3. Add the orange segments and juice, mangoes, goji berries, and lime juice. Add the coconut milk dressing and toss the ambrosia with a large spoon. Serve in small bowls, garnished with mint.

Note: You can find dried goji berries in health food stores, many large supermarkets, and online.

# STRAWBERRY & HONEY YOGURT POPS

**MAKES 8 TO 12 POPS (DEPENDING ON THE SIZE OF THE MOLDS)**

These frozen pops highlight the beautiful natural flavor of strawberries, and it's my go-to recipe when strawberries are in season and perfectly ripe. This is a simple dessert to make; it's not overly sweet and there's just a tiny bit of ginger for spice. Such a refreshing way to end a summer meal—and kids love them.

**FOR THE SIMPLE SYRUP**

⅔ **cup water**

⅔ **cup packed light brown sugar**

**1 vanilla bean, cut in half lengthwise and pod scraped**

¼ **teaspoon ground ginger**

Note: You can find ice-pop molds in kitchenware stores, department stores, and online.

**FOR THE POPS**

**1½ pounds fresh strawberries, hulled**

**1 cup plain nonfat yogurt**

**5 teaspoons honey**

**4 teaspoons fresh lemon juice**

**1 ice-pop mold (see Note) or 8 mini paper cups and 8 Popsicle sticks**

**MAKE THE SIMPLE SYRUP**

1. Bring the water, sugar, vanilla seeds and pod, and ginger to a boil in a small saucepan over medium-high heat. Stir until the sugar dissolves completely. Remove the vanilla pod. Transfer the syrup to a small bowl, cover with plastic wrap, and refrigerate until cold, at least 1 hour.

**MAKE THE POPS**

2. Puree the strawberries in a food processor until smooth. Transfer the puree to a large pitcher and whisk in the simple syrup, yogurt, honey, and lemon juice.

3. Pour into the ice-pop molds. Top with the mold cover. If you're using paper cups, fill them and freeze for a few hours before inserting the Popsicle sticks. Freeze the pops until firm, at least 8 hours or overnight.

4. Dip the bottom of the mold into hot water for 10 to 15 seconds to loosen the pops. Remove the pops from the molds and serve. If using paper cups, kids can peel the paper right off the pop.

# BUTTERMILK SORBET

**MAKES ABOUT 1 PINT**

This sorbet pleases my tongue more than any ice cream. It has the richness of ice cream, but the acidity of the buttermilk makes it taste light and refreshing. It's particularly good served with pumpkin pie or chocolate cake, where it cuts through the sweetness.

¼ cup water
Grated zest and juice of 1 lemon
1 vanilla bean, cut in half lengthwise
    and pod scraped
3 cardamom pods
1 (½-inch) piece ginger, crushed
1¾ cups sugar
2 cups buttermilk

*Don't throw that ginger away. Keep it in the refrigerator and use it to make ginger tea or a vinaigrette. Or toss it with sugar and dry it on a piece of parchment for spicy ginger candy.*

1. Bring the water, lemon zest and juice, vanilla bean seeds and pod, cardamom, ginger, and sugar to a boil in a saucepan. Stir to make sure the sugar is dissolved and simmer for 2 minutes. Strain into a heatproof bowl and refrigerate until cold, at least 1 hour.

2. Stir the syrup into the buttermilk. Transfer to an ice-cream maker and follow the manufacturer's instructions to freeze. When it is frozen, transfer the sorbet to an airtight container and freeze for at least 1 hour before serving.

# GINGER SIMPLE SYRUP

One of the things about being a chef is that you know the benefits of having little culinary extras like this syrup around the house. I don't know another ingredient more linked to good health throughout the world than ginger.

This potent ginger syrup can be drizzled over ice cream or berries and stone fruits—particularly early in the season when the fruit's a little tart. Spoon it over pancakes or brush it on a pound cake when it comes out of the oven.

It has a spicy kick that also makes for a terrific soda. Pour ¼ cup syrup into a tall glass and top with cold seltzer or club soda. Stir to combine.

Put 2 cups water, 1 cup light corn syrup, 3¾ cups sugar, and a 3-inch piece of ginger that you've peeled and chopped into a large saucepan over medium-high heat. Bring to a boil, stirring frequently to dissolve the sugar. Reduce the heat to low and simmer very gently for 15 minutes. The syrup will thicken and reduce slightly. Remove from the heat and let cool. Strain the syrup into a clean jar or other container. It will keep indefinitely in the refrigerator. This makes about 3 cups.

# INDEX

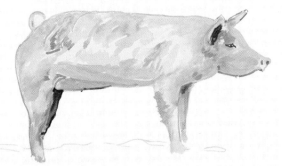